Svapnavāsavadatta of Bhāsa

श्रीः

महाकवि–भासप्रणीतं

स्वप्नवासवदत्तम्।

SVAPNAVĀSAVADATTA OF BHĀSA

Edited with a short Sanskrit Commentary, English Translation and Critical Notes

By

M.R. KALE

and

with an Introduction by

M.R. KALE *and* L.S. BHANDARE

MOTILAL BANARSIDASS PUBLISHING HOUSE • DELHI

Email: mlbd@mlbd.in • Website: www.mlbd.in

8th Reprint : Delhi, ***2022***
Third Edition : Delhi, 1982
Second Revised Edition : Bombay, 1945

ISBN: 978-93-91024-11-6 (Hardcover)
ISBN: 978-93-91024-12-3 (Paperback)

Printed & Published by
Rajendra P Jain *for*
Motilal Banarsidass Publishing House
A-44, Naraina Industrial Area, Phase I,
New Delhi–110 028 (INDIA)
Email: mlbd@mlbd.in
Website: www.mlbd.in

PREFACE.

This edition of the Svapnavāsavadatta is prepared on the same lines as of the other plays edited by me, being based on the printed editions of the same, the best readings being chosen where available. In this an attempt is made to supply the University student with a text-book calculated to meet his usual wants. In the com., necessarily brief, are given the prose order of the ślokas, the solutions of the more difficult compounds, derivations of important words, &c. The notes are meant to be exhaustive. All controversial points have been discussed in the Intro. For ready reference a glossary of important words has been added at the end. I have consulted the editions M. M. Gaṇpati Sāstrī and Professors Bhide and Devadhar and to them my thanks are due for whatever help I have derived from them. My thanks are due to Dr. Sukthankar, Mr. B. R. Hiwargaokar and other scholars, whose articles on Bhāsa were of great help to me in writing the introduction. My thanks are also due to my friend Mr. L. S. Bhāndāre B. A., S.T.C. to whom, owing to long continued ill health, I had to leave the work of completing the Introduction written in part by me, and which he has done in a manner creditable to him. My thanks are due to D. V. Mulgaonkar Esq., the managing Proprietor of the firm of Messrs Gopal Narayen & Co., Book-sellers & Publishers, but for whose patronage the book would not have seen light this year.

Bombay,
May 1929.

M. R. KA'LE.

पद्यानां सूचिः ।

INTRODUCTION.

THE SANSKRIT DRAMA.[1]

We shall begin with a brief outline of the general structure and arrangement of the Sanskrit Drama, as developed by the later writers on dramaturgy.[2] Poetry in Sanskrit, from its inherent nature, as apart from its intrinsic merit, is divided into two kinds—दृश्य 'what is capable of being seen or exhibited' and श्रव्य 'what can only be heard or chanted.' The drama falls under the first division. 'Rúpaka' is the general term in Sanskrit for all dramatic compositions, which also comprises a subordinate class called *Uparúpaka.* The Rúpaka,[3] which has Rasa or sentiment for its substratum, is divided into ten classes, *viz* नाटकं सप्रकरणं भाणः प्रहसनं डिमः । व्यायोगसमवकारौ वीथ्यङ्केहामृगा इति ॥. Of the Uparúpakas or Minor Dramas there are eighteen species, the most important of which are *Nâṭikas,* such as the Ratnâvalî, Viddhaśâlabhañjikâ &c., *Troṭakas* such as the Vikramorvaśîya, &c.

Having thus disposed of the divisions into which the whole of the scenic art is capable of falling, we turn to the principle of division among the *Rûpakas* themselves, which is threefold[4]—(1) वस्तु or the Plot of the play: (2) नेता or the Hero; and (3) रस or the Sentiment.

---

1 This Section is the same as that prefixed to my ed. of the Ratnâvalî with some changes and omissions.

2 The information given here has been mainly culled from the Das'arūpaka.

3 अवस्थानुकृतिर्नाट्यं रूपं दृश्यतयोच्यते । रूपकं तत्समारोपाद्दशधैव रसाश्रयम् ॥ D.—P. रूप्यतेऽभिनयैर्यत्र वस्तु तद्रूपकं विदुः । नाटकाद्यैर्दशविधम्. *Nâtya* is another and perhaps a wider term for the drama or the dramatic art, and is so called because it represents the different situations in (the scenes presented by) life. The sage Bharata is the founder of the science of music and dramaturgy and his work is styled the *Nâṭya Śâstra.* *Nâṭya* is also called *Rûpa* inasmuch as it has *dṛiśyatâ* or the capability of being seen, and *Rûpaka* inasmuch as its subject-matter is represented by actors assuming particular characters.

4 वस्तु नेता रसस्तेषां भेदकः ।

These three are the essential constituents, nay, the very life-blood, of every dramatic piece. Each of these we shall succinctly deal with in its order.

---

1 VASTU OR THE PLOT.

Vastu is primarily of two kinds: आधिकारिक or 'principal' and प्रासंगिक or 'accessory.' The Principal is that which relates to the chief characters or the persons concerned with the essential interest of the piece, and pervades the whole arrangement. The Accessory is that which appears in furtherance of the main topic, and is concerned with characters other than the Hero and the Heroine. This latter is of two kinds, *viz*. *Patâkâ* and *Prakarî*. *Patâkâ* or 'banner' is an episode by which the progress of the plot is illustrated, furthered or hindered (so as to give additional interest to it). It is of considerable length and sometimes extends to the very end of a play. The *Prakarî* is also an episodical incident—of limited duration and minor importance—one in which the principal characters take no part. Besides these two, there are three other elements requisite for the development of the plot. These are बीज or the seed, बिन्दु or the drop, and कार्य or the final issue. *Bîja*[1] is the circumstance leading to the ultimate end briefly stated, which, as the plot develops bears multifarious results and which is, as it were, the seed of the plot. *Bindu*[2] is what cements a break in the plot caused by the introduction of some other incident. *Kârya* is the final object of the plot, which being attained the whole is finished. These five are technically called Arthaprakṛitis (अर्थप्रकृतयः).

The *Vastu*, which is thus divided into five classes, may again be divided into three classes according to the source of its derivation. It may be borrowed from history or tradition, or it may be fictitious, or mixed *i. e.*, partly drawn from history and partly the creation of the poet's fancy. A *Nāṭaka* belongs to the first class, a *Prakaraṇa* to the second.

As regards its development a dramatic plot has five stages or conditions called *Avasthâs*. They are (1) आरम्भ beginning or setting

---

1 स्वल्पोद्दिष्टस्तु तद्धेतुर्बीजं विस्तार्यनेकधा ।

2 अवान्तरार्थविच्छेदे बिन्दुरच्छेदकारणम्.

on foot of the enterprise, (2) यत्न effort, (3) प्राप्त्याशा prospect of success, (4) नियताप्ति certain attainment through the removal of obstacles, and (5) फलागम obtainment of the desired object. While these five stages are in progress, there must be some links to connect them with the principal and subordinate parts of the main action (the episodes and incidents). These are called the *Saṃdhis* or junctures. They are five in number, answering to the five *Arthaprakṛitis*, each of which they join with its corresponding stage, *viz*, मुख (Protasis or the opening juncture), प्रतिमुख (Epitasis). गर्भ (catastasis), अवमर्श (Peripeteia), and निर्वहण (Catastrophe), also called उपसंहृति or उपसंहार. Thus *Mukhasaṃdhi* is the combination of the Bîja and Ârambha, *i. e.* wherein the seed is sown, so to speak, with all its *Rasas*. In the *Pratimukha* there is the means (*yatna*) to the chief end, as originally implied by the Bîja in the Mukha which herein sprouts up. In the *Garbha* there is attainment and non-attainment of the desired end, implying a further sprouting up of the original Bîja. There are impediments, but the main plot gains ground under resistance. The *Avamarśasaṃdhi* is that in which the seed attains a more luxuriant growth than in the *Garbha*, being accompanied by *Niyatâpti* of the end, but whose final result is postponed further off by fresh impediments of various sorts, as in the Śâkuntala the King's forgetting Śak. after marriage owing to Durvâsas' curse. The *Nirvahana* or consummation is the harmonious combination of all the aforesaid parts in the final catastrophe.

The subject-matter, whether historical, fictitious, or mixed, is from its inherent nature capable of a twofold division. It is divided into (1) सूच्य—deserving to be suggested or implied only, as being of a dry and otherwise unfit character; and (2) दृश्यश्रव्य-fit to be represented and heard as being highly sentimental and pleasing. The suggestions or implications are made in five ways—विष्कम्भचूलिकाङ्कास्याङ्कावतारप्रवेशकैः। (1) For *Viṣkambha* see Notes, Act I. (2) *Chûlikâ* is the suggestion of some incident from behind the scenes (नेपथ्ये). (3) An अङ्कास्य[1] is one wherein is suggested by the actors at the time of their departure the connexion between the Act finished and the one to be commenced, which otherwise would look disconnected, as the

1 अङ्कान्तपात्रैरङ्कास्यं छिन्नाङ्कस्यार्थसूचनात् ।.

speech of Kāmandakî and others at the end of the 3rd Act of the Mâl.-Mâdh. (4) अङ्कावतार[1] consists in implanting the seed of the subject-matter of an Act in the previous Act before it has drawn to its close, so that the Act following is a continuation of the one preceding; *e. g*, the sixth Act of the Śâk., the germ of which is cast at the end of the fifth Act; Mâlav. II. and Mâl.-Mâd. II, are other instances. (5) For प्रवेशक see notes Act IV.

The subject-matter is further divided into three kinds—**सर्वश्राव्यं** or **प्रकाशं**, **अश्राव्यं** or **स्वगतं** and **नियतश्राव्यम्.** The last is of two kinds, जनान्तिक and अपवारितक or अपवार्य. Independent of these divisions there is one called आकाशभाषित (आकाशे) or speech from the void which is explained in the Notes.

The styles or modes of action (वृत्तय:) to be followed in a drama are four in number *viz.* शृङ्गारे कैशिकी वीरे सात्वत्यारभटी पुनः । रसे रौद्रे च बीभत्से वृत्तिः सर्वत्र भारती ॥. Cî. these the Kaiśikî has four *aṅgas, viz.* (1) नर्म or polite pleasantry, (2) नभःस्फूर्ज० (स्फञ्ज according to D.–R.) or development of love, (3) नर्मस्फोट or the distant indication of love, and (4) नर्मगर्भ or covert action for the furtherance of love (यथा मालतीमाधवे सखीरूपधारिणा माधवेन मालत्या मरणव्यवसायवारणम्).

NETÂ OR THE HERO.

The Hero is required to be modest, decorous, comely, munificent civil, of sweet address, eloquent, sprung from a noble family, &c.[2] Heroes are mentioned to be of four kinds, *viz.*, **धीरोदात्त**, **धीरललित**, **धीरशान्त** and **धीरोद्धत.** *Dhîralalita,'* or Hero who is graceful and firm, is defined as निश्चिन्तो मृदुरनिशं कलापरो धीरललितः स्यात् (Sāh. D. III. 23) *i. e,* one who is free from cares, ever gentle and always given to the arts, like Vatsarâja. We are not concerned with the other three classes of Heroes here. Each of these Heroes may be of one or other of four sorts. He may be, **दक्षिण** or 'gallant,' *i. e.* equally devoted to many women, though principally attached to one; or **शठ** 'sly' *i. e.,* one who being attached to one lady, covertly acts

1 अङ्कावतारस्त्वङ्कान्ते पातोऽङ्कस्याविभागतः ।

2 नेता विनीतो मधुरस्त्यागी दक्षः प्रियंवदः । रक्तलोकः शुचिर्वाग्मी रूढवंशः स्थिरो युवा ॥ बुद्ध्युत्साहस्मृतिप्रज्ञाकलामानसमन्वितः । शूरो दृढश्च तेजस्वी शास्त्रचक्षुश्च धार्मिकः ॥ भेदैश्चतुर्धा ललितशान्तोदात्तोद्धतैरयम् ॥

in a way unpleasant to her; or he may be धृष्ट 'bold,' openly making his professions to another, and not ashamed even when reproached, or lastly he may be अनुकूल 'favourable,' devoted to one Heroine only. The धीरोदात्त Hero has eight manly qualities—शोभा, विलास, माधुर्य, गाम्भीर्य, धैर्य, तेजस्, लालित्य and औदार्य.

Among the assistants of the Hero the principal is पीठमर्द, the hero of the Patâkâ or episode, clever in discourse, devoted to his master, and a little inferior to him in qualities. Next comes the Vidûṣaka, his constant companion, whose business consists in the repartees of wit, in helping his friend in his love-intrigues, and thus assisting in the general *dénouement* of the play.

The Nâyikâ or the Hiroine who must be possessed of qualities similar to those of the Hero is of three kinds.[1] She may be the wife of the hero (स्वीया), as Sîtâ in the Uttar.; or one belonging to another (अन्या or परकीया), or a common woman (सामान्या or साधारणस्त्री) as Vasantasenā in the Mṛich. The परकीया may be a maiden (so called because she is in the power of her guardian) or the wife of another. But the latter must not be introduced as the Heroine in a play[2]. The maiden's love, however, better helps the *rasa* and is, therefore, the most favourite theme with many Sanskrit poets. Further divisions and subdivisions of the *Nâyikâ* are not introduced here, as they have very little to do with the construction of the drama. For her assistants the Heroine may have a सखी, दासी, धात्रेयी, प्रतिवेशिका and others, possessing qualities corresponding to those of the friends of the Hero.

---

3 RASA OR SENTIMENT.

Rasa is that lasting impression of feeling produced to his overwhelming delight in a man of poetic susceptibility by the proper action of the *Vibhâvas*, and *Anubhâvas*, as well as the *Sâttvika* bhâvas and the *Vyabhichâribhâvas*, Bhâva (भाव) or 'feeling' is

---

1 स्वान्या साधारणस्त्रीति तद्गुणा नायिका त्रिधा ।.

2 अन्यस्त्री कन्यकोढा च नान्योढाङ्गिरसे क्वचित्. "We may observe however, to the honour of Hindu drama, that the *Parakîyâ* or she who is the wife of another person, is never to be made the object of dramatic intrigue; a prohibition that would have sadly cooled the imagination, and curbed the wit, of Dryden and Congreve" Wilson: Select Specimens. Vol. I. p. 45,

the complete pervasion of the heart by any emotion, whether of pleasure or of pain, arising from the object under sight. **Vibhâva** (विभाव) or an Excitant is that which being perceived nourishes the main sentiment. It is divided into (1) ***Âlambana***, that which is, as it were, the support or substratum of the Rasa–the person or thing with reference to whom or which a sentiment arises—such as the Hero or the Heroine, and (2) ***Uddîpana*** or what excites or enhances (adds to the development of) the sentiment, such as the moon, the beauties of the vernal season, &c.; beauty, decorations, &c. of the principal characters, in the case of श्रृङ्गार. ***Anubhâva*** or an Ensuant is the outward manifestation of the internal feeling through the eyes, face &c. The Sâttvika or natural *bhâvas* are a subdivision of *Anubhâva*, and are mentioned as eight in number–स्तम्भप्रलयरोमाञ्चाः स्वेदो वैवर्ण्यवेपथू । अश्रु वैस्वर्यमित्यष्टौ ।. The *Vyabhichârîs* or the Accessories are those *bhâvas* which are not strictly confined to any *Rasa*, but appearing and disappearing, like waves in the ocean, they serve as feeders to the prevailing sentiment and strengthen it in different ways. *Sthâyibhâva* (स्थायिभाव) or the Permanent Sentiment[2] of a composition 'is one—the ocean melting all salt into water—which not being interrupted by any sentiment contrary or akin to its nature occurring at intervals, converts all of them into its own nature' Now a *Rasa* would prove contrary to another if the आश्रय or substratum of both were the same. But as अङ्गी (principal) and अङ्ग (subordinate) a रस may be mixed with one or more of others.

There are eight Sthâyibhâvas, रति, हास, शोक, क्रोध; उत्साह, भय, जुगुप्सा, and विस्मय on which are based respectively the sentiments–शृङ्गार the Erotic, हास्य the Comic, करुण the Pathetic, रौद्र the Furious, वीर the Heroic, भयानक the Terrible, बीभत्स the Loathsome, and अद्भुत the Marvellous. There is a ninth sentiment, that of शान्त the Quietistic, having शम or tranquility for its Sthâyibhâva. But it is not suited to dramatic purposes

---

1 विभावैरनुभावैश्च सात्त्विकैर्व्यभिचारिभिः। आनीयमानः स्वाद्यत्वं स्थायीभावो रसः स्मृतः । सुखदुःखादिकैर्भावैर्भावस्तद्भावभावनम् । ज्ञायमानतया तत्र विभावो भावपोषकृत् ॥ आलम्बनोद्दीपनत्वप्रभेदेन स च द्विधा । अनुभावो विकारस्तु भावसंसूचनात्मकः ॥

2 विरुद्धैरविरुद्धैर्वा भावैर्विच्छिद्यते न यः । आत्मभावं नयत्यन्यान्स स्थायी लवणाकरः ॥

and rarely occurs as a main sentiment in a drama. Of these eight sentiments शृङ्गार and हास्य, वीर and अद्भुत, बीभत्स and भयानक, and रौद्र and करुण are akin to each other as they proceed from the same condition of the mind. As we are here mainly concerned with the Erotic, that being the prevailing sentiment in most Sans. plays, we will say something about it here. शृङ्गार is mainly divided into विप्रलम्भ or Love in-separation and संभोग or Love in-union. The former the Daśarūpaka subdivides into two kinds, अयोग the Non-consummation of marriage, and विप्रयोग the separation of the lovers deep in love after marriage. The former, when arises from the dependent position of one or the other of the parties or through distance or through the intervention of adverse fate, has ten stages, अभिलाष, चिन्ता and others. चिन्ता occurs through मान, प्रवास or some such cause; मान 'jealous anger,' arises from a breach in the duties of love (प्रणयभङ्ग) and may be on both sides (rarely however, the Nâyaka is *Mânî*). This मान has several varieties, such as ईर्ष्यामान, आनुमानिकमान &c. It is capable of being dispelled in six ways: साम्ना भेदेन दानेन नत्युपेक्षा-रसान्तरैः—and is called गुरु, लघु or मध्यम according to the greatness or the smallness of the effort required to make the Nâyikâ give it up. संभोग is when the two lovers are in the enjoyment of each other's company, engaged in looking at each other, kissing each other, &c.

THE GENERAL CONDUCT OF THE NÂṬAKA.

Every dramatic piece opens with a Prelude or Prologue (प्रस्तावना) which is itself introduced by what is called the *Nândî*. This *Nândî* according to some must suggest the gist of the whole plot. The Sûtradhâra may sometimes retire after the recital of the Nândî, in which case another actor, called स्थापक (for he *establishes* as it were the topic of the play), takes his place. In the Prelude, which may begin with a brief allusion to the poet's literary attainments, his genealogy, &c., the Sûtradhâra or the Sthâpaka suggests the subject in the form of the Bîja, or by a simple beginning, or by naming the character about to enter, as in the Śâkuntala. He must please the audience with sweet songs descriptive of some season and couched in the Bhâratî vritti. The प्रस्तावना is of two kinds—(1) प्ररोचना as in the Rat., and (2) आमुख, in which the Sûtradhâra holds conversation with the actress or his assistants, bearing on the subject to be introduced.

This latter is of three kinds, of which one is प्रयोगातिशय. When the entry of a character is directly indicated by the Sūtradhâra, saying 'Here he enters,' that is Prayogâtiśaya.

The Prelude being over, the piece is commenced, being hereafter arranged and exhibited in the manner indicated in the three foreoging Sections. The whole matter should be well determined and divided into Acts and Scenes. A Nâṭaka may consist of from five to ten acts. The Hero should be of the Dhîrodātta class. The Sentiment should be शृङ्गार or वीर (or sometimes करुण), others being introduced as conducive to its development. Nothing should be introduced into the play, which either misbeseems the Hero or is discordant with the main sentiment. An Act must not be tiresomely long, should be full of *Rasa,* and introduced by *Viṣkambhaka,* &c, according to necessity. Its close is marked by the exit of all characters. Such incidents as journeys, massacres, wars &c, should not be represented in a play, they may only be indicated. The death of the Hero must never be exhibited. This accounts for the somewhat monotonous character of Sanskrit plays, and the absence of tragedies in Sanskrit[1]. The play should end, as it began, with a Benediction or prayer, called the Bharatavâkya, which is repeated by the principal personage, not in his dramatic character but as a member of the dramatic party (भरत) and contains an expression of their wishes for general prosperity and happiness. The unity of interest or action must be maintained throughout.

As regards the language to be used in a piece, the Hero and the higher characters speak in classical Sanskrit, while females and the

---

1 Wilson observes—They (the Hindu plays) never offer a calamitous conclusion, which, as Johnson remarks, was enough to constitute Tragedy in Shakespeare's days; and although they propose to excite all the emotions of the human breast. terror and pity included, they never effect this object by leaving a painful impression upon the mind of the spectator. The Hindus in fact have no Tragedy........ The absence of tragic catastrophe in the Hindu dramas is not merely an unconscious omission; such a catastrophe is prohibited by a positive rule. The conduct of what may be termed the classical drama of the Hindus is exemplary and dignified. Nor is its moral purport neglected; and one of their writers declares, in an illustration familiar to ancient and modern poetry, that the chief end of the Theatre is to disguise, by the insidious sweet, the unpalatable, but salutary bitter, of the cup.

minor characters speak in the different Pràkrit dialects.

The student will see from the foregoing sketch that the characteristic peculiarities of the Indian Drama are mainly three: (1) Its peculiar structure; (2) the absence of the distinction between Comedy and Tragedy; and (3) the diversity of language to be spoken by the characters. The above-mentioned general characteristics of a Nâṭaka belong with certain modifications to the other divisions of the Rûpaka as well.

BHĀSA'S PLAYS.

(CONTROVERSIES REGARDING BHĀSA'S PLAYS.)

In the history of Sanskrit Literature, a more interesting event than the discovery of thirteen dramas about the year 1909-10, by the late Mm. Ganapati Shastri of Trivandrum, has not happened. It seemed that the lost treasure of the plays of the famous dramatist Bhâsa was recovered and Bhâsa ceased to be a mere name. The names of these thirteen plays are:— (1) मध्यमव्यायोग (2) पञ्चरात्र (3) दूतवाक्य (4) दूतघटोत्कच (5) कर्णभार (6) ऊरुभङ्ग (7) प्रतिमा (8) अभिषेक (9) बालचरित (10) प्रतिज्ञायौगन्धरायण (11) स्वप्नवासवदत्त (12) अविमारक and (13) चारुदत्त. The first six of these are based on the Mahâbhârata, प्रतिमा and अभिषेक on the Râmâyaṇa, बालचरित on Harivanśa, प्रतिज्ञायौगन्धरायण and स्वप्नवासवदत्त are based on the stories of Vatsarâja and Vāsavadattā, which were current in the poet's time. The sources of अविमारक and चारुदत्त cannot be definitely traced. Unfortunately, in none of the manuscripts the name of the writer of these plays is mentioned. Mr. Ganapati Shastri, however, after having subjected these dramas to critical examination came to the conclusion that all the thirteen dramas were written by one author and that author was Bhâsa of great fame, so highly praised by Kâlidâsa and other poets. This Bhāsa theory propounded by Ganapati Shastri and supported by scholars like Mr. S. M. Paranjape, Hiwargaokar, Keith, Thomas, has been strongly contested by eminent scholars like Mr. P. V. Kane, Rangacharya Raddy, Bhattanath Shastri, Dr. Barnett and Messrs Krishna Pisharodi and Rama Pisharodi. Between these two extremes stand Dr. Sukthankar and Prof. Winternitz, who accept the Bhāsa theory with reserve, as in their opinion the evidence so far adduced is not quite conclusive.

Most of these scholars agree that all the thirteen plays are written by one and the same author. The grounds on which the common authorship of the plays has been established may be briefly stated thus:–

(1) All these plays begin with the stage-direction नान्द्यन्ते, ततः प्रविशति सूत्रधारः, whereas the classical dramas begin with the नान्दी.

(2) In these plays the word स्थापना is used for the prologue, whereas in the classical dramas the word प्रस्तावना is used.

(3) In none of these plays the name of the dramatist is mentioned, whereas in the classical plays the name of the dramatist and his family history are given.

(4) In most of these dramas the names of the chief Dramatic Personage are mentioned in the opening verse. This is technically called मुद्रालंकार.

(5) The भरतवाक्यs of the plays are almost the same. 'इमामपि महीं कृत्स्नां राजसिंहः प्रशास्तु नः is repeated with a slight variation in many plays.

(6) Striking similarity in the language and style of the plays. The use of the same imagery, the repetition of the same peculiar words, expressions, sentences, stanzas and quadrants of verses.

(7) In these plays grammatical solecisms or archaisms (आर्षप्रयोगs) are very common.

(8) In most of these plays a dramatic device called पताकास्थान (*i. e.* a sort of dramatic irony) is used.

The principal arguments which Ganapati Shastri has advanced to support his Bhāsa theory may be briefly stated thus:—

(1) The technique of all these plays, such as the commencement made by the सूत्रधार, the non-mention of the poet in the introductory part of the dramas &c. shows that the poet lived in times before the practice of beginning with the (नान्दी) and the mentioning of the poet's name came into vogue.

(2) The numerous grammatical archaisms (आर्षप्रयोगs) in disregard of Pāṇini's rules shows that the author of these plays should have lived long before Pâṇini.

(3) The disregard that is shown to certain rules found in the *Nâṭyaśâstra* in these plays, shows that their author was an ancient poet.

(4) These plays are characterised by an intensity of *Rasa* and by a marvellously exquisite flow of language and an all round grace of poetical elegance common only to the archaic compositions of the sages like *Vâlmîki* and *Vyâsa.* This shows that the author of these plays was an archaic poet of renown and lived in times when Sanskrit was the spoken language.

(5) Tradition ascribes the authorship of the *Swapnavâsavadattâ,* one of these thirteen plays, to Bhâsa. Therefore the author of the Sv. and the other closely similar plays should be Bhâsa himself, who has been extolled by Kâlidâsa and Bâṇa.

(6) Kalidasa has borrowed some expressions and ideas from some of these plays. A poet like Kālidâsa would imitate only a great poet like Bhâsa, whom he has highly praised and placed at the head of the ancient poets of great renown.

These arguments are on the whole sound. Only an exception may be taken to the assertion that Bhāsa is prior to Pâṇini.

We now propose to deal in detail with the evidence that has been adduced in favour of and against the authenticity of these thirteen plays.

(1) The great poet Bāṇa (7th century A. D.) pays compliment to Bhāsa in the following verse:—

'सूत्रधारकृतारम्भैर्नाटकैर्बहुभूमिकैः ।
सपताकैर्यशो लेभे भासो देवकुलैरिव ॥'

Genapati Shastri argues that Bâṇa by using the expression सूत्रधारकृतारम्भैः points out the distinguishing charucteristic of Bhāsa's plays, that they are begun by सूत्रधार. But the opponents of the Bhàsa theory contend that Bâṇa uses the expression सूत्रधारकृतारम्भैः, because it applies also to temples (देवकुलैः) to which Bhâsa's plays are compared. The expression is not used to point out any distinguishing quality of Bhāsa's plays. Again even if the Trivandrum group of thirteen plays answer the description सूत्रधारकृतारम्भैः they do not answer the test indicated by the expressions बहुभूमिकैः (with many roles) and सपताकैः (rich in episodes). Again this feature of these plays that they are begun with सूत्रधार does not belong to them alone. As Dr. Barnett has pointed out the मत्तविलासप्रहसन by महेन्द्रविक्रमवर्मन् (620 A. D.) begins with सूत्रधार. Other plays like the तपतीसंवरण and सुभद्राधनंजय by कुलशेखरवर्मन् (11th century A. D.) also begin in the same way. Hence this particular feature of these plays is not a proot of its antiquity.

(2) Daṇḍin (6th century A, D.) in his काव्यादर्श quotes the line लिम्पतीव तमोऽङ्गानि वर्षतीवाञ्जं नभः ' which is found in the बालचरित and the चारुदत्त.

(3) Vâkpati (800 A, D.) in his गउडवहो says that he finds pleasure in Bhāsa, friend of fire, the author of Raghuvanśa, Subandhu and Hārichandra—' भासम्मि जलणमित्ते कुंतीदेवे अ जस्स रघुआरे । सौबंधवे अ बंधम्मि हारीयंदे अ आणदो ' (भासे ज्वलनमित्रे कुन्तीदेवे च यस्य रघुकारे । सौबन्धवे च बन्धे हारीचन्द्रे च आनन्दः ।) Here Vâkpati calls Bhāsa ' a friend of fire ' and this epithet is significant. In many of Bhāsa's plays a conflagration or a fire incident is mentioned, वाक्पति has probably in his mind the fire in the play of स्वप्नवासवदत्त, when he calls Bhāsa ' friend of fire. '

(4) Bhâmaha (800 A. D) in his काव्यालंकार (Chap, IV) illustrates न्यायविरोध by describing the incidents in the life of Vātsarāja. The subject of Bhâmaha's criticism is found in the *Pratijnânâṭikâ*. Moreover the Prākrit sentences " अणेण मम भादा हदो, अणेण मम पिदा, अणेण मम सुदो " in the first act of *Pratijnânâṭikâ* are quoted in the form of a verse, " हतोऽनेन मम भ्राता मम पुत्रः पिता मम " by Bhâmaha in his discussion on *Nyâyavirodha*. Bhâmaha neither mentions the play nor the writer of the play, The subject of Bhâmaha's criticism is also found in the *Brihatkathâ*. Hence the opponents of the Bhāsa theory argue that Bhāmaha might have in his mind the बृहत्कथा when he illustrated न्यायविरोध. The passage " हतोऽनेन &c. " might as well have occurred in the बृहत्कथा. But this argument of the opponents has very little strength or meaning in it.

(5) Wāmana (900 A. D.) in his काव्यालंकारसूत्रवृत्ति (Adhi. V. chap. 3) quotes as an instance of व्याजोक्ति the following verse:—

' शरच्छशाङ्कगौरेण वाताविद्धेन भामिनि ।
काशपुष्पलवेनेदं साश्रुपातं मुखं मम ॥ '

This verse occurs in the Swapnavāsavadattā, Act. IV. In the same work Wāmana quotes ' यो भर्तृपिण्डस्य कृते न युध्येत् । It is the 4th line of a śloka in *Pratijnânâṭikâ*. Again Wāmana in the same work (Adhi. V. chap. I) quotes the verse,

' यासां बलिर्भवति मद्गृहदेहलीनां
हंसैश्च सारसगणैश्च विलुप्तपूर्वः ।
तास्वेव पूर्वबलिरूढयवाङ्कुरासु
बीजाञ्जलिः पतति कीटमुखावलीढः ॥ '

This verse occurs in the *Chârudatta* and the *Mrichhakaṭika.* The opponents of the Bhāsa theory say that the verse is quoted from the Mrichhakaṭika and not from the Chārudatta, because Wāmana also quotes the passage "द्यूतं हि नाम पुरुषस्य सिंहासनं राज्यम्" which occurs only in the Mrichhakaṭika.

(6) Rājaśekhara (9th century A. D.) refers to Bhāsa's plays in the following verse:—

'भासनाटकचक्रेऽपि च्छेकैः क्षिप्तैः परीक्षितुम ।
स्वप्नवासवदत्तस्य दाहकोऽभून्न पावकः ॥'

In this verse Rajaekśhara clearly hints that स्वप्नवासवदत्त was the best and most popular of all Bhāsa's plays, in his time. In the present group of 13 plays, the Sv. is surely the best. Hence it can be concluded that the author of our Sv. is Bhāsa. And as the whole group of 13 plays is the production of one author, Bhāsa is proved to be the author also of the other 12 plays.

(7) Abhinavagupta (10th century A. D.), in his भरतनाट्यवेदविवृति refers to the स्वप्नवासवदत्त in the passage, 'क्वचित् क्रीडा यथा स्वप्नवासवदत्तायाम.' In our Sv. Padmāwatî is represented as playing with a ball (Act II). So we can conclude that Abhinavagupta referred to our Sv. (Trivandrum Series).

(8) Bhojadev (11th century A. D.) in his शृङ्गारप्रकाश refers to the स्वप्नवासवदत्त in the following passage:—स्वप्नवासवदत्ते पद्मावतीमत्रस्थां द्रष्टुं राजा समुद्रगृहकं गतः । पद्मावतीरहितं च तदवलोक्य तस्या एव शयने सुष्वाप । वासवदत्तां च स्वप्नवदस्वप्ने ददर्श । स्वप्नायमानश्च वासवदत्तामाबभाषे । स्वप्नशब्देन चेह स्वापो वा स्वप्नदर्शनं वा स्वप्नायितं वा विवक्षितम ।

This is an exact summary of the incidents described in the fifth act of the Sv. of the Trivandrum grup.

(9) Sarvānanda (1159 A. D.) in his commentary on अमरकोश comments on the शृंगार rasa, and divides it into three classes and refers to the स्वप्नवासवदत्त in the following passage thus:—

त्रिविधः शृंगारः धर्मार्थकामभिन्नः । तत्राद्यो यथा नन्दयन्त्यां ब्राह्मणभोजनम । द्वितीयः स्वदिग्रामासात्कर्तुमुदयनस्य पद्मावतीपरिणयोऽर्थशृङ्गारः । तृतीयः स्वप्नवासवदत्ते तस्यैव वासवदत्तापरिणयः कामशृङ्गारः ।

In this passage Sarvānanda says that the theme of the Swapnavāsavadattā is the marriage of Udayana with Vāsavadattā. But the theme of the Sv. of the Trivandrum Series, is the grief of Udayana for his wife Vāsavadattā and his marriage with Padmāvatî and not his marriage with Vāsavadattā. Bhattanath Swami* argues on this

* Indian Antiquary, December 1916.

ground that the Sv. mentioned by Sarwānanda is a play different from that published in the Trivandram Series. It is however possible to answer Bhattanath Swami's contention. In Sarvānand's passage, अर्थश्रृङ्गार is not illustrated by the mention of any play. as धर्मश्रृङ्गार and कामश्रृङ्गार are. This may happen owing to some mistake in the order of the words in the passage. It may therefore be contended that Sarvānanda has illustrated both the अर्थश्रृङ्गार and कामश्रृङ्गार by the same play. For both the varieties of शृङ्गार are illustrated by the present Sv.

(10) Shardatanaya (12th century A. D.). in his भावप्रकाश defines प्रशान्त नाटक and mentions the Swapnavāsavadattā as belonging to this class and proceeds to point out the stages in the development of the action corresponding to the five सन्धिs mentioned by सुबन्धु:—

स्वप्नवासवदत्ताख्यमुदाहरणमत्र तु ।
आच्छिद्य भूपाद् व्यसनाद् देवी मागधिकाकरे ॥
न्यस्ता यतस्ततो न्यासान् मुखसंधिरयं भवेत् ।
न्यासस्य च प्रतिमुखं समुद्भेद उदाहृतम् ।
पद्मावत्या मुखं वीक्ष्य विशेषकविभूषितम् ।
जीवत्यावन्तिकेत्येतद् ज्ञातं भूमिभुजा यथा ॥
उत्कण्ठितेन सोद्वेगं बीजोक्तिर्नामकीर्तनम् ।
एहि वासवदत्तेति क यासीत्यादि दृश्यते ॥
सद्भावस्थितयोरेकं प्राप्यान्यस्य गवेषणम् ।
दर्शनस्पर्शनालापैरेतत्स्याद् बीजदर्शनम् ॥
(अत्रोदाहरणम्) चिरप्रसुप्तः कामो मे वीणया प्रतिबोधितः ।
तां तु देवीं न पश्यामि यस्या घोषवती प्रिया ॥
किं ते भूयः प्रियं कुर्यामिति वाग्यत्र नोच्यते ।
तमनुद्दिष्टसंहारमित्याहुर्भरतादयः ॥

In the above passage five things are mentioned as occurring in the Swapnavasavādattā—(1) That Vāsavadattā was rescued and entrusted to the care of Padmāvatī. This is the first stage called न्यास (We find this in Act I of our Sv.). (2) that Vatsarāja came to know from the beautiful तिलक on Padmāvatī's face that Vāsavadattā was alive. This is the second stage called न्याससमुद्भेद. (This does not correspond to the second *sandhi* in our play—Act V) (3) that the king in deep sorrow exclaimed " Come, Vāsavadattā, come, " This is the third stage called बीजोक्ति. (This is also found in our play in Act V). (4) That the king having obtained the lute *Ghoṣavatī* searched for Vāsavadattā, its beloved companion and talked about her. This is the fourth stage called बीजदर्शनम . (This as well as the śloka ' चिरप्रसुप्तः कामो मे ' &c. quoted in illustration of the सन्धि is found in our play, Act VI.) (5) Such words as ' किं ते भूयः प्रियं कुर्याम् ' are not mentioned at the close of the drama. This is the fifth stage called अनुद्दिष्टसंहार. (This peculiarity is also found in our play,) The opponents of the Bhāsa theory say that the Trivandrum Sv. is not the same as the Sv. mentioned by Sharadatanaya, because there is no correspondence between the second *sandhi* of the one and the second *sandhi* of the other. We think that this argument of the opposit ionists is not quite sound. If all the *sandhis* described by Sarvānanda correspond to those in the Trivandrum play except only one, we can reasonably conclude that the play reviewed by the commentator is the same as the one in our possession.

(11) In a work on dramaturgy called नाट्यदर्पण by Rāmachandra and Guṇachandra, (12th century A. D.) there is a reference to the Swapnavāsavadattā with an explicit mention of its author. The reference is as follows :—

यथा भासकृते स्वप्नवासवदत्ते शेफालिकाशिलातलमवलोकय ।

वत्सराजः— पादाक्रान्तानि पुष्पाणि सोष्म चेदं शिलातलम् ।

नूनं काचिदिहासीना मां दृष्ट्वा सहसा गता ॥

This verse is not found in the Trivandrum Swapnavāsavadattā and therefore Prof. Sylvain Levi* concludes that the author of the Trivandrum play is not Bhāsa. But the absence of a verse or passage in a work cannot be taken as a proof that the work is not authentic. For a verse or passage might be left out by the oversight of a copyist. The verse that is omitted in the Trivandrum Sv. has a proper place for it in the play in the first scene of the fourth act. In our present edition the verse is thus inserted after the stage direction, उभावुपविशतः, occurring after the third verse. It may as well be inserted immediately after the stage direction, तथा कुर्वन्ति, occurring after the second verse.

---

* Prof. Sylvain Levi has reviewed Nāṭyadarpaṇa and Sâgarnandin's Nataka-laksaṇa-ratna-kośa in Journal Asiatique, Oct. Dec. 1923.

(12) Sāgarnandin in his work on dramaturgy entitled नाटकलक्षणरत्नकोश, while discussing the manner of transition from the prologue to the main scene makes the following reference to the Swapnavāsavadattā:—

"यथा स्वप्नवासवदत्ते नेपथ्ये सूत्रधारः उत्सारणां श्रुत्वा पठति अये कथं तपोवनेऽप्युत्सारणा। (विलोक्य) कथं मन्त्री यौगन्धरायणो वत्सराजस्य राज्यप्रत्यानयनं पद्मावतीयजनेनोत्सार्यते। इत्युत्सारणाशब्दोऽत्र पूर्वकप्रयोगमुत्सार्य नाटकार्थसूचक इति प्रयोगातिशयः।"

The extract from the Sv. in the above passage does not exactly agree with the introductory portion in the Trivandrum Sv. Hence Prof. Levi and other opponents of the Bhāsa theory conclude that the Trivandrum Sv. is not the authentic work of Bhȃsa. We do not think that this conclusion is correct. For the two passages are identical in sense though there is some difference in language. Sāgarnandin does not seem to have quoted the passage. word for word, from the Sv. The passage in question seems to be a summary of the introductory portion in the Sv. The passage in our Sv. is fuller in details and written in a more elegant language than the extract in Sāgarnandin's work.

(13) Abhinavagupta in his commentary on ध्वन्यालोक quotes the following *áryà* as occurring in the Swapnavāsavadattā—

संचितपक्ष्मकपाटं नयनद्वारं स्वरूपतडनेन।
उद्घाटय सा प्रविष्टा हृदयगृहं मे नृपतनूजा॥

The verse is not found in the Trivandrum Sv. Therefore the opponents of the Bhāsa theory conclude that there must be another Sv. of which the Trivandrum Sv. is an altered version. Now it must be admitted that the verse quoted by Abhinavagupta cannot have a place in the present edition of our Sv. Because the verse expresses the feeling of a lover on first beholding his beloved. There is no occasion for such an effusion in the present play, inasmuch as its main theme is the sorrow of Vatsarāja for his wife Vāsavadattā with whom he had enjoyed many years of conjugal felicity. It is not, however, necessary to assume the existence of another Swapnavāsavadattā The commentator might have made a mistake in mentioning the source of the verse.

(14) Viśwanāth (1500 A. D.) in his साहित्यदर्पण (Parc. VI) quotes the following verse as occurring in the Bālacharita.:—

उत्साहातिशयं वत्स ! तव बाल्यं च पश्यतः।
मम हर्षविषादाभ्यामाक्रान्तं युगपन्मनः॥

This verse is not found in the Trivandram Bālacharita. The commentator of the साहित्यदर्पण says that the verse is addressed by Paraśu Rāma to Śrī Rāma. The play referred to in the Sāhityadarpaṇa evidently deals with the life of Śrī Rāma. The Trivandrum play deals with the childhood of Śrī Kṛiṣṇa and therefore is a different play from the former. There is no evidence to prove that the Bālacharitra from which this verse is quoted was the work of Bhàsa.

(15) In sanskrit anthologies there are 13 stanzas ascribed to Bhāsa. None of these stanzas is found in the Trivandrum plays attributed to Bhāsa. Mr. Ramavatar Sarma and other opponents of the Bhāsa theory make this an argument for denying the authorship of Bhāsa to these plays. But this argument is not sound. Though none of these stanzas are found in any of the thirteen plays hitherto discovered, plays may yet be discovered in which some of these stanzas may be found. Again in these anthologies the names of the authors are often wrongly quoted. The verses attributed even to Kālidāsa and other well-known dramatists are not found in their works. One of these thirteen stanzas that are ascribed to Bhāsa:

पेया सुरा प्रियतमामुखमीक्षणीयं
ग्राह्यः स्वभावललितो विकटश्च वेषः ।
येनेदमीदृशमदृश्यत मोक्षवर्त्म
दीर्घायुरस्तु भगवान् स पिनाकपाणिः ॥

is found in the मत्तविलासप्रहसन of Mahendratrivikramawarman, who lived in the earlier part of the 7th century A. D.

(16) The Chārudatta, one of the Trivandrum group of plays, has been a subject of sharp controversy among scholars. The close similarity between the Chārudatta and the Mṛichchakaṭika and many identical and analogous passages in the two plays indisputably establish a genetic relationship between two plays. This has raised the question which of the two is the original. Dr. Sukthankar, Dr. Belwalkar, Dr. Keith and other scholars have dealt with this question and come to the conclusion that the Chārudatta is prior to the Mṛichchakaṭika and is the original on which the latter is based. Mr. Kane, Raddy Shastri, Bhattanath Swamin and others take the opposite view and maintain that the Chārudatta is a mean product of plagiarism. We agree with Dr. Sukthankar and his adherents and hold that the Chārudatta is the original, which has been worked up into the magnificent play of the Mṛichchakaṭika by Śudraka.

(17) Two Malayalam scholars, Mr. A. K. Pisharodi and Mr. K.

R. Pisharodi, have propounded a theory that these thirteen plays are compilations made from different sources by the Chakkyars of Kerala to meet the demand for dramas suitable for the reformed Kerala stage. These Chakkyars are a class hereditary actors, who stage Sanskrit plays on occasions of temple festivals. Select scenes and acts from these thirteen dramas are reported to have been staged by these Chakkyars. The principal arguments by which the Pisharodis base their theory are—That there was a large demand for dramas suitable for the reformed Kerala stage, that dramas were compiled to meet this demand, that there is a tradition that such compilations were made in ancient times and that select acts from some of these thirteen plays were staged by the Chakkyars. But where is the evidence to prove that the Trivandrum group of plays are compilations made by the Chakkyars? The above arguments prove nothing regarding the thirteen plays except that select acts from some of them were staged by the Chakkyars.

We have thus examined the evidence adduced and the arguments set forth by the protagonists and opponents of the Bhāsa theory. We maintain that the evidence in favour of the Bhāsa theory is much stronger and we are led to the conclusion that the author of the Sv. group of plays is the ancient poet Bhāsa of great fame in Sanskrit literature.

THE DATE OF BHĀSA.

The date of Bhāsa, like that of many other Sanskrit writers is very difficult to determine for want of sufficient data and of reliable chronology to draw our conclusion from. It is not possible to accurately fix the date of Bhāsa. All that we can do with the help of the scanty materials at our disposal is to fix approximately the limits of the period during which the poet must have flourished. That Bhāsa is an ancient poet. much anterior to Kàlidàsa, is a fact established beyond doubt by the very reference to him by that poet in the prologue of the Málavikágnimitra. The internal evidence of his style which is absolutely free from the artificiality of the Kávya literature, the presence of a number of a archaic forms and uncouth constructions in his works, the old-world atmosphere in which his characters move—all these point to his great antiquity. But it is necessary to determine to what period of antiquity our poet belonged.

We shall first proceed to fix the date later than which Bhāsa could not have lived. The earliest direct reference to Bhāsa is, as stated above, by Kālidāsa in his Māl, and it has been almost settled that Kāli. flourished in the first century B. C. From this it is evident that Bhāsa was recognised as an ancient poet of established fame in the first century B. C.; and it will not be unreasonable to suppose that at least a century must have elapsed before Bhāsa came to be so recognised in Kālidāsa's time. We can, therefore, safely conclude that Bhāsa could not have lived at a period later than the 2nd century B. C. The Mṛchchakaṭika enables us to push this date still further back. Before the discovery of Bhāsa's plays the Mṛch. of Śūdraka was supposed to be the earliest extant drama. But now that Bhāsa's Chārudatta is discovered, the Mṛch. on close examination and comparison appears to be an adaptation and amplification of the former. Now according to Vincent A. Smith S'ūdraka ascended the throne in 220 B. C. and died in 197 B. C. The question whether Mrch was written by him or by his court poets Saumilla and Rāmila, in the name of their patron, has nothing to do with the date of the play. The Mṛch., therefore, must have been composed in the second or more probably in the 3rd century B. C. But Kauṭilya's Arthaśātra enables us to place Bhāsa in times still prior to this Kauṭilya, who is the same as Chāṇakya, the famous minister of Chandragupta (the year of whose accession to the throne is determined to be 321 B. C.) cites in his Arthaśāstra as an authority, the verse—

नवं शरावं सलिलैः सुपूर्णं सुसंस्कृतं दर्भकृतोत्तरीयम् ।
तत्तस्य मा भून्नरकं स गच्छेद्यो भर्तृपिंडस्य कृते न युध्येत् ॥ (Kau. A. 10. 3)

The words अपीह श्लोकौ भवतः which precede the verse in the Artha, show that it is quoted from some other work. And the verse, as we know now, is in its proper place in the Pratijnāyaugandharāyaṇa (IV, 3). Now at least a period of half a century must be allowed to Bhāsa to have acquired such a celebrity to be quoted as an authority by such a great personage as Chāṇakya. Hence it follows that Bhāsa lived in a period earlier than that of Chāṇakya, *i. e.* 4th century (about 370 B. C.) B. C. This conclusion is supported by the fact that Bhāsa mentions the Arthaśāstra of Bṛhaspati in his Pratimânâṭaka*

* " भोः काश्यपगोत्रोऽस्मि साङ्गोपाङ्गं वेदमधीये, मानवीयं धर्मशास्त्रं, माहेश्वरं योगशास्त्रं, बार्हस्पत्यमर्थशास्त्रं, मेधातिथेर्न्यायशास्त्रं प्राचेतसं श्राद्धकल्पं च "

In this passage, which is addressed by Rāvaṇa to Rāma, the Nyāyaśāstra of Medhātithi is mentioned. The opponents of the Bhāsa

(p. 79) and does not seem to be aware of the existence of Chāṇakya's Arthaśāstra, which he would have surely referred to, had he lived after Chāṇakya. The Mahābhārata (Śānti p. 59) tells us that Bṛhaspati was a writer on Arthaśāstra, who epitomised the original Daṇḍanīti composed by Brahmā. Kauṭilya too acknowledges Bṛihaspati as his predecessor as a writer on Artha. It follows, therefore, that Chāṇa.'s Artha. was not in existence in Bhāsa's time. So we fix 370 or thereabout as the downward date for Bhāsa.

The internal evidence furnished by two of Bhāsa's plays enables us to fix the upward limit that can be assigned to Bhāsa. The two plays are the Pratijñānāṭikā and the Svapnavāsavadattā, which are based on historical events. The three kings that figure in these plays are historical characters. King Udayana or Vatsa of Kauśambi, King Pradyota of Ujjayinī, and King Darśaka of Rājagṛha (Magadha) are mentioned both in the Purāṇas and in the Buddhistic and Jain works. The genealogies given in the Viṣṇu and Vāyu Purāṇas warrant us in concluding that Udayana and Pradyota were contemporaries, while the Buddhistic and Jain works tell us that Pradyota and Ajātaśatru were contemporaries of Buddha and Mahāvīra. (See Rhys David's Buddhist India p. 3).

Now we know from the Vāyu and other Purāṇas that Darśaka was the immediate successor of Ajātaśatru. Putting together the statements of the Buddhistic and Jain works and Bhāsa's treatment of Pradyota and Darśaka as contemporaries we come to the conclusion that Ajāta. died before Pradyota and his successor was thus a younger contemporary of that King. Thus Udayana, Pradyota and Darśaka were all contemporaries of Buddha and Mahāvīra. And according to Vincent A. Smith the dates of the reigns of Darśaka and his immediate

---

theory maintain that the Nyāyaśāstra of Medhātithi here mentioned is Medhātithi's commentary on Manu and therefore the author of these plays must have lived after the 10th century. For Medhātithi, Manu's commentator, lived in the 10th century. But the author, whoever he might be, would not mention Medhātithi along with the names of such ancient sages as Manu, Maheśwar, Bṛihaspati and Prachetas. Dr. Sukthankar has argued that the Nyāyaśāstra must be an independent work and of the same order as the other śāstras. The boast of Rāvaṇa that he has studied Medhātithi's commentary would be such a ludicrous anachronism that even a plagiarist of the 10th century would not commit such an absurd mistake.

successor are 475 and 450 B. C. (Early His. of India pp. 38-39) It follows therefore that Darśaka, Udayana and Pradyota must have been contemporaries at least in the period between 475 and 450 B. C. These dates give us the limit on other side, *i. e.* the limit before which Bhāsa could not have lived. We feel therefore justified in fixing 450 B. C. as the superior and 370 as the inferior limit to the period between which Bhāsa must have lived and flourished.

BHĀSA'S MERITS AS A DRAMATIST.

Bhāsa was certainly a talented dramatist judging from the number and variety of his dramas. The principal characteristics of his plays that strike the reader most are their simplicity in construction, naturalness in style, and realism in description as well as the dramatic qualities of vigour, life and action and sharpness of characterisation. The plot of each drama is unfolded in a few effective situations that follow each other in their natural sequence and that are calculated to bring out the sentiment in hand. The style is simple, clear and sweet.* It is free from all artificiality and rhetorical devices noticeable in the later Sanskrit drama. The words are simple and apt. Long compounds and elaborate figures of speech so common in the later Sanskrit literature are conspicuous by their absence. The compounds used by Bhāsa consist at the most of six or seven words and these too are rarely used. Sometimes we come across an artificial style with the use

---

*(1) गुणानां वा विशालानां सत्काराणां च नित्यशः ।
कर्तारः सुलभा लोके विज्ञातारस्तु दुर्लभाः ॥ (Sv. Act. IV-9)

(2) काष्ठादग्निर्जायते मथ्यमानाद् भूमिस्तोयं खन्यमाना ददाति ।
सोत्साहानां नास्त्यसाध्यं नराणां मार्गारब्धाः सर्वयत्नाः फलन्ति ॥
(Praty. Act-I-18).

(3) शिक्षा क्षयं गच्छति कालपर्ययात् सुबद्धमूला निपतन्ति पादपाः ।
जलं जलस्थानगतं च शुष्यति हुतं च दत्तं च तथैव तिष्ठति ॥
(Karṇâbhara S'l. 19)

(4) कथं लम्बसटः सिंहो मृगेण विनिपात्यते ।
गजो वा सुमहान् मत्तः शृगालेन निहन्यते ॥ (Abh. Act. III-19

of alliteration and Yamakas.. The figures that commonly embellish his style are the Upamâ and Utprekṣâ. Far-fetched conceits are never indulged in. In spite of its simplicity, Bhāsa's style is sometimes obscure. Sentences are sometimes elliptical and it is difficult to get at their meaning unless we supply the ellipsis. Sometimes the connection between sentences is left by the poet to be found out by their reader. It is his compressed style that makes some part of Bhāsa's writing obscure; and the reader in order to clear up the obscurities must have recourse to a comparison with his originals, the Râmâyaṇa and the Mahâbhârata as well as his own works. Another feature of Bhāsa's style that contributes to its obscurity is his use of forms of words and expressions that became obsolete in the later Sanskrit literature. These archaic or ungrammatical forms and constructions clearly show that the style of Bhāsa was greatly influenced by the style of the epics. Bhāsa no doubt drew his inspiration from the Epics and the dominating influence of the Epics is clearly seen everywhere in his dramas. Along with many beautiful expressions and ideas of the epics, along with their naturalness and simplicity of diction Bhāsa seems to have unconsciously adopted even the solecisms from his great originals. Or more probably Sanskrit being the living tongue in his time, Bhāsa did not like later writers feel obliged to use forms and constructions strictly in conformity with the hard and fast rules of Pâṇini's grammar.

Bhāsa's descriptions are simple, natural and straight-forward. He aims more at producing cumulative effect by grouping together striking details than finishing his pictures with a few suggestive strokes. His descriptions. beautiful and realistic as they are, are never touched with the glow of imagination, and are never lifted into the sphere of the sublime like those of Kâlidâsa and Bhavabhūti.

---

‡(1) रघुकुलप्रदीपस्य सर्वलोकनयनाभिरामस्य च सुविपुलमहाग्रीवस्य सुग्रीवस्य च &c. (Abhiśeka).

(2) निहतपतितगजतुरगनररुधिरकलिलभूमिप्रदेशस्य विक्षिप्तवर्मचर्मातपत्रचामरतोमरशरकुन्त &c. (Ūrubhanga P. 90).

(3) सम्प्राप्ता हरिवरबाहुसम्प्रगुप्ता
किष्किन्धा तव नृप बाहुसम्प्रगुप्ता । (Abhiṣeka I–7).

(4) शून्यः प्राप्तो यदि रथो भग्नो मम मनोरथः ।
नूनं दशरथं नेतुं कालेन प्रेषितो रथः ॥ (Pratimā. II–11).

Bhāsa's characters are sharply distinguished or individualised. Every character is strongly marked with its own individuality, and made to help the development of the plot each in its way. The predominance of male characters and the martial spirit exhibited by most of them is a notable feature of Bhāsa's dramas. The dramas clearly reflect the spirit of an heroic age.

One of the striking features of Bhāsa's dramas is the use of a dramatic device called पताकास्थान in order to excite astonishment. In the *Prâtijnânâṭaka* (Act, II), Mahāsena, father of Vāsavadattā and his queen are speaking about the merits of several suitors of Vāsavadattā. The King then asks his queen, "Which of these, do you think, is worthy of our daughter?" Presently a chamberlain enters and says, 'Vatsarāja.' He brings the joyful tidings of Vātsarāja's capture and being unable to contain himself with joy bursts out "Vatsarāja." Similarly in the Abhiṣeka (Act V), when Rāvaṇa taunts Sītā and says to her, "When that wretch of a mortal together with his brother Lakṣmaṇa is killed by Indrajit, by whom wilt thou be set free?" A Rākṣasa enters and says, "By Rāma."

Lastly a word about the influence of Bhāsa on the later Sanskrit literature. The influence of Bhāsa is most seen in the dramas of Kālidāsa. We find that Kālidāsa refers with great respect to Bhāsa in his Mālavikāgnimitra¶ as an illustrious Sanskrit poet, probably conscious of the debt he owed to his great predecessor Sometimes the coincidence of the descriptions of the same scenes and events is so striking that we cannot but feel that Kālidāsa drew his inspiration from Bhāsa,‖ As Ganapati Shastri, the most enthusiastic admirer of Bhāsa says, "That the dramatic excellence of Bhāsa has been a model for Kālidāsa could well be established from the fact that the S'ākuntala is mostly adorned with the ideas and expressions peculiar to Bhāsa." However it must not be forgotten that whatever Kālidāsa borrowed bears the unmistakable stamp of his individuality and conclusively proves the immense superiority of the premier poet of India over his illustrious predecessor.

¶ प्रथितयशसां भाससौमिल्लकविपुत्रादीनां प्रबन्धानतिक्रम्य वर्तमानकवेः कालिदासस्य क्रियायां कथं परिषदो बहुमानः ।

‖ Cf. the description of अशोकवन in the *Abhiṣeka* with Kaṇva's address to the creepers in the fourth act of the S'ākuntala and the descriptions of the earth as it appears to Meghanāda descending down from above in the *Avimâraka* and to Duṣyanta coming down from heaven to Hemakūṭa in the S'ākuntala.

THE SVAPNAVĀSAVADATTA.

(A FEW CRITICAL REMARKS.)

The Svapnavāsavadattā is undoubtedly the poet's masterpiece and the fruit of his mature genius. That it was considered the best among Bhāsa's works in Rājaśekhara's time (9th century A D.) is proved from the well-known verse of that poet, "भासनाटकचक्रेऽपि च्छेकैः क्षिप्ते परीक्षितुम् । स्वप्नवासवदत्तस्य दाहकोऽभून्न पावकः ॥ ". The play has been commented upon and citations have been made from it by celebrated writers on rhetoric like Wāmana, Rāmachandra, Abhinavagupta, Shāradātanaya and others. The plot of the drama is drawn from the romantic stories about Udayana and Vāsavadattā, which were current in the poet's time and which seem to have captivated popular imagination. The Svapnavāsavadatta forms in substance the sequel of the Pratijnāyaugandharāyaṇa. The main theme of the drama is the sorrow of Udayana for his wife Vāsavadattā, believed by him to have perished in a conflagration. In the legend that has come down to us in the Kathāsaritsāgara, which is said to be a faithful version of the Bṛihatkathā, Udayana is allowed to suspect that Vāsavadattā might be alive. But Bhāsa with his true dramatic genius depicts him as having not the least hope that he might be re-united with his beloved wife. The poet shows considerable skill in working out the plot of the drama. In Act I, the device of introducing a Brahmachārin is effectively used to acquaint the audience with the reported death of Vāsavadattā and the minister in a fire at Lâvaṇaka. In Act V, the incidents are cleverly contrived to bring the king who is asleep and Vāsavadattā together. The situation, in which Vâsavadattâ mistakes the sleeping king for Padmāvatî, is naturally evolved, for the chamber in which he was sleeping was very dimly lighted and she was naturally unwilling to disturb her mistress, who she hoped had fallen into deep slumber. The vision of Vâsavadattâ, which the king gets in his sleep, is a natural outcome of the state of his mind, which is ever haunted by the agonizing thought of her destruction in the fire. In Act VI, the king's grief rises to its climax on the discovery of the lute Ghoṣavatî and the catastrophe of the drama is reached. The Swapnavāsavadattā, like the other play of Bhāsa, is remarkable for the swiftness of its action. These are no impediments in the way. Every incident in the drama has a direct bearing on the catastrophe. As Dr. Sukthankar says, " A studied unity of purpose runs through the drama. binding all its component parts closely together. The action is kept free from all trace of melodramatic surprise: the movement is smooth, measured and characterized by classic dignity."

The interest in the story of the play does not so much lie in the incidents as in the development of the principal characters in it. The hero of the play, Udayana, is of an exalted character. He is a faithful, devoted husband and not the gay, careless if courteous gentleman of Harsa's dramas. Vāsavadattā is a devoted, unselfish wife, who cheerfully suffers martyrdom for the good of her husband. very different from the jealous if high-minded wife of Harsa's plays. Of all the dramas based on the legends about Udayana the Swapnavāsavadatta is by far the best. As Dr. Sukhthankar observes. "The picture painted in it in broad outline is as different from the scenes of petty intrigue, gallant adventure and shallow sentimentality of plays like the Priyadarśikâ and the Ratnāvali as the grand mural frescoes of Ajanta are from the miniature paintings of a later age."

The prevailing sentiment (रस) in the Svapnavāsavadatta is विप्रलम्भश्रृङ्गार (Love-in-separation) and with it is associated करुणरस (the sentiment of pathos). The अर्थश्रृङ्गार which is revealed in Udayana's marrying Padmāvatī, with the intention of recovering his lost territories, is subordinate to the central sentiment. The sentiment of विप्रलम्भश्रृङ्गार is intensified by the aid of irony, which the poet so effectively and frequently employs in the Swapnavāsavadatta. A striking instance of it is seen in Act III of the play, where Vāsavadattā is asked to weave the wedding-garland for Padmāvati, her rival, on the score of her noble birth and skill in the art.

The Svapnavāsavadatta is a noble creation of the poet's brain. It depicts conjugal love in a most exalted form and is a noble heritage left to us by the great poet. As Dr. Sukhthankar observes:—"The aim of the dramatist is to portray on the one hand the complete self-abnegation of the noble queen, who suffers martyrdom for the sake of her lord with cheerful resignation, and on the other hand to depict her husband as at heart true to his love, while unwillingly submitting to the exigencies of the life of a king. The burden of the story is the triumph of stead-fast, unfaltering, undying Love for which no sacrifice is too great."

THE PRINCIPAL CHARACTERS IN THE PLAY.

VATSARĀJA (HERO).

Udayana, known as Vatsarāja, is a prince of exalted character. He is dearly loved and highly honoured by the people. The Brahmachārin, who comes from Lāvâṇaka to the hermitage at the same time as Yaugandharāyaṇa and Vâsavadattā, reports to them that Lāvāṇaka lost all charm on the departure of the king from it and became too lonely to live in. Vatsarāja is a faithful, devoted husband unlike the hero of Harṣa's Ratnāvali or Priyadarśikā, who is ever ready to engage in a new love intrigue. When he was informed that his beloved queen and minister perished in the village conflagration he was ready to sacrifice his life in the same fire. It was chiefly out of political motives that he married Padmāvatî, sister of the king of Magadha. His love for his beloved Vāsavadattā, whom he imagines lost, is as deep and constant as ever. Padmâvati, his new beautiful queen never supersedes in his heart old beloved Vâsavadattâ, whose memory he cherishes with the tenderest affection. He confesses this to his companion Vidūṣaka, " पद्मावती बहुमता मम यद्यपि रूपशीलमाधुर्यैः । वासवदत्ताबद्धं न तु तावन्मे मनो हरति ॥ " (Act VI-4). Most touching is the manner in which he mourns for Vāsavadattâ. He is moved to tears whenever he talks about her. As he says to the Vidûṣaka, " It is difficult to cast off deep-rooted love; grief revives at each fresh remembrance. It is the course of nature that on shedding tears in this world the mind obtains relief, having paid off the debt. " (Act IV-6). His grief is inconsolable. He never forgets Vāsavadattā and never ceases to mourn for her. When the lute Ghoṣawatī is discovered, his grief reaches its climax and he falls into a swoon. When the chamberlain from the king of Ujjain comes to him with a congratulatory message and tries to console him, he replies, " महासेनस्य दुहिता शिष्या देवी च मे प्रिया । कथं सा न मया शक्या स्मर्तुं देहान्तरेष्वपि ॥ " (Act VI-11) Thus Vatsarāja passes through a prolonged period of sorrow and suffering, because of his deep and sincere love for Vâsavadattâ. The vision, that he gets of Vâsavadattâ while sleeping in the Sea Mansion, is the natural outcome of the state his mind, haunted by the agonizing thought of her supposed loss. His love and sorrow, however, chasten and elevate his character and call forth all the innate nobility of his nature.

VĀSAVADATTĀ.

Vāsavadatta is a devoted, selfless wife, who sacrifices her feelings for the sake of her lord. She readily agrees to help the minister in his scheme, though it involves immense sorrow and suffering to her. Her self-abnegation and self-sacrifice are beyond all praise. What an irony of fate that this noble queen was entrusted to the care of a young princess, who ere long was to be wedded to her own lord! When the king weds Padmāvatī she involuntarily exclaims, "आर्यपुत्रोऽपि नाम परकीयः संवृत्तः" She however behaves with great respect and affection towards her young guardian and co-wife. She exercises admirable self-restraint during the period of her life in disguise. When from the jasmin-bower she hears the king declare to the Vidūṣaka that Padmāvatī has not been able to wean his heart from his beloved Vāsavadatta, she feels supremely happy and says, "दत्तवेतनमस्य परिखेदस्य। अहो अज्ञातवासोऽप्यत्र बहुगुणः संपद्यते." When Padmāvatī falls ill, she feels very sorry because her husband, distressed with separation, lost thereby a source of consolation. As she says, "अहो अकरुणाः खल्वीश्वरा मे। विरहपर्युत्सुकस्यार्यपुत्रस्य विश्रमस्थानभूतेयमपि नाम पद्मावत्यस्वस्था जाता". (p. 47) All through the long period of separation from her lord she shows calm resignation to her lot. No repining, no outburst of ill temper mars the serenity and dignity with which she endures her suffering.

PADMĀVATĪ.

Padmāvatī is a beautiful, innocent, high-minded princess, who desires to marry Vatsarája because he is known to be tender-hearted (सानुक्रोश). Though young she accepts the guardianship of such an elderly lady as Vāsavadattā, to keep her promise which was implied in her proclamation. Her simplicity and innocence impart a charm to her character. She is perfectly highminded and absolutely free from jealousy. When from the jasmin-bower, she hears the king tell the Vidūsaka in confidence that he still loves Vāsavadattā, she does not at all feel offended and rebukes her maid who finds fault with the king saying, "सदाक्षिण्य एवार्यपुत्रो य इदानीमप्यार्याया वासवदत्ताया गुणान् स्मरति ॥" (p. 35) When the chamberlain of Mahāsena, King of Ujjain and the nurse of Vāsavadattā were announced, she said to the king, "आर्यपुत्र प्रियं मे ज्ञातिकुलस्य कुशलवृत्तान्तं श्रोतुम्।" (p. 55). When the picture-board, on which the portraits of the king and Vāsavadatta, were painted, is presented to the king, Padmāvatī looking at the board. shows her respect to the portrait of Vāsavadattā by saying, " आर्यपुत्र चित्रगतं गुरुजनं दृष्ट्वाभिवादयितुमिच्छामि । " (p. 60). Lastly when the lady entrusted to her care is discovered to be Vāsavadattā, Padmāvatī falls at her feet, begging to be pardoned for having treated her as a friend, in ignorance of her true character (आर्ये सखीजनसमुदाचारेणाजानत्यातिक्रान्तः समुदाचारः । तच्छीर्षेण प्रसादयामि । " p. 64)

The Vidūṣaka.

In most of the Sanskrit plays the Vidūṣaka is introduced as a constant, trusty companion of the King, the hero. He is a Brāhmaṇ He excites laughter by his strange, ugly appearance and funny remarks. His business is to help the King in his love intrigues. He is a glutton and always speaks of dainties. In our play, however, the Vidūṣaka is comparatively more serious and less comical. But he is a glutton, since he complains that he cannot digest food, does not get sleep and is afflicted with gout. As the King is not engaged in any love intrigue, the Vidūṣaka has not to play his usual part in any such affair. His chief duty is to console the king in his distress at the supposed loss of his beloved Vāsavadattā. He shows cleverness and presence of mind on more occasions than one. While the king and the Vidūṣaka were conversing about Vāsavadattā in the Pramadāvana, the king's eyes were filled with tears and the Vidusaka went to bring water for washing the king's face. While coming back with water he met Padmāvatī, who questioned him as to why he was carrying water. He replied with ready wit that the king's face was full of tears, owing to the pollen of Kāśa flowers being wafted into his eyes by the wind (p. 39). Again when he found that the king was in a awkward situation at the sudden appearance of Padmāvatī on the scene while the king was in a sorrowful mood, he relieved the king of his embarrassment by reminding him that it was time for him to move, since he must be ready to receive the king of Magadha in the afternoon (p. 39–40).

THE PLOT OF THE DRAMA.

Yaugandharāyaṇa the minister of Udayana is anxious to recover for his master all the territories of which he was deprived by a king named Aruṇi. This necessitates and alliance with the king of Magadha. The minister is therefore anxious that his master should wed Padmāvati, sister of the king of Magadha. But Udayana is too deeply attached to his queen Vāsavadattā to entertain any such proposal. The minister therefore forms a scheme and induces Vāsavadattā to help him in it. During the king's absence on hunting a expedition, the minister spreads a report that he and Vāsavadattā have perished in the fire that consumed the village of Lāvāṇaka, in which they resided, Yaugandharāyaṇa and Vāsavadattā then leave the village in disguise and arrive at a hermitage where Padmāvati, the Magadha princess happens to come. Yaugandharāyaṇa who is in the disguise of a recluse gives Vāsavadattā in charge of Padmāvati, representing that she is his sister, whose husband has gone on a journey. Vāsavadattā lives with Padmāvati under the assumed name of Awantikà. After some time the King is persuaded to marry Padmāvati, who is a beautiful, high-minded princess. But the King's love for Vāsavadattā is as strong and as fresh as ever He mourns for Vāsavadattâ whom he imagines lost. Once while the king and the Vidūṣaka were in the pleasure garden, the king in the course of conversation confessed to his friend that he still cherished love for Vāsavadatta. Padmāvati and Vāsavadattā heard all this conversation from the jasmin bower. Afterwards Padmāvati is seized by a severe headache and it is arranged that she should sleep in the Ocean Pavilion. The king goes there to comfort her but finds that she is not there. He lies down on the bed spread for Padmāvati and soon falls fast asleep. In the meanwhile Vāsavadattā comes to comfort Padmā-vatī. She mistakes the sleeping form for that of her mistress and sits on the bed. The king begins to address Vāsavadattā in a dream. Vāsavadattā knowing her mistake goes away, but not without replacing the king's hand which was hanging down from the couch. After the king has awakened from his sleep he receives the joyful news that the enemy's forces were scattered and that he must now be ready to deal the finishing stroke and destroy Aruṇi. One day the king's sorrow for Vāsavadattā is renewed and rises to the highest pitch on the discovery of the lute Ghoṣavatī, her beloved companion. That very day a messenger comes from Mahāsena of Ujjain and his queen with a message of congratulation to Udayana on his complete victory over his enemy and a present of the picture of the nuptials of himself and Vāsavadattā. Padmāvati recognizes in the lady painted in the picture the features of the sister left in her charge by the Brahman recluse. Yaugandharâyaṇa soon arrives on the scene to explain how he had devised the whole plan to promote the interests of his master.

THE GEOGRAPHY OF THE PLAY.

कौशाम्बी—The chief scene of the play is laid at Kauśâmbi, the capital of king Udayana who ruled over the Vatsa country. Vatsa is thus described in the Kathas.—अस्ति वत्स इति ख्यातो देशो दर्पोपशान्तये । स्वर्गस्य निर्मितो धात्रा प्रतिमल्ल इव क्षितौ ॥. The city of Kauśambi was very famous in ancient times, being mentioned in the Rāmāyana of Vālmiki. The Kathās. describes its grandeur as लक्ष्मीविलासवसतिर्भूतलस्येव कर्णिका. (II 1-5). It was founded by Kauśāmba (son of Kusa), ten in descent from Pururavas It is now reduced to an insignificant village called Kosam, on the river Jamnà, near Allahabad.

मगध—The country of Magadha corresponds roughly to the southern part of the modern province of Bihar. Its capital राजगृह has been identified with the modern Rajgir. It was Bimbasāra (528 B C.—500 B. C.) who built राजगृह and made it his capital.

काम्पिल्य—Kāmpilya is the name of a town in the country of the Pānchālas, where the स्वयंवर of Draupadī was held. It corresponds to the Kâmpilla of modern times, situated between Badāūn and Farrkhābâd.

लावाणक—Lāvāṇaka was the name of a village adjacent to Magadha, and was probably situated on the south bank of Jamnā, near its confluence with the Ganges.

Abbreviations of the names of Works &c.

Abh. Sāk.—Abhijnāna Śākuntala.
Ab. Sl.—Abhiṣekanātaka.
Ak.—Amarakosa.
Anar. R—Anarghyarāghava.
Avi.—Avimāraka.
Bâl-bh.—Bāla-bhārata.
Bāl. Ch.—Balacharita.
Bh. N.—Bharata's Nātyaśastra.
Bh. Pr.—Bhâvaprakáśa.
Brh. K. M.—Bṛhatkathāmanjarī.
Chá. D.—Chārudatta.
Com.—Commentary.
Das. Ch.—Daśakumāracharita.
Das. R.—Daśa-rūpaka.
Dut. gh.—Dūtaghatotkacha.
Dū. V.—Dutavākya.
Har. Ch.—Harṣacharita.
Kad.—Kádambarī.
K. Bh.—Karṇa-bhava.
K. M.—Karpūramanjarī.
Kat. S.—Kathāsaritsāgara.
Kâv. D.—Kàvyádarśa.
Kâ. Sūt.—Kāvyālamkāra sūtra.
Kum.—Kumārasammbhava.
May.—Madhyamavyâyoga.
M. bhâ.—Mahàbhàrata.
Māl. Mād.—Màlatī-Mādhava.
Māl.—Mālavikāgnimitra,
Meg.—Meghadūta.
Mṛch. K.—Mṛichchakaṭika.
Mud.—Mudrārākṣasa.
Nāg.—Nâgânanda.
Naṭ. d.—Naṭyadarpaṇa.
Pan. vā.—Pañchatantra.
Prat. Yau.—Pratijnāyaugandharayaṇa.
Prati.—Pratimā.
Priy.—Priyadarśikā.
Ragh.—Raghuvaṃśa.
Rat.—Ratnâvalī.
Śāk,—Abhi.-Śākuntala.
Sid. K.—Siddhānta-Kaumudī.
Śiś.—S'iśupālavadha (Māgha-kâvya).
Sv.—Svpnavāsavadatta.
Uru.—Urubhanga.
Uttar.—Uttararāmacharita.
Vid.—Viddhaśālabhanjika,
Vik.—Vikramorvaśīya.

॥ श्रीः ॥

स्वप्नवासवदत्तम् ।

(नान्द्यन्ते ततः प्रविशति सूत्रधारः ।)

सूत्रधारः—

उदयनवेन्दुसवर्णावासवदत्ताबलौ बलस्य त्वाम् ।
पद्मावतीर्णपूर्णौ वसन्तकम्रौ भुजौ पाताम् ॥ १ ॥

यत्पादपङ्कजनिषेवणवीतदोषा
भक्तोत्तमा यमधिकाधिकभक्तियोगात् ।
अन्यदृशा हृदि विभाव्य विचिन्तयन्ति
श्रीदत्तमिष्टफलदं तमुपाश्रयेऽहम् ॥
पूर्वटीकाः समालोक्य तत्सदुक्तीर्विभाव्य च ।
स्वप्नवासवदत्तस्य टिप्पणीयं विरच्यते ॥

अथ तत्रभवान्भासो नाम महाकविः स्वप्नवासवदत्ताख्यं नाटकं प्रणिनीषुः कृते प्रत्यूहपरिहारिणि नान्दीरूपमङ्गले सूत्रधारप्रवेशं तावन्निर्दिशति—**नान्द्यन्ते** । ततः प्रविशतीति । स्वप्ने दृष्टा वासवदत्ता स्वप्नवासवदत्ता । सा एवाभेदोपचारात्तदाख्यं नाटकम् । नान्दीपदनिरुक्तिस्तु नन्दयतीति नन्दः । पचाद्यच् । नन्द एव नान्दः । प्रज्ञादित्वादण् । ततः 'टिड्ढाणञ्' इति ङीप् । अस्या लक्षणम्—'आशीर्वचनसंयुक्ता स्तुतिर्यस्मात्प्रयुज्यते । देवद्विजनृपादीनां तस्मान्नान्दीति संज्ञिता ॥ सा च यन्नाट्य-वस्तुनः पूर्वं रङ्गविघ्नोपशान्तये । कुशीलवाः प्रकुर्वन्ति पूर्वरङ्गः स उच्यते ॥ प्रत्या-हारादिकान्यङ्गान्यस्य भूयांसि यद्यपि । तथाप्यवश्यं कर्तव्या नान्दी विघ्नोपशान्तये ॥' इत्युक्तेरवश्यं कर्तव्या सूत्रधारेणैव । तदुक्तं—'सूत्रधारः पठेन्नान्दीं मध्यमस्वरमा-स्थितः ।' इति । अतः तस्या अन्ते तां कृत्वेत्यर्थः । ततः नान्दीसमापनानन्तरमेवेति क्रियान्तरवारणार्थं तत इति पदम् । **सूत्रधारः**—सूत्रं धारयतीति सूत्रधारः । 'नाट्यस्य यदनुष्ठानं तत्सूत्रं स्यात्सबीजकम् । रङ्गदैवतपूजाकृत्सूत्रधार उदीरितः ॥' इति तल्लक्षणम् । संगीतसर्वस्वे च—'वर्तनीयतया सूत्रं प्रथमं येन सूच्यते । रङ्गभूमिं समाक्रम्य सूत्रधारः स उच्यते ॥' इति । अथ 'आशीर्नमस्क्रिया वस्तुनिर्देशो वापि तन्मुखम् ।' इति वचनादाशीर्वचनपूर्वं नाट्यवस्तु प्रस्तौति—**उदयनेति** । उदयनवेन्दुसवर्णौ आस-वदत्ताबलौ पद्मावतीर्णपूर्णौ वसन्तकम्रौ बलस्य भुजौ त्वां पाताम् । इत्यन्वयः । बलस्य बलभद्रस्य कृष्णाग्रजस्य भुजौ त्वां युष्मान्सभ्यानित्यर्थः । पाताम् । कीदृशावित्याह । उदये यो नवो नूतनः इन्दुः । द्वितीयाचन्द्र इत्यर्थः । तेन समानः वर्णो ययोः तौ । दत्तमासवं मद्यं यस्यै सा आसवदत्ता । वाहिताग्न्यादिषु इत्यतो दत्तशब्दस्य परनि-

एवमार्यमिश्रान् विज्ञापयामि । अये ! किंनु खलु मयि विज्ञापनव्यग्रे शब्द इव श्रूयते ? अङ्ग ! पश्यामि ।

(नेपथ्ये ।)

उत्सरतोत्सरतार्याः ! उत्सरत । [उस्सरह उस्सरह अय्या ! उस्सरह ।]

सूत्रधारः—भवतु विज्ञातम् ।

भृत्यैर्मगधराजस्य स्निग्धैः कन्यानुगामिभिः ।
धृष्टमुत्सार्यते सर्वस्तपोवनगतो जनः ॥ २ ॥

(निष्क्रान्तः ।)

स्थापना ।

पातः । आसवदत्ता अबला याभ्यां तौ आसवदत्ताबलौ । यद्वा आसवेन पीतेन मद्येन । पानातिरेकादित्यर्थः । दत्तमबल बलाभावो याभ्यां तौ तथोक्तौ । पुनश्च पद्मायाः श्रिया अवतीर्णेनावतारेण । भावे क्तः । पूर्णौ लक्ष्मीसनाथौ । पुनश्च वसन्त इव कम्रौ मनोज्ञौ । वसन्ते वसन्तेन वा कम्रौ इति व्याख्याने तयोः कादाचित्कं मनोरमत्वं प्रसज्येत ॥

अत्र कविना श्लेषेण प्रधानपात्राणामुदयनवासवदत्तापद्मावतीवसन्तकानां नामनिर्देशः कृतः । तथा च वासवदत्तोपकृतस्य पद्मावतीलाभेन परिपूर्णबलस्योदयनस्य भुजौ पातामित्यनेन । शत्रुहृतस्वराज्यस्य पुनःप्राप्तिरूपमन्तिमकार्यमपि सूचितम् । इति मुद्रालंकारोऽयम् । तदुक्तं–' सूच्यर्थसूचनं मुद्रा प्रकृतार्थपरैः पदैः । ' इति । आर्यावृत्तम् । तल्लक्षणम्–' यस्याः पादे प्रथमे द्वादश मात्रास्तथा तृतीयेऽपि । अष्टादश द्वितीये चतुर्थके पञ्चदश साऽऽर्या ॥ ' इति ।

एवमार्यमिश्रानिति । एवं मनःस्थितप्रकारेण । आर्याः च ते मिश्राश्च आर्यमिश्राः । आर्याः सभ्याः । 'आर्यसभ्यसज्जनसाधवः' इत्यमरः । यद्वा आराद्याता दूरं गता ग्राम्यत्वादिदोषेभ्य इत्यार्याः । सुकुलादिसम्पन्ना वा । यदाह भरतः–'कुलं शीलं दया दानं धर्मः सत्यं कृतज्ञता । अद्रोह इति येष्वेतत्तानार्यान्संप्रचक्षते ॥ इति । मिश्राः पूज्याः । पूज्ये मिश्रपदं नित्यं बहुवचनान्तम् । 'मरीचिमिश्रैर्दक्षेण' इति विष्णुपुराणात् । इति मालतीमाधवटीकायां जगद्धरः । अत्रान्तरे नेपथ्ये शब्दं श्रुत्वाह–**अये** इति । अये इति विषादे आश्चर्ये वा । किंनु खलु इति जिज्ञासायाम् । विज्ञापनव्यग्रे विज्ञापनचिन्तापरे । शब्द इव न तु निश्चयेन इदंपरतया जान इत्यर्थः । अङ्ग इति सम्बोधने सम्भ्रमे वा । पश्यामि यथार्थस्वरूपेण ज्ञास्यामीत्यर्थः । **भृत्यैरिति** । मगधानां राजा मगधराजः तस्य स्निग्धैः । न तु तटस्थैः । तेषामेव राजकन्यानुसरणयोग्यत्वात् । कन्या पद्मावती तामनुगच्छन्तीति तैः । भृत्यैः । तपःप्रधानं तपःसाधनं वा वनं तपोवनं । शाकपार्थिवादिः । तत्रतः सर्वोऽपि जनः स्त्रीबालसहितोऽपीत्यर्थः । धृष्टमुद्धतं यथा तथा उत्सार्यते दूरीक्रियते । अनेनानन्तर-

अथ प्रथमोऽङ्कः ।

(प्रविश्य[1] ।)

भटौ[2]—उत्सरतोत्सरतार्याः ! उत्सरत । [उस्सरह उस्सरह अय्या ! उस्सरह ।]

(ततः प्रविशति परिव्राजकवेषो यौगन्धरायण आवन्तिकावेषधारिणी वासवदत्ता च ।)

यौगन्धरायणः—(कर्णं दत्त्वा[3]) कथमिहाप्युत्सार्यते ? कुतः

धीरस्याश्रमसंश्रितस्य वसतस्तुष्टस्य वन्यैः फलै-
र्मानार्हस्य जनस्य वल्कलवतस्त्रासः समुत्पाद्यते ।
उत्सिक्तो विनयादपेतपुरुषो भाग्यैश्चलैर्विस्मितः
कोऽयं भो ! निभृतं तपोवनमिदं ग्रामीकरोत्याज्ञया ॥ ३ ॥

पात्रप्रवेशः सूचितः । स्थापना स्थाप्यते कथावस्त्वाद्यस्यामिति स्थापना । इयमेवामुखं प्रस्तावनेति नाम्ना च कालिदासादिकृतनाटकेषु व्यवह्रियते । भासकृतनाटकेषु चेयं स्थापनेति संज्ञयोपलभ्यते दर्शयति च भासस्य प्राचीनत्वम् । एतस्याः कर्तापि स्थापक इत्युच्यते । तदुक्तं भरतेन—'स्थापकः प्रविशेत्तत्र सूत्रधारगुणाकृतिः । प्रसाद्य रङ्गं विधिवत्कवेर्नाम च कीर्तयेत् । प्रस्तावनां ततः कुर्यात्काव्यप्रस्थापनाश्रयाम् ॥' इति । अस्याश्च पञ्च भेदा उक्ताः साहित्यदर्पणे । यथा—'उद्घात्यकः कथोद्घातः प्रयोगातिशयस्तथा । प्रवर्तकावलगिते पञ्च प्रस्तावनाभिदाः ।' अत्र च—'यदि प्रयोग एकस्मिन्प्रयोगोऽन्यः प्रयुज्यते । तेन पात्रप्रवेशश्चेत्प्रयोगातिशयस्तदा ॥' इत्युक्तेः सूत्रधारेणानन्तरपात्रप्रवेशसूचनात्प्रयोगातिशयः । एषामामुखभेदानामेकं कंचित्प्रयोजयेत् ।' तेनार्थमथ पात्रं वा समाक्षिप्यैव सूत्रधृक् । प्रस्तावनान्ते निर्गच्छेत्ततो वस्तु प्रयोजयेत् ॥' परित्यज्य सर्वं व्रजति इति परिव्राजकः । ण्वुल् । तस्य इव वेषो यस्य सः । युगन्धरस्यापत्यं पुमान्यौगन्धरायणः । 'नडादिभ्यः फक्' इति फक् । उदयनस्य राज्ञः प्रधानमन्त्री । अवन्त्यां जाता आवन्तिका । 'मनुष्यतत्स्थयोर्वुञ्' इति वुञ् । तस्या वेषं धारयतीति । वासवदत्ता उदयनस्य पत्नी । इहापि उत्सारणानर्हे तपोवनेऽपि । **धीरस्येति** । धीरस्य स्थिरप्रज्ञस्य । विषयैरनाकृष्टस्येति यावत् । आसमन्ताच्छ्राम्यन्ति तपोव्रतादिनेति आश्रमः । तं संश्रितस्तस्य । वन्यैः फलैस्तुष्टस्य वसतः । मानमर्हतीति मानार्हस्तस्य वल्कलवतः चीरवाससः जनस्य त्रासः भयं समुत्पाद्यते । अतः भो उत्सिक्त उद्धतः; चलैर्भाग्यैर्विस्मितो गर्वितः विनयादपेतश्चासौ पुरुषश्च विनयादपेतः पुरुषः । विनयादपेताः पुरुषा यस्येति वा । कोऽयं निभृतं शान्तं तपोवनमाज्ञया ग्रामीकरोति ग्राम्यजनोचितोत्सारणक्रियया ग्रामसमतां नयति ? शार्दूलविक्रीडितं वृत्तम् । 'सूर्याश्वैर्यदि मः सजौ सततगाः

---

१ ततः प्रविशतः साधारणौ. २ साधारणौ. ३ एतन्नास्ति पुस्तकान्तरे.

वासवदत्ता—आर्य ! क एष उत्सारयति ? [अय्य ! को एसो उस्सारेदि !]

यौगन्धरायणः—भवति । यो धर्मा[1]दात्मानमुत्सारयति ।

वासवदत्ता—आर्य ! न ह्येवं वक्तुकामा । अहमपि ना[2]मोत्सारयितव्या भवामीति । [अय्य ! ण हि एव्वं वत्तुकामा । अहं वि णाम उस्सारइदव्वा होमि त्ति ।]

यौगन्धरायणः—भवति । एवमनिर्ज्ञाता[3]नि दैवतान्यप्यवधूयन्ते ।

वासवदत्ता—आर्य ! तथा परिश्रमः परिखेदं नोत्पादयति यथायं परिभवः । [अय्य ! तह परिस्समो परिखेदं ण उप्पादेदि जह अअं परिभवो ।]

यौगन्धरायणः—भुक्तोज्झित एष विषयोऽत्रभवत्या । [4]नात्र चिन्ता कार्या । कुतः

पूर्वं त्वयाप्यभिमतं गतमेवमासी-
च्छ्लाघ्यं गमिष्यसि पुनर्विजयेन भर्तुः ।
कालक्रमेण जगतः परिवर्तमाना
चक्रारपंक्तिरिव गच्छति भाग्यपङ्क्तिः ॥ ४ ॥

भटौ[5]—उत्सरतार्याः ! उत्सरत । [उस्सरह अय्या ! उस्सरह ॥]

शार्दूलविक्रीडितम् ।' इति तल्लक्षणम् ॥ ३ ॥ भवति मन्ये । य आत्मानं धर्मात्पुण्यादुत्सारयति प्रच्यावयति स उत्सारयतीति योजना । पाठान्तरे अधर्मे अपुण्यकर्मणि । उभयत्र एवमकार्यं कुर्वन्नित्यर्थः । **एवं वक्तुकामा**-एवं वक्तुं कामो यस्याः सा वक्तुकामा न । 'तुं काममनसोरपि । लुम्पेदवश्यं मः कृत्ये ' इति मकारलोपः । नायं मम प्रश्नस्याशयः । अहमपि वत्सराजमहिष्यपि उत्सारणार्हा भवामि किमिति मया पृष्टम् । नाम संभावनायाम् । अनिर्ज्ञातानि यथार्थतोऽज्ञातानि । अवधूयन्ते परिभूयन्ते । एष विषयः परिजनकृतोत्सारणारूपोऽर्थः । **पूर्वमिति** । त्वयापि पूर्वं स्वराज्यवर्तिन्येत्यर्थः । एवमभिमतमिष्टं गतमासीत् । भर्तुर्विजये पुनरपि श्लाघ्यं परिजनश्लाघायुक्तं गमिष्यसि । उक्तमर्थं सामान्येन समर्थयते—**कालक्रमेणेति** । जगतः भाग्यपंक्तिः दैवनिबन्धना सुखदुःखादिश्रेणिः कालक्रमेण अनुकूलप्रतिकूलकालपरिपाट्या चक्रारपंक्तिः चक्रस्य अराणां पंक्तिरिव परिवर्तमाना भ्रमन्ती गच्छति । अस्यानुरूपभावो मेघदूते-'कस्यात्यन्तं सुखमुपनतं दुःखमेकान्ततो वा नीचैर्गच्छत्युपरि च दशा चक्रनेमिक्रमेण' ॥ इति । वसन्ततिलका छन्दः । तल्लक्षणम् । 'उक्ता वसन्ततिलका तभजा जगौ गः' इति ॥ ४ ॥

---

१ अधर्म आत्मानं विनियोजयति. २ तावत् (दाव). ३ अविज्ञा०. ४ नात्रभवत्या. ५ साधा०.

(ततः प्रविशति काञ्चुकीयः ।)

काञ्चुकीयः—सम्भषक ! न खलु न खलूत्सारणा । पश्य

परिहरतु भवान् नृपापवादं
न परुषमाश्रमवासिषु प्रयोज्यम् ।
नगरपरिभवान् विमोक्तुमेते
वनमभिगम्य मनस्विनो वसन्ति ॥ ५ ॥

उभौ—आर्य ! तथा । [अय्य ! तह ।]

(निष्क्रान्तौ ।)

यौगन्धरायणः—हन्त सविज्ञानमस्य दर्शनम् । वत्से ! उपसर्पाव-स्तावदेनम् ।

वासवदत्ता—आर्य ! तथा । [अय्य ! तह ।]

यौगन्धरायणः—(उपसृत्य ।) भोः ! किंकृतेयमुत्सारणा ?

काञ्चुकीयः—भोस्तपस्विन् !

यौगन्धरायणः—(आत्मगतम् ।) तपस्विन्निति गुणवान् खल्वयमालापः । अपरिचयात्तु न श्लिष्यते मे मनसि ।

काञ्चुकीयः—कञ्चुकी । अत्र छण् कथंचित्साध्यः । एतल्लक्षणं मातृगुप्ताचार्यैरुक्तम्–'ये नित्यं सत्यसम्पन्नाः कामदोषविवर्जिताः । ज्ञानविज्ञानकुशलाः काञ्चुकीयास्तु ते स्मृताः ॥' इति । अन्यच्च–'अन्तःपुरचरो वृद्धो विप्रो गुणगणान्वितः । सर्वकायार्थकुशलः कञ्चुकीत्यमिधीयते ॥' **परिहरत्विति** । भवान् नृपापवादं भवत्कृत्या नृपस्य जायमानां निन्दां परिहरतु वर्जयतु । आश्रमवासिषु परुषं निष्ठुरं वाक्यं न प्रयोज्यम् । हि एते प्रशस्तं मन एषामस्तीति मनस्विनः नगरपरिभवान् नगरे जायमाना विमानना: मोक्तुं परिहर्तुं वनमभिगम्य वसन्ति। अत्रापि परिभूयेरंश्चेद्युक्तायुक्तविचाराज्ञानदोषो नृपस्य प्रसज्येतेति भावः। पुष्पिताग्रा वृत्तम्। 'अयुजि नयुगरेफतो यकारो युजि च नजौ जरगाश्च पुष्पिताग्रा ।' इति लक्षणम् ॥५॥ हन्तेति हर्षे । उत्सारणानिराकृत्या स्वप्रवेशसौलभ्याद्धर्षः । विशिष्टेन ज्ञानेन युक्तायुक्तविवेकेन सहितं सविज्ञानं दर्शनं बुद्धिः । पर्यालोचनं वा । तपस्विन् यतिवेषदर्शनात्तथामन्त्रणम् । आत्मगतमन्यैः श्रवणानर्हं स्वस्मिन्नेव चिन्त्यमानं स्वगतम् । तदुक्तं–'सर्वश्राव्यं प्रकाशं स्यादश्राव्यं स्वगतं मतम् ।' गुणवान् योग्यतया श्लाघ्यः । रमणीय इति यावत् । अपरिचयादसंस्तुतत्वात् । नवीनत्वादित्यर्थः । न श्लिष्यते अभिमतत्वेन न श्लिष्टो भवति । परस्मैपदे प्राप्तेऽपि आत्मनेपदं । ओदनः संगतो

---

१ भवाद्धि. २ साधा०.

काञ्चुकीयः—भोः ! श्रूयताम् । एषा खलु गुरुभिरभिहितनामधेयस्यास्माकं महाराजदर्शकस्य भगिनी पद्मावती नाम । सैषा नो महाराजमातरं महादेवीमाश्रमस्थामभिगम्यानुज्ञाता तत्रभवत्या राजगृहमेव यास्यति । तदद्यास्मिन्नाश्रमपदे वासोऽभिप्रेतोऽस्याः । तद् भवन्तः

तीर्थोदकानि समिधः कुसुमानि दर्भान्
स्वैरं वनादुपनयन्तु तपोधनानि ।
धर्मप्रिया नृपसुता न हि धर्मपीडा-
मिच्छेत् तपस्विषु कुलव्रतमेतदस्याः ॥ ६ ॥

यौगन्धरायणः—(स्वगतम् ।) एवम् । एषा सा मगधराजपुत्री पद्मावती नाम या पुष्पकभद्रादिभिरादेशिकैरादिष्टा स्वामिनो देवी भविष्यतीति । ततः

प्रद्वेषो बहुमानो वा संकल्पादुपजायते ।
भर्तृदाराभिलाषित्वादस्यां मे महती स्वता ॥ ७ ॥

वासवदत्ता—(स्वगतम् ।) राजदारिकेति श्रुत्वा भगिनिकास्नेहोऽपि मेऽत्र संपद्यते । [राअदारिअत्ति सुणिअ भइणिआसिणेहो वि मे एत्थ संपज्जइ ।]

(ततः प्रविशति पद्मावती सपरिवारा चेटी च ।)

चेटी—ऐत्वेतु भर्तृदारिका इदमाश्रमपद प्रविशतु । [एदु एदु भट्टिदारिआ इदं अस्समपदं पविसदु ॥]

पच्यते इतिवत् कर्मवत्कर्मणा तुल्यक्रिय इति कर्मवद्भावात्समर्थनीयम् । गुरुभिः पूज्यैः पित्रादिभिः । नाम एव नामधेयम् । तत्रभवत्या पूज्यया महादेव्या । राजगृहं मगधदेशराजधानी । अभिप्रेतो रुचितः । **तीर्थोदकानीति** । तस्माद्भवन्तः तपोधनानि तपसो धनानि उपकारकाणि तीर्थोदकानि समिधः कुसुमानि दर्भान् वनात्स्वैरं स्वेच्छयोपनयन्तु । धर्मः प्रियो यस्याः सा धर्मप्रिया नृपसुता तपस्विषु धर्मपीडां धर्मक्रियोपरोधं नेच्छेत् । एतदस्याः कुलव्रतम् । वसन्ततिलका वृत्तम् । लक्षणं तूक्तम् ॥६॥ आदिशन्ति भविष्यदर्थमित्यादेशिका दैवज्ञाः तैः । स्वामिनः उदयनस्य । **प्रद्वेष इति** । कस्यापि विषये प्रद्वेषः बहुमानो वा सङ्कल्पः अनिष्ट इष्टो वा मनोव्यापारस्तस्मादुपजायते । भर्तुः दाराः भर्तृदाराः । भावप्रधानो निर्देशः । भर्तृदारत्वेन इयं मम भर्तुर्दारा भवेदित्यभिलाषः । सोऽस्यास्तीति भर्तृदाराभिलाषी तस्य भावः भर्तृदाराभिलाषित्वं तस्मात् । अस्यां मे महती स्वतात्मीयबुद्धिरस्ति ॥७॥ अनेन आरम्भो नाम कार्यस्य प्रथमावस्था सूचिता । तदुक्तं— 'औत्सुक्यमात्रमारम्भः' इति । अत्र पद्मावत्याम् । भगिनिकास्नेहोऽपि न केवलं भर्तुर-

१ इत इतः (इदो इदो).

(ततः प्रविशत्युपविष्टा तापसी ।)

तापसी—स्वागतं राजदारिकायाः । [साअदं राअदारिआए ।]

वासवदत्ता—(स्वगतम् ।) इयं सा राजदारिका । अभिजनानुरूपं खल्वस्या रूपम् । [इयं सा राअदारिआ । अभिजणाणुरूवं खु से रूवं ।]

पद्मावती—आर्ये ! वन्दे । [अय्ये ! वंदामि ।]

तापसी—चिरं जीव । प्रविश जाते ! प्रविश । तपोवनानि नामातिथिजनस्य स्वगेहम् । [चिरं जीव । पविस जादे ! पविस । तवोवणाणि णाम अदिहिजणस्स सअगेहं ॥]

पद्मावती—भवतु भवतु । आर्ये ! विश्वस्तास्मि । अनेन बहुमानवचनेनानुगृहीतास्मि । [भोदु भोदु । अय्ये ! विस्सत्थम्हि । इमिणा बहुमाणवअणेण अणुग्गहिदम्हि ।]

वासवदत्ता—(स्वगतम् ।) न हि रूपमेव वागपि खल्वस्या मधुरा । [ण हि रूवं एव्व वाआ वि खु से महुरा ।]

तापसी—भद्रे ! इमां तावद् भद्रमुखस्य भगिनिकां कश्चिद् राजा न वरयति । [भद्दे ! इमं दाव भद्दमुहस्य भइणिअं कोवि राआ ण वरेदि ।]

चेटी—अस्ति राजा प्रद्योतो नामोज्जयिन्याः । स दारकस्य कारणाद् दूतसंपातं करोति । [अत्थि राआ पज्जोदो णाम उज्जइणीए । सो दारअस्स कारणादो दूदसम्पादं करेदि ।]

वासवदत्ता—(आत्मगतम् ।) भवतु भवतु । एषा चात्मीयेदानीं संवृत्ता । [भोदु भोदु । एसा अ अत्तणीआ दाणिं संवुत्ता ॥]

तापसी—अर्हा खल्वियमाकृतिरस्य बहुमानस्य । उभे राजकुले महत्तरे इति श्रूयते । [अर्हा खु इअं आइदी इमस्स बहुमाणस्स । उभआणि राअउळाणि महत्तराणि त्ति सुणीअदि ।]

भ्युदयहेतुतयाभिमता सपत्नीति । अभिजनस्योदारवंशस्यानुरूपं सदृशम् । जाते वत्से । अतति गच्छतीति अतिथिः । इथिन् । अतिथीनां जनः समूहः अतिथिजनस्तस्य । भद्रे इति चेटीं प्रति सम्बोधनम् । न वरयतीति प्रश्नः । दारकस्य स्वसुतस्य कारणाद्विवाहसम्बन्धहेतोः । दूतसंपातं दूतसम्प्रेषणम् । आत्मीया सम्बन्धिनी स्वभ्रात्रर्थं वरणात् ।

---

१ विश्वासिहि (विस्ससिहि). २ कोपि (कोवि).

पद्मावती—आर्य ! किं दृष्टो मुनिजन आत्मानमनुग्रहीतुम् ? अभिप्रेतप्रदानेन तपस्विजन उपनिमन्त्र्यतां तावत् कः किमत्रेच्छतीति । [अय्य ! किं दिट्ठो मुणिजणो अत्ताणं अणुग्गहीदुं ? अभिप्पेदप्पदाणेण तवस्सिजणो उवणिमंतीअदु दाव को किं एत्थ इच्छदि त्ति ।]

काञ्चुकीयः—यदभिप्रेतं भवत्या । भो भो आश्रमवासिनस्तपस्विनः ! श्रृण्वन्तु श्रृण्वन्तु भवन्तः । इहात्रभवती मगधराजपुत्र्यनेन विस्रम्भेणोत्पादितविस्रम्भा धर्मार्थमर्थेनोपनिमन्त्रयते ।

कस्यार्थः कलशेन को मृगयते वासो यथानिश्चितं
दीक्षां पारितवान् किमिच्छति पुनर्देयं गुरोर्यद् भवेत् ।
आत्मानुग्रहमिच्छतीह नृपजा धर्माभिरामप्रिया
यद् यस्यास्ति समीप्सितं वदतु तत्कस्याद्य किं दीयताम् ॥ ८ ॥

यौगन्धरायणः (आत्मगतम् ।) हन्त दृष्ट उपायः[१] । (प्रकाशम् ।) भोः अहमर्थी ।

पद्मावती—दिष्ट्या सफलं मे तपोवनाभिगमनम् । [दिट्ठिआ सहळं मे तवोवणाभिगमणं ।]

तापसी—सन्तुष्टतपस्विजनमिदमाश्रमपदम् । आगन्तुकेनानेन[३] भवितव्यम् । [संतुट्ठतपस्सिजणं इदं अस्समपदं । आअंतुएण इमिणा होदव्वं ।]

आत्मानमनुग्रहीतुमात्मनोऽनुग्रहार्थम् । अभिमतस्येष्टस्य प्रदानेन प्रदानप्रतिश्रुत्या । उपनिमन्त्र्यतामुपच्छन्द्य प्रतिग्रहाभिमुखीक्रियताम् । विस्रम्भो विश्वासः । धर्मायेदं धर्मार्थं तद्यथा तथा । **कस्येति** । कस्य तपस्विजनस्य कलशेन । एतत्पात्रोपलक्षणम् । अर्थः प्रयोजनम् । को वासो वस्त्रं मृगयते वाञ्छतीत्यर्थः । कः पुनः । यथानिश्चितं निश्चितं कर्तृत्वेनाध्यवसितमर्थमनतिक्रम्य यथानिश्चितं दीक्षां वेदाध्ययनादिव्रतं पारितवान् किमिच्छति यद्गुरोर्देयं भवेत् । गुरुदक्षिणात्वेनेति यावत् । एवं पृच्छन्ती धर्मे अभिरमन्ते इति धर्माभिरामाः । ते प्रिया यस्याः सा धर्माभिरामप्रिया । यद्वा धर्मोऽभिरामः प्रियश्च यस्याः सा तथोक्ता । नृपसुतेह आत्मानुग्रहमिच्छति । भवद्भिरभिलषितकथनेनेति शेषः । अतः यस्य यत्समीप्सितं स तद्वदतु । अद्य कस्य किं दीयताम् । तदुच्यतामिति शेषः । शार्दूलविक्रीडितं वृत्तम् । लक्षणमुक्तम् ॥ ८ ॥ उपायः स्वाभिलषितसिद्धेरित्यर्थः । दिष्ट्येत्यानन्दे । 'दिष्ट्या समुपजोषं चेत्यानन्दे' । इत्यमरः । आगन्तु-

---

१ यद्यद्यस्य. २ अस्मात्परं भवतु । एवं तावत्करिष्ये इत्य०. ३ केनाप्य० (एण वि).

काञ्चुकीयः—भोः ! किं क्रियताम् ?

यौगन्धरायणः—ईयं मे स्वसा । प्रोषितभर्तृकामिमामिच्छाम्यत्रभवत्या कंचित् कालं परिपाल्यमानाम् । कुतः

कार्यं नैवार्थैर्नापि भोगैर्न वस्त्रै-
र्नाहं काषायं वृत्तिहेतोः प्रपन्नः ।
धीरा कन्येयं दृष्टधर्मप्रचारा
शक्ता चारित्रं रक्षितुं मे भगिन्याः ॥ ९ ॥

वासवदत्ता—हम् । इह मां निक्षेप्तुकाम आर्ययौगन्धरायणः । भवतु अविचार्य क्रमं न करिष्याति । (आत्मगतम् ।) [हं । इह मं णिक्खिविदुकामो अय्ययोगंधरायणो । होदु अविआरिअ कमं ण करिस्सदि ।]

काञ्चुकीयः—भवति । महती खल्वस्य व्यपाश्रयणा । कथं प्रतिजानीमः ? कुतः

सुखमर्थो भवेद् दातुं सुखं प्राणाः सुखं तपः ।
सुखमन्यद् भवेत् सर्वं दुःखं न्यासस्य रक्षणम् ॥ १० ॥

पद्मावती—आर्य ! प्रथममुद्घोष्य कः किमिच्छतीत्ययुक्तमिदानीं विचारयितुम् । यदेषे भणति तदनुष्ठत्वार्यः । [अय्य पढमं उग्घोसिअ को किं इच्छदित्ति अजुत्तं दाणिं विआरिदुं । जं एसो भणादि तं अणुचिट्ठदु अय्यो ।]

केन नत्वत्रत्येन अर्थिताविष्करणात् । प्रोषितो देशान्तरगतो भर्ता यस्याः सा प्रोषितभर्तृका । नद्यृतश्च इति कप् । **कार्यमिति** । मम अर्थैर्नैव कार्यं नापि भोगैर्न वस्त्रैः । वृत्तिहेतोः जीविकार्थे अहं काषायं न प्रपन्नः । मया प्रव्रज्या न गृहीतेत्यर्थः । इयं धीरा मनस्विनी दृष्टः धर्मस्य प्रचार आचरणं यस्या यस्यां वा सा दृष्टधर्मप्रचारा मम भगिन्याः चरित्रमेव चारित्रं शीलम् । प्रज्ञादिभ्यश्च इत्यण् । रक्षितुं शक्ता । अनया परिपाल्यमानया अस्याश्चारित्रभङ्गाय न कोऽपि प्रवर्तेतेति यावत् । अत्र शक्तेत्यस्य धीरा दृष्टधर्मप्रचारेति पदयोर्हेतुत्वात्काव्यलिङ्गमलङ्कारः । वैश्वदेवी वृत्तम् । 'बाणाश्वैश्छिन्ना वैश्वदेवी ममौ यौ ।' इति तल्लक्षणम् ॥ ९ ॥ निक्षेप्तुकामो न्यासीकर्तुमिच्छुः । क्रमं कर्मप्रवृत्तिम् । व्यपाश्रयणाश्रयार्थमभ्यर्थनेति यावत् । प्रतिजानीमोऽभ्युपगम्याङ्गीकुर्मः । **सुखमिति** । अर्थः द्रव्यं सुखं यथा तथा दातुं भवेत् । शक्य इति शेषः । प्राणा दातुं सुखं भवेयुः । तपो दातुं सुखं भवेत् । अन्यत्सर्वं दातुं सुखं भवेत् । किंतु न्यासस्य रक्षणं दुःखं दुःसम्पाद्यम् ॥१०॥ प्रथममित्यादिनास्या महानुभावत्वमाज्ञापयतीत्यनेन

---

१ श्रूयताम् । इयं ... प्रोषितभर्तृका तामि०. २ सः भ०. ३ किमत्र (किं एत्थ). ४ एष आज्ञापयति (आणवेदि).

काञ्चुकीयः—अनुरूपमेतद्भवत्याभिहितम् ।

चेटी—चिरं जीवतु भर्तृदारिकैवं सत्यवादिनी । [चिरं जीवदु भट्टिदारिआ एवं सच्चवादिणी ।]

तापसी—चिरं जीवतु भद्रे ! । [चिरं जीवदु भद्दे ! ।]

काञ्चुकीयः—भवति तथा । (उपगम्य ।) । भोः ! अभ्युपगतमत्रभवतो भगिन्याः परिपालनमत्रभवत्या ।

यौगन्धरायणः—अनुगृहीतोऽस्म्यत्रभवत्या । वत्से ! उपसर्पात्रभवतीम् ।

वासवदत्ता—(आत्मगतम् ।) का गतिः ? एषा गच्छामि मन्दभागा । [का गई ? एसा गच्छामि मंदभाआ ।]

पद्मावती—भवतु भवतु । आर्यात्मीयेदानीं संवृत्ता । [भोदु भोदु । अय्या अत्तणीआ दाणिं संवुत्ता ।]

तापसी—या ईदृश्यस्या आकृतिरियमपि राजदारिकेति तर्कयामि । [जा ईदिसी से आइदी इयं वि राअदारिअत्ति तक्केमि ।]

चेटी—सुष्ठु आर्या भणति । अहमप्यनुभूतसुखेति पश्यामि । [सुट्ठु अय्या भणादि । अहं वि अणुहूदसुहत्ति पेक्खामि ।]

यौगन्धरायणः—(आत्मगतम् ।) हन्त भोः ! अर्धमवसितं भारस्य । यथा मन्त्रिभिः सह समर्थितं तथा परिणमति । ततः प्रतिष्ठिते स्वामिनि तत्रभवतीमुपनयतो मे इहात्रभवती मगधराजपुत्री विश्वासस्थानं भविष्यति । कुतः

पद्मावती नरपतेर्महिषी भवित्री
दृष्टा विपत्तिरथ[२] यैः प्रथमं प्रदिष्टा ।

विनयश्च दर्शितः । मन्दो भागः भाग्यस्य यथा सा मन्दभागा । **पद्मा०**—भवतु भवत्विति वीप्सा परितोषं दर्शयति । हन्तेति हर्षे । भारस्याध्यवसितगुरुकार्यस्येत्यर्थः । समर्थितं संमन्त्र्य निश्चितम् । प्रतिष्ठिते स्वराज्ये स्वामिनि वत्सराजे । मगधराजपुत्री पद्मावती । विश्वासस्थानं स्वामिनः प्रत्ययजनने विश्वासहेतुः । **पद्मावतीति** । पद्मावती नरपतेरुदयनस्य महिषी कृताभिषेका पत्नी भवित्री भविता । अत्र कः प्रत्यय इत्याह—**दृष्टेति** । यैः आदेशिकैः प्रथमं विपत्तिः अस्मत्स्वामिन इत्यर्थात् ।

---

१ तत्रभवत्या. २ रपि.

तत्प्रत्ययात् कृतमिदं न हि सिद्धवाक्या-
न्युत्क्रम्य[1] गच्छति विधिः सुपरीक्षितानि ॥ ११ ॥

(ततः प्रविशति ब्रह्मचारी ।)

ब्रह्मचारी—(ऊर्ध्वमवलोक्य ।) स्थितो मध्याह्नः । दृढमस्मि परिश्रान्तः । अथ कस्मिन् प्रदेशे विश्रमयिष्ये ? (परिक्रम्य ।) भवतु, दृष्टम् । अभितस्तपोवनेनानेन भवितव्यम् । तथाहि—

विस्रब्धा[2] हरिणाश्चरन्त्यचकिता देशागतप्रत्यया[3]
वृक्षाः पुष्पफलैः समृद्धविटपाः[4] सर्वे दयारक्षिताः ।
भूयिष्ठं कपिलानि गोकुलधनान्यक्षेत्रवत्यो दिशो
निःसंदिग्धमिदं तपोवनमयं धूमो हि बह्वाश्रयः ॥ १२ ॥

यावत् प्रविशामि ! (प्रविश्य ।) अये ! आश्रमविरुद्धः खल्वेष जनः । (अन्यतो विलोक्य ।) अथवा तपस्विजनोऽप्यत्र । निर्दोषमुपसर्पणम् । अये ! स्त्रीजनः ।

प्रदिष्टा सा दृष्टा प्रत्यक्षीकृता । अस्माभिरिति शेषः । तत्प्रत्ययादादेशिकवाक्यविश्वासादिदं पद्मावत्यां वासवदत्तान्यसनादिकं कृतम् । विधिः सुपरीक्षितानि सिद्धवाक्यानि उत्क्रम्योलंघ्य न गच्छति । तदनुसारेण वर्तते इत्यर्थः ॥ वसन्ततिलका वृत्तम् ॥११॥ अत्र वत्सराजस्य पद्मावतीप्राप्तिहेतुर्यौगन्धरायणव्यापारो बीजम् । तदुक्तं-'स्वल्पोद्दिष्टस्तु तद्धेतुर्बीजं विस्तार्यनेकधा ।' इति । अथाभीष्टविवाहस्य प्रधानहेतुभूतस्य पद्मावत्या नायकेऽभिलाषस्योदयनगतगुणप्रशंसया बीजारोपणार्थं तद्वृत्तान्तं प्रस्तोतुं ब्रह्मचारिप्रवेशं निर्दिशति—**ततः प्रविशतीति** । ब्रह्म वेदस्तदध्ययनार्थं व्रतं वा तच्चरतीति ब्रह्मचारी । दृढमत्यन्तम् । **विस्रब्धेति** । देशात् निर्भयत्वेन परिचितात्स्थानादागतो विश्वासस्तस्मात् पाठान्तरे देशागतः प्रत्ययो येषाम् । विस्रब्धा अतोऽचकिता अविविग्ना हरिणाः चरन्ति । दयया रक्षिताः संवर्धिताः सर्वे वृक्षाः पुष्पफलैः समृद्धा विटपा येषां ते **समृद्धविटपाः** पूर्णशाखाः । यद्वा समृद्धविटपाः सर्वे वृक्षा दयारक्षिताः । न तु **कठोरस्पर्शेन** रभसाद्वा भग्नशाखाः । गोकुलानि गोवृन्दानि धनानीव भूयिष्ठं कपिलानि । **कपिलानामेव** गवां प्राशस्त्यात् । तथा च स्मृतिः-' अग्निचित्कपिला सत्री राजा भिक्षुर्महोदधिः । दृष्टमात्राः पुनन्त्येते तस्मात्पश्येत नित्यशः ॥' इति । क्षेत्राण्यासां विद्यन्ते इति **क्षेत्रवत्यः** । यथा ग्रामेषु । न क्षेत्रवत्यः अक्षेत्रवत्यः दिशः । अतःनिःसंदेशमसंशयमिदं **तपोवनम्** । हि यस्मादयं धूमः बह्वाश्रयः, बहूनि समिद्घृततिलादीनि आश्रयो यस्य स **तथा** । स्वभावोक्तिः काव्यलिङ्गं च । शार्दूलविक्रीडितं वृत्तम् ॥ **१२** ॥ अये **इत्याश्चर्ये** ।

---

१ उद्भ्रम्य. २ [illegible]ब्धाः, ३ प्रत्ययात्. ४ विभवाः.
२ विस्रब्धाः, विस्रब्धं

काञ्चुकीयः—स्वैरं स्वैरं प्रविशतु भवान्। सर्वजनसाधारणमाश्रमपदं नाम।

वासवदत्ता—हम्। [हं।]

पद्मावती—अम्मो! परपुरुषदर्शनं परिहरत्यार्या। भवतु। सुपरिपालनीयः खलु मन्न्यासः। [अम्मो! परपुरुसदंसणं परिहरदि अय्या। भोदु। सुपरिवाळणीओ खु मण्णासो।]

काञ्चुकीयः—भोः! पूर्वं प्रविष्टाः स्मः प्रतिगृह्यतामातिथिसत्कारः।

ब्रह्मचारी—(आचम्य।) भवतु भवतु। निवृत्तपरिश्रमोऽस्मि।

यौगन्धरायणः—भोः! कुत आगम्यते क्व गन्तव्यं क्वाधिष्ठानमार्यस्य?

ब्रह्मचारी—भोः! श्रूयताम्। राजगृहतोऽस्मि। श्रुतिविशेषणार्थं वत्सभूमौ लावाणकं नाम ग्रामस्तत्रोषितवानस्मि।

वासवदत्ता—(आत्मगतम्।) हा! लावाणकं नाम। लावाणकसंकीर्तनेन पुनर्नवीकृत इव मे संतापः। [हा! ळावाणअं णाम। ळावाणअसंकित्तणेण पुणो णवीकिदो विअ मे संदावो।]

यौगन्धरायणः—अथ परिसमाप्ता विद्या?

ब्रह्मचारी—न खलु तावत्।

यौगन्धरायणः—यद्यनवसिता विद्या किमागमनप्रयोजनम्?

ब्रह्मचारी—तत्र खल्वतिदारुणं व्यसनं संवृत्तम्।

यौगन्धरायणः—कथमिव?

ब्रह्मचारी—तत्रोदयनो नाम राजा प्रतिवसति।

यौगन्धरायणः—श्रूयते तत्रभवानुदयनः। किं सः?

आश्रमविरुद्धः। नगरवासीत्यर्थः। एष जनः काञ्चुकेयमुद्दिश्येयमुक्तिः। स्त्रीजनः पद्मावत्यादिः। स्वैरं यथारुचि। अशङ्कितमिति यावत्। साधारणं समानप्रवेशार्हम्। हमिति शब्दोऽरुचौ। अम्मो इति आनन्दे आश्चर्ये वा।। परपुरुषदर्शनं स्वयमेव परिहरति अतः सुपरिपालनीयः। अस्याः शीलरक्षणार्थे मया नातिचिन्ता कार्येति भावः। श्रुतिविशेषणार्थं श्रुतेर्वेदस्य विशिष्टाध्ययनार्थम्। नवीकृतः सर्वस्य वृत्तान्तस्य स्मृत्युपस्थितत्वात्। संतापः प्रियवियोगादिजन्मा। अनवसिताऽसमाप्ता। व्यसनमापत्। ‘व्यसनं

ब्रह्मचारी—तस्यावन्तिराजपुत्री वासवदत्ता नाम पत्नी दृढमभिप्रेता किल ।

यौगन्धरायणः—भवितव्यम् । ततस्ततः ?

ब्रह्मचारी—ततस्तस्मिन् मृगयानिष्क्रान्ते राजनि ग्रामदाहेन सा दग्धा ।

वासवदत्ता—(आत्मगतम्) अलीकमलीकं खल्वेतत् । जीवामि मन्दभागा । (अलिअं अलिअं खु एदं । जीवामि मंदभाआ ।)

यौगन्धरायणः—ततस्ततः ?

ब्रह्मचारी—ततस्तामभ्यवपत्तुकामो यौगन्धरायणो नाम सचिवस्तस्मिन्नेवाग्नौ पतितः ।

यौगन्धरायणः—सत्यं पतित इति । ततस्ततः ?

ब्रह्मचारी—ततः प्रतिनिवृत्तो राजा तद्वृत्तान्तं श्रुत्वा तयोर्वियोगजनितसंतापस्तस्मिन्नेवाग्नौ प्राणान् परित्यक्तुकामोऽमात्यैर्महता यत्नेन वारितः ।

वासवदत्ता—(आत्मगतम् ।) जानामि जानाम्यार्यपुत्रस्य मयि सानुक्रोशत्वम् । (जाणामि जाणामि अय्यउत्तस्स मइ साणुक्कोसत्तणं ।)

यौगन्धरायणः—ततस्ततः ?

ब्रह्मचारी—ततस्तस्याः शरीरोपभुक्तानि दग्धशेषाण्याभरणानि परिष्वज्य राजा मोहमुपगतः ।

सर्वे—हा ।

वासवदत्ता—(स्वगतम् ।) सकाम इदानीमार्ययौगन्धरायणो भवतु । [सकामो दाणिं अय्यजोअंधराअणो होदु ।]

चेटी—भर्तृदारिके ! रोदिति खल्वियमार्या । (भट्टिदारिए ! रोदिदि खु इअं अय्या ।)

पद्मावती—सानुक्रोशया भवितव्यम् । (साणुक्कोसाए होदव्वं ।)

यौगन्धरायणः—अथ किमथ किम् ? प्रकृत्या सानुक्रोशा मे भागिनी । ततस्ततः ?

तिवल्लभा । विपदि भ्रंशे ' इत्यमरः । किलेति वार्तायाम् । अलीकमसत्यम् । अभ्यवपत्तुं व्यसनादुद्धर्तुं कामो यस्य । 'व्यसनसाहाय्यमभ्यवपत्तिः' इति कौटिल्यः । तुंकाममनसोरपि ।' इति मलोपः । अनुक्रोशेनानुकम्पया सह सानुक्रोशः तस्य भावः सानुक्रोशत्वम् । परिष्वज्याश्लिष्य । सकामः सम्पन्नमनोरथः । पैर्यथावृत्तस्याज्ञातत्वाल्लोके संचारितार्थस्य परमार्थत्वेन गृहीतत्वाच्च । **अथ किमथ किमिति** । इयमुदयनसम्बद्धा

---

१ अथ भोः.

ब्रह्मचारी—ततः शनैः शनैः प्रतिलब्धसंज्ञः संवृत्तः ।

पद्मावती—दिष्ट्या ध्रियते । मोहं गत इति श्रुत्वा शून्यमिव मे हृदयम् । [दिट्ठिआ धरइ । [1]मोहं गदो त्ति सुणिअ सुण्णं विअ मे हिअअं ।]

यौगन्धरायणः—ततस्ततः ?

ब्रह्मचारी—ततः स राजा महीतलपरिसर्पणपांसुपाटलशरीरः सहसोत्थाय 'हा वासवदत्ते ! हा अवन्तिराजपुत्रि ! हा प्रिये ! हा प्रियशिष्ये !' इति किमपि किमपि बहु प्रलपितवान् । किं बहुना

नैवेदानीं तादृशाश्चक्रवाका
नैवाप्यन्ये स्त्रीविशेषैर्वियुक्ताः ।
धन्या सा स्त्री यां तथा वेत्ति भर्ता
भर्तृस्नेहात् सा हि [2]दग्धाप्यदग्धा ॥ १३ ॥

यौगन्धरायणः—अथ भोः ! तं तु पर्यवस्थापयितुं न कश्चिद्यत्नवानमात्यः ?

ब्रह्मचारी—अस्ति रुमण्वान्नामामात्यो दृढं प्रयत्नवांस्तत्रभवन्तं पर्यवस्थापयितुम् । स हि

अनाहारे तुल्यः [3]प्रततरुदितक्षामवदनः
शरीरे संस्कारं नृपतिसमदुःखं परिवहन् ।

स्यात्किमिति संशयनिरासार्थं ससम्भ्रमोक्तिः । प्रकृत्या स्वभावतः, न तु केनचित्सम्बन्धेन । ध्रियते जीवति । शून्यं विषादाद्विगतचेतनम् । महीतले परिसर्पणेन पांसुभिः धूल्या पाटलं श्वेतरक्तं शरीरं यस्य स तथा । **नैवेदानीमिति** । इदानीं प्रियाविरहशोकार्ते उदयने चक्रवाकाः तादृशा उदयन इव विरहशोकाकुला न । स्त्रीषु विशेषाः स्त्रीविशेषाः, आभिजात्यलावण्यादिगुणविशिष्टाः स्त्रिय इत्यर्थः । तैः वियुक्ता अन्येऽपि तथा न। सा स्त्री वासवदत्तेति यावत् । धन्या यां भर्ता तथाऽविस्मरणीयगुणतया शोच्यामेव वेत्ति । सा हि दग्धापि भर्तृस्नेहात् भर्त्रा अनुरागाविष्करणाददग्धा एव । न खलु सोपरता यस्या भर्ता स्मरतीति भावः । शालिनीवृत्तम् । 'मातौ गौ चेच्छालिनी वेदलोकैः' इति तल्लक्षणम् ॥ ३ ॥ प्रत्यवस्थापयितुं प्रकृतिस्थं कर्तुम् । यत्नवान् कृतयत्नः । **अनाहार इति** । अनाहारे आहाराग्रहणे तुल्यः, नरपतिनेति शेषः । यद्वा नृपतौ अनाहारे अविद्यमान आहारो यस्य तादृशे सति अयमपि तत्तुल्यः, आहारग्रहणं न करोतीत्यर्थः । सततं यद्रुदितं तेन क्षामं वदनं यस्य स तथा । नृपतिवदिति शेषः । तथा च नृपतिना समं दुःखं यस्मिन्कर्मणि तद्यथा तथा नृपतिरिव दुःखेन । कथंकथमपि इत्यर्थः । नृपतिसमं दुःखं यस्मिन्निति संस्कारविशेषणं वा । शरीरे संस्कारं स्नानगन्ध-

---

१ मोहगतः (मोहगदो). २ अग्निदग्धा. ३ सतत.

दिवा वा रात्रौ वा परिचरति यत्नैर्नरपतिं
नृपः प्राणान् सद्यस्त्यजति यदि तस्याप्युपरमः ॥ १४ ॥

वासवदत्ता—(स्वगतम् ।) दिष्ट्या सुनिक्षिप्त इदानीमार्यपुत्रः । [दिट्ठिआ सुणिक्खित्तो दाणिं अय्यउत्तो ।]

यौगन्धरायणः—(आत्मगतम् ।) अहो महद्भारमुद्वहति रुमण्वान् । कुतः

सविश्रमो ह्ययं भारः प्रसक्तस्तस्य तु श्रमः ।
तस्मिन् सर्वमधीनं हि यत्राधीनो नराधिपः ॥ १५ ॥

(प्रकाशम् ।) अथ भोः ! पर्यवस्थापित इदानीं स राजा ।

ब्रह्मचारी—तदिदानीं न जाने । ' इह तया सह हसितम् , इह तया सह कथितम्, इह तया सह पर्युषितम् , इह तया सह कुपितम्, इह तया सह शायितम्, ' इत्येवं विलपन्तं तं राजानममात्यैर्महता यत्नेन तस्माद् ग्रामाद् गृहीत्वापक्रान्तम्[1] । ततो निष्क्रान्ते[2] राजनि प्रोषितनक्षत्र-चन्द्रमिव नभोऽरमणीयः संवृत्तः स ग्रामः । ततोऽहमपि निर्गतोऽस्मि ।

तापसी—स खलु गुणवान् नाम राजा य आगन्तुकेनाप्यनेनैवं प्रशस्यते । [सो खु गुणवंतो णाम राआ जो आअंतुएण वि इमिणा एव्वं पसंसीअदि ।]

माल्यधारणादिकं परिवहन् । दिवा वा रात्रौ वा । वा समुच्चये । सर्वकालमित्यर्थः । यत्नैः नरपतिं परिचरति शुश्रूषते । नृपः सद्यः प्राणांस्त्यजति चेदस्यापि सद्य एव उपरमो जीवितावसानं भवेत् । नृपतिमरणे क्षणमपि प्राणान्न धारयेदित्यर्थः । शिखरिणीवृत्तम् । अस्य लक्षणं 'रसै रुद्रैश्छिन्ना यमनसभला गः शिखरिणी ।' इति ॥१४॥ सुनिक्षिप्तः सुरक्षकहस्ते न्यस्तः । महाभारं यः प्रजानां पालयिता तस्यापि पालनरूपम् । **सुविश्रम इति** । अयं मयात्मनि विन्यस्तः नराधिपभार्यारक्षणरूपः सविश्रमः विश्रमेण विश्रान्त्या सहितः । तस्य रुमण्वतः । श्रमस्तु प्रसक्तः सततः । हि यतो यस्मिन्नराधिपः अधीनः आयत्तः तस्मिन्सर्वमधीनम् । राजरक्षितव्यस्य सर्वस्य रक्षणं तस्मिन्प्रसक्तमिति निरतिशयश्रमोऽयं रुमण्वतो भार इत्यर्थः ॥ १५ ॥ पर्यवस्थापितः समाश्वासनेन प्रकृतिस्थः कृतः । हसितं मयेति शेषः । एवं सर्वत्र । प्रोषितानि निर्गतानि । अन्तर्हितानीति यावत् । नक्षत्राणि चन्द्रश्च यस्मात्तत् । आगन्तुकेन पथिके-

---

१ पक्रान्तमपश्यम्. २ अपक्रान्ते.

चेटी—भर्तृदारिके ! किं नु खल्वपरा स्त्री तस्य हस्तं गमिष्यति ? [भट्टिदारिए ! किं णु खु अवरा इत्थिआ तस्स हत्थं गमिस्सदि ?]

पद्मावती—(आत्मगतम् ।) मम हृदयेनैव सह मन्त्रितम् । [मम हिअएण एव्व सह मंतिदं ।]

ब्रह्मचारी—आपृच्छामि भवन्तौ । गच्छामस्तावत् ।

उभौ—गम्यतामर्थसिद्धये ।

ब्रह्मचारी—तथास्तु । (निष्क्रान्तः ।)

यौगन्धरायणः—साधु । अहमपि तत्रभवत्याभ्यनुज्ञातो गन्तुमिच्छामि ।

काञ्चुकीयः—तत्रभवत्याभ्यनुज्ञातो गन्तुमिच्छति किल ।

पद्मावती—आर्यस्य भगिनिकार्येण विनोत्कण्ठिष्यते । [अय्यस्स भइणिआ अय्येण विना उक्कंठिस्सदि ।]

यौगन्धरायणः—साधुजनहस्तगतैषा नोत्कण्ठिष्यति । (काञ्चुकीयमवलोक्य ।) गच्छामस्तावत् ।

काञ्चुकीयः—गच्छतु भवान् पुनर्दर्शनाय ।

यौगन्धरायणः—तथास्तु । (निष्क्रान्तः ।)

काञ्चुकीयः—समय इदानीमभ्यन्तरं प्रवेष्टुम् ।

पद्मावती—आर्ये ! वन्दे । [अय्ये ! वंदामि ।]

तापसी—जाते ! तव सदृशं भर्तारं लभस्व । [जादे ! तव सदिसं भत्तारं ळभेहि ।]

वासवदत्ता—आर्ये ! वन्दे तावदहम् । [अय्ये ! वंदामि दाव अहं ।]

तापसी—त्वमप्यचिरेण भर्तारं समासादय । (तुवं पि अइरेण भत्तारं समासादेहि ।)

वासवदत्ता—अनुगृहीतास्मि । (अणुग्गहीदम्हि ।)

नापि । अत्र गुणाख्यानाद्विलोभनं नाम मुखसन्धेरङ्गमुक्तम् । किं नु खलु कश्चिदेतत्स्यात् । तस्यैवं भार्यानुरक्तस्य । यदि गच्छेत्सा धन्या भवेदित्यभिसन्धिः । ममेति मम हृद्गतो भाव एवोक्त इत्यर्थः । अनेन हावलक्षणो विकार उक्तः । भावादीषत्प्रकाशो यः स हाव इति कथ्यते । इति । आपृच्छामि आमन्त्रये ॥ परस्मैपदं चिन्त्यम् । 'आङि नुप्रच्छयोः' इति आत्मनेपदं स्यात् । अर्थसिद्धये श्रुतिविशिष्टाध्ययनरूपाभिलषितसिद्धिर्भवत्वित्यर्थः ।

---

१ साधयामः. २ आर्ये गच्छामि. ३ लभेहि.

काञ्चुकीयः—तदागम्यताम् । इत इतो भवत्यः । संप्रति हि

खगा वासोपेताः सलिलमवगाढो मुनिजनः
प्रदीप्तोऽग्निर्भाति प्रविचरति धूमो मुनिवनम् ।
परिभ्रष्टो दूराद्रविरपि च संक्षिप्तकिरणो
रथं व्यावर्त्यासौ प्रविशति शनैरस्तशिखरम् ॥ १६ ॥

(निष्क्रान्ताः सर्वे ।)

इति **प्रथमोऽङ्कः** ।

अथ द्वितीयोऽङ्कः ।

(ततः प्रविशति चेटी ।)

चेटी—कुञ्जरिके कुञ्जरिके ! कुत्र कुत्र भर्तृदारिका पद्मावती ? किं भणसि एषा भर्तृदारिका[1] माधवीलतामण्डपस्य पार्श्वतः[2] कन्दुकेन क्रीडतीति ? यावद् भर्तृदारिकामुपसर्पामि । (परिक्रम्यावलोक्य ।) अम्मो ! इयं भर्तृदारिका उत्कृतकर्णचूलिकेन व्यायामसंजातस्वेदबिन्दुविचित्रितेन परि-

---

उत्कण्ठिष्यते उत्सुका भविष्यति । **खगा इति** । खगा विहगा वासं स्ववसतिस्थानमुपेताः ! मुनिजनः सलिलं जलमवगाढः स्नानार्थं प्रविष्टः । प्रदीप्तोऽग्निर्भाति प्रकाशते । धूमः मुनिवनं तपोवनं प्रविचरति । असौ दूराद्वियतः परिभ्रष्टः संक्षिप्तकिरणः रविरपि रथं व्यावर्त्य परावर्त्य शनैः अस्ताचलस्य शिखरं प्रविशति । सायंसन्ध्यासमयो जात इत्यर्थः । शिखरिणी वृत्तम् ॥ १६ ॥ निष्क्रान्ताः सर्वे इति अङ्कसमाप्तिः । अङ्कलक्षणमादिभरते-'अङ्क इति रूढिशब्दो भावैश्च रसैश्च रोहयत्यर्थान् । नानाविधानयुक्तो यस्मात्तस्माद्भवेदङ्कः ॥ यत्रार्थस्य समाप्तिर्यस्य च बीजस्य भवति संहारः । किंचिदवलग्नबिन्दुः सोऽङ्क इति सदावगन्तव्यः ॥' इत्यादि ॥

अथ प्रथमाङ्कसूचितस्य पद्मावत्या उदयनविषयकस्याभिलाषस्य परिपोषार्थं तथा च पद्मावतीभ्रात्रोदयनाय पद्मावतीदानं तस्या हस्ते कौतुकबन्धनमित्यादिविषयप्रतिपादनाय द्वितीयाङ्कमारभमाणः पद्मावत्याः प्रवेशं सूचयितुं प्रवेशकं रचयितुमिच्छंस्तदनुगुणं चेटीप्रवेशमुपक्षिपति-**ततः प्रविशतीति** । कुञ्जरिके इत्यादिचेटीभाषणमत्र आकाशे इति द्रष्टव्यम् । तदुक्तं—'किं ब्रवीष्येवमित्यादि विना पात्रं ब्रवीति यत् । श्रुत्वेवानुक्तमप्येकस्तत्स्यादाकाशभाषितम् ॥' इति । कर्णे चूलिका आभरणविशेषः कर्णचूलिका । उत्कृता ऊर्ध्वं कृता कर्णचूलिका यस्मिन् तेन इति मुखविशेषणम् ।

---

१ °रिका पद्मावती. २ पार्श्वगता.

श्रान्तरमणीयदर्शनेन मुखेन कन्दुकेन क्रीडन्तीत एवागच्छति । यावदुपसर्प्स्यामि । (कुञ्जरिए कुञ्जरिए ! कहिं कहिं भट्टिदारिआ पदुमावदी । किं भणासि 'एसा भट्टिदारिआ माहवीळदामंडवस्स पस्सदो कंदुएण कीळदि' त्ति ? जाव भट्टिदारिअं उवसप्पामि । अम्मो ! इअं भट्टिदारिआ उक्करिदकण्णचूळिएण वा आमसंजादसेदबिंदुविइत्तिदेण परिस्संतरमणीअदंसणेण मुहेण कंदुएण कीळंदी इदो एव्व आअच्छदि । जाव उवसप्पिसं ॥)

(निष्क्रान्ता ।)

प्रवेशकः ।

(ततः प्रविशति कन्दुकेन क्रीडन्ती पद्मावती सपरिवारा वासवदत्तया सह ।)

वासवदत्ता—हला ! एष ते कन्दुकः । (हळा ! एसो दे कंदुओ ।)

पद्मावती—आर्ये ! भवत्विदानीमेतावत् । (अय्ये ! भोदु दाणिं एत्तअं ।)

वासवदत्ता—हला ! अतिचिरं कन्दुकेन क्रीडित्वाधिकसंजातरागौ परकीयाविव ते हस्तौ संवृत्तौ । (हळा ! अदिचिरं कंदुएण कीळिअ अहिअसंजादराआ परकेरआ विअ दे हत्था संवुत्ता ।)

चेटी—क्रीडतु क्रीडतु तावद् भर्तृदारिका । निर्वर्त्यतां तावदयं कन्याभावरमणीयः कालः । (कीळदु कीळदु दाव भट्टिदारिआ । णिव्वत्तीअदु दाव अअं कण्णाभावरमणीओ काळो ।)

पद्मावती—आर्ये ! किमिदानीं मामपहसितुमिव निध्यायसि ? (अय्ये ! किं दाणिं मं ओहसिदुं विअ णिज्झाअसि ?)

व्यायामेन सञ्जाता ये स्वेदबिन्दवस्तैर्विचित्रितेन । परिश्रान्तेन परिश्रान्त्या रमणीयं दर्शनं यस्य तेन मुखेनोपलक्षितेत्यर्थः । **प्रवेशकः**—तल्लक्षणं—'तद्वदेवानुदात्तोक्त्या नीचपात्रप्रयोजितः । प्रवेशोऽङ्कद्वयस्यान्तः शेषार्थस्योपसूचकः ॥ ' इति । हलेति सखीं प्रत्याह्वाने । 'हण्डे हञ्जे हलाह्वाने नीचां चेटीं सखीं प्रति ।' इत्यमरः । भूमिपतितं कन्दुकमुद्गृह्यार्पयन्त्याह-**अयं ते कंदुक इति**। एतावत्क्रीडनमिति शेषः। अतःपरं क्रीडितुं नेच्छामीति भावः । परकीयाविव कन्दुकप्रहरणासामर्थ्यात्स्वेच्छाननुवर्तित्वादित्यर्थः इति मन्ये इति शेषः । अधिके वरे सञ्जातो रागोऽनुरक्तिर्ययोस्तावतः परकीयौ इत्यपि ध्वनिः । निर्वर्त्यतां स्वैरमुपयुज्यताम् । कन्याभावेन अपराधीनत्वाद्रमणीयः मनोहरः ।

---

१ उपसर्पामि (उपसप्पामि). २ आवन्तिकावेषधारिणी वासवदत्ता च. ३ हला किंनिमित्तं वारयसि (किं णिमित्तं वारेसि) इत्यधि.

वासवदत्ता—नहि नहि । हला अधिकमद्य शोभसे[1] । अभित इव तेऽद्य वरमुखं पश्यामि । (णहि णहि । हला अधिअं अज्ज सोहसि । अभिदो विअ दे अज्ज वरमुहं पेक्खामि ।)

पद्मावती—अपेहि । मेदानीं मामुपहस (अवेहि । । मा दाणिं मं ओहस ।)

वासवदत्ता—एषास्मि तूष्णीका भविष्यन्महासेनवधूः । (एसाम्हि तुण्हीआ भविस्सम्महासेणवहू ।)

पद्मावती—क एष महासेनो नाम ? (को एसो महासेणो णाम ।)

वासवदत्ता—अस्त्युज्जयिनीयो राजा प्रद्योतो नाम । तस्य बलपरिमाण-निर्वृत्तं नामधेयं महासेन इति । (अत्थि उज्जइणीओ राआ पज्जोदो णाम । तस्य बळपरिमाणणिव्वुत्तं णामहेअं महासेणो त्ति ।)

चेटी—भर्तृदारिका तेन राज्ञा सह संबन्धं नेच्छति । (भट्टिदारिआ तेण रञ्ञा सह संबंधं णेच्छदि ।)

वासवदत्ता—अथ केन खल्विदानीमाभिलषति ? (अह केण खु दाणिं अभिळसदि ?)

चेटी—अस्ति वत्सराज उदयनो नाम । तस्य गुणान् भर्तृदारिका-भिलषति । (अत्थि वच्छराओ उदअणो णाम । तस्स गुणाणि भट्टिदारिआ अभिळसदि ।

वासवदत्ता—(आत्मगतम् ।) आर्यपुत्रं भर्तारमभिलषति । (प्रकाशम् ।) केन कारणेन ? (अय्यउत्तं भत्तारं अभिळसदि । केण कारणेण ?)

चेटी—सानुक्रोश इति । [साणुक्कोसो त्ति ।]

वासवदत्ता—(आत्मगतम् ।) जानामि जानामि । अयमपि जन एव-मुन्मादितः । [जाणामि जाणामि । अअं वि जणो एव्वं उम्मादिदो ।]

निध्यायसि निर्वर्णयसि । शोभते इति पाठे भवतीत्यध्याहार्यम् । श्लेषेणाह अभित इव सर्वत इव ते वरं रमणीयं मुखं वरमुखं पश्यामि निरीक्षे । अपि च ते त्वामभिता वरमुखं त्वां वरयितुर्यूनो मुखं पश्यामि । तव विवाहोऽचिरभावीति पश्यामीति भावः । उपहस परिहासं मा कुरु । भविष्यन्ती महासेनस्य वधूः स्नुषा तत्सम्बुद्धिः । बलपरिमाणेन सेनाया महापरिमाणेन निर्वृत्तं संजातम् । महती सेना यस्येति । सम्बन्धं वैवाहिकम् । अभिलषति तद्गुणाकृष्टा तस्मिन्बद्धभावा वर्तते इति यावत् । सानुक्रोशो भार्यायां

---

1 शोभवे (शोहदि).

चेटी—भर्तृदारिके ! यदि स राजा विरूपो भवेत् । [भट्टिदारिए ! जदि सो राआ विरूवो भवे ।]

वासवदत्ता—नहि नहि । दर्शनीय एव । [णहि णहि । दंसणीओ एव्व]

पद्मावती—आर्ये ! कथं त्वं जानासि ? । [अय्ये ! कहं तुवं जाणासि ?]

वासवदत्ता—(आत्मगतम् ।) आर्यपुत्रपक्षपातेनातिक्रान्तः समुदाचारः । किमिदानीं करिष्यामि ? (प्रकाशम्) भवतु दृष्टम् । हला ! एवमुज्जयिनीयो जनो मन्त्रयते । [अय्यउत्तपक्खवादेण अदिक्कंदो समुदाआरो । किं दाणिं करिस्सं ? होदु दिट्ठं । हळा ! एव्वं उज्जइणीओ[1] जणो मंतेदि ।]

पद्मावती—युज्यते । न खल्वेष उज्जयिनीदुर्लभः । सर्वजनमनोभिरामं खलु सौभाग्यं नाम । [जुज्जइ । ण खु एसो उज्जइणीदुल्ळहो । सव्वजणमणोभिरामं खु सोभग्गं णाम ।]

(ततः प्रविशति धात्री ।)

धात्री—जयतु भर्तृदारिका । भर्तृदारिके ! दत्तासि । [जेदु[2] भट्टिदारिआ । भट्टिदारिए ! दिण्णासि ।]

वासवदत्ता—आर्ये ! कस्मै ? [अय्ये ! कस्स ?]

धात्री—वत्सराजायोदयनाय । [वच्छराअस्स उदअणस्स ।]

वासवदत्ता—अथ कुशली स राजा ? [अह कुसळी सो राआ ?]

धात्री—कुशली स[3] इहागतः । तस्य भर्तृदारिका प्रतीष्टा च । [कुसळी सो इह आअदो । तस्स भट्टिदारिआ पडिच्छिदा अ ।]

वासवदत्ता—अत्याहितम् । [अच्चाहिदं ।]

धात्री—किमत्रात्याहितम् ? [किं एत्थ अच्चाहिदं ?]

वासवदत्ता—न खलु किंचित् । तथा नाम संतप्योदासीनो भवतीति । [णं हु किंचि । तह णाम संतप्पिअ उदासीणो होदि त्ति ।]

सानुकम्पः । अयमपि जनोऽहमपि उन्मादित उन्मत्तीकृतः । कथं त्वं जानासि परपुरुषदर्शनपरिहारिणीति भावः । अतिक्रान्तः परपुरुषस्य पद्मावतीदृष्टया सौन्दर्यवर्णनात् । दृष्टं यद्वक्तुमुचितमित्यर्थः । उज्जयिनीय उज्जयिन्यां भवः । सर्वजनाभिरामं न केवलमात्मीयजनानाम् । दत्ता वाग्दत्तेत्यर्थः । तस्य तेनेत्यर्थः । प्रतीष्टा स्वीकृता । अत्याहितं अतिरभसकृतं कर्म । अत्र कन्यास्वीकरणे । तथा नाम ब्रह्मचार्युक्तप्रकारेण । उदासीनः वासवदत्तां प्रति निःस्नेहो भवतीति ।

---

१ ° इणीजणो. २ जेदु जेदु. ३ स आ०.

धात्री—आर्ये ! आगमप्रधानानि सुलभपर्यवस्थानानि महापुरुषहृदयानि भवन्ति । [अय्ये ! आअमप्पहाणाणि सुळहपय्यवत्थाणाणि महापुरुसहिअआणि होंति[1] ।]

वासवदत्ता—आर्ये ! स्वयमेव तेन वरिता ? [अय्ये ! सअं एव्व तेन वरिदा ।]

धात्री—नहि नहि । अन्यप्रयोजनेनेहागतस्याभिजनविज्ञानवयोरूपं दृष्ट्वा स्वयमेव महाराजेन दत्ता । णहि णहि । अण्णप्पओअणेण इह आअदस्स अभिजणविञ्ञाणवओरूवं पेक्खिअ सअं एव्व महाराएण दिण्णा ।]

वासवदत्ता—(आत्मगतम् ।) एवम् । अनपराद्ध इदानीमत्रार्यपुत्रः । [एव्वं । अणवरद्धो दाणिं एत्थ अय्यउत्तो ।]

(प्रविश्यापरा ।)

चेटी—त्वरतां त्वरतां तावदार्या । अद्यैव किल शोभनं नक्षत्रम् । अद्यैव कौतुकमङ्गलं कर्तव्यमित्यस्माकं भर्त्री भणति । [तुवरदु तुवरदु दाव अय्या[2] अज्ज एव्व किळ सोभणं णक्खत्तं । अज्ज एव्व कोदुअमंगळं कादव्वं त्ति अम्हाणं भट्टिणी भणादि ।]

वासवदत्ता—(आत्मगतम् ।) यथा यथा त्वरते तथा तथान्धीकरोति मे हृदयम् । [जह जह तुवरदि तह तह अंधीकरेदि[3] मे हिअअं ।]

धात्री—एत्वेतु भर्तृदारिका । [एदु[4] एदु भट्टिदारिआ ।]

(निष्क्रान्ताः सर्वे ।)

इति द्वितीयोऽङ्कः ।

आगमः शोकस्येत्यर्थः । प्रधानः येषां तानि । शोकस्य प्रथमापाते विह्वलानि भवन्ति । तेषां मृदुत्वात् । यद्वा आगमः शास्त्रं तदुपदेश इति यावत् । अनित्यानि शरीराणि तत्र का परिदेवना इत्यादिरूपः प्रधानं येषां तानि । अतः सुलभपर्यवस्थापनं प्रकृतावस्थापनं येषां तानि तथाभूतानि । महान्तो हि विवेकात्स्वदुःखं निगृह्णन्तीति भावः । अभिजनश्च उच्चैः कुलं च विज्ञानं च वयः नवं च रूपं चेत्येतेषां समाहारः °रूपम् । ' मोक्षे धीर्ज्ञानमन्यत्र विज्ञानं शिल्पशास्त्रयोः । ' इत्यमरः । महाराजेन दर्शकेन । अनपराद्धः स्वयमप्रार्थितायाः पद्मावत्याः स्वीकारात् । स्वयमेव तामवरिष्यच्चेन्मयि सापराधोऽभविष्यत् । न तु तथा कृतवानित्याशयः । शोभनं मङ्गलकरम् । कौतुकमङ्गलं कौतुकं विवाहसूत्रं तस्य बन्धनरूपं मङ्गलम् । ' कौतुकं

---

१ होन्ति सोअसूण्णाणि (शोकशून्यानि) इत्य०. २ भटिदारिआ. ३ अन्धआरेण पिहिदं विअ (अन्धकारेण पिहितमिव) ४ पविसदु दाव अब्भन्तरं भट्टिदारिआ.

अथ तृतीयोऽङ्कः ।

(ततः प्रविशति विचिन्तयन्ती वासवदत्ता ।)

वासवदत्ता—विवाहामोदसंकुले अन्तःपुरचतुःशाले परित्यज्य पद्मावतीमिहागतास्मि प्रमदवनम् । यावदिदानीं भागधेयनिर्वृत्तं दुःखं विनोदयामि । (परिक्रम्य ।) अहो अत्याहितम् । आर्यपुत्रोऽपि नाम परकीयः संवृत्तः । यावदुपविशामि । (उपविश्य ।) धन्या खलु चक्रवाकवधूः या विरहिता न जीवति । न खल्वहं प्राणान् परित्यजामि । आर्यपुत्रं पश्यामीत्येतेन मनोरथेन जीवामि मन्दभागा । [विवाहामोदसंकुले अंतेउरचउस्साळे परित्तजिअ पदुमावदिं इह आअदम्हि पमदवणं । जाव दाणिं भाअधेअणिव्वुत्तं दुःखं विणोदेमि । अहो अच्चाहिदं । अय्यउत्तो वि णाम परकेरओ संवुत्तो । जाव उवविसामि । धञ्ञा खु चक्कवाअवहू जा विरहिदा ण जीवइ । ण खु अहं पाणाणि परित्तजामि । अय्यउत्तं पेक्खामि त्ति एदिणा मणोरहेण जीवामि मंदभाआ ।]

(ततः प्रविशति पुष्पाणि गृहीत्वा चेटी ।)[3]

चेटी—क्व नु खलु गता आर्यावन्तिका ? (परिक्रम्यावलोक्य ।) अम्मो ! इयं चिन्ताशून्यहृदया नीहारप्रतिहतचन्द्रलेखेवामण्डितभद्रकं वेषं

त्वभिलाषे स्यादुत्सवे नर्महर्षयोः । ' विवाहसूत्रगीतादिभोगयोरपि न द्वयोः । ' इति मेदिनी । स्वामिनी दर्शकस्त्री । ' राजस्त्रियस्तु संभाष्याः सर्वाः परिजनेन तु । भट्टिनी स्वामिनीत्येवम् । ' इत्यमरः । त्वरते राजपत्नीति शेषः । अन्धीकरोति शोकान्धकारग्रस्तं करोतीत्यर्थः । अनेनोत्तराङ्कार्थस्योपक्षेपः कृतः ।

अथ पूर्वाङ्कोपक्षिप्तस्य विवाहमङ्गलस्य निवृत्त्यर्थे तृतीयाङ्कमारभते । तत्रादौ विषण्णाया वासवदत्तायाः प्रवेशः । विवाहस्यामोदेन प्रमोदेन महोत्सवेनेति यावत् । सङ्कुले नानाकार्यव्यग्रबन्धुजनाकुले । अन्तःपुरचतुःशाले अन्तःपुरसम्बद्धे चतुःशाले । चतस्रः शालाः समाहृताः चतुःशालमन्योन्याभिमुखशालाचतुष्टयगृहम् । आवन्तो वा इति वा क्लीबत्वम् । प्रमदानां प्रमदोचितं वा वनं प्रमदवनम् । 'स्यादेतदेव प्रमदवनमन्तःपुरोचितं ।' इत्यमरः । भागधेयनिर्वृत्तं दैवप्राप्तम् । अत्याहितं महानिष्टम् । आर्यपुत्रोऽपि नाम तथा मयि प्रकृष्टप्रेमवानपि । परकीयः पद्मावतीपतित्वेन । चिन्तयाध्यानेन शून्यं निर्व्यापारं हृदयं यस्याः । नीहारेति । नीहारेण हिमेन प्रतिहता छन्नप्रभा

---

१ सचिन्ता. २ अण्णोण्णवि. ३ पुष्पहस्ता.

धारयन्ती प्रियङ्गुशिलापट्टके उपविष्टा । यावदुपसर्पामि । (उपसृत्य ।) आर्ये आवन्तिके ! कः कालः त्वामन्विष्यामि ? (कहिं णु खु गदा अय्या आवंतिआ ! अम्मो ! इअं चिंतासुञ्ञहिअआ णीहारपडिहदचंदलेहा विअ अमंडिदभद्दअं वेसं धारअंदी पिअंगुसिलापट्टए उवविट्ठा । जाव उवसप्पामि । अय्ये आवंतिए ! को कालो तुमं अण्णेसामि ?)

वासवदत्ता—किंनिमित्तम् ? (किंणिमित्तं ?)

चेटी—अस्माकं भट्टिनी भणति महाकुलप्रसूता स्निग्धा निपुणेति इमां तावत् कौतुकमालिकां गुम्फत्वार्या । (अम्हाअं भट्टिणी भणादि ' महाकुळप्पसूदा सिणिद्धा णिउणा[2] ' त्ति इमं दाव कोदुअमाळिअं गुम्हदु[3] अय्या ।)

वासवदत्ता—अथ कस्मै किल गुम्फितव्यम् ? (अह कस्सं किळ गुम्मिदव्वं ?)

चेटी—अस्माकं भर्तृदारिकायै । (अम्हाअं भट्टिदारिआए ।)

वासवदत्ता—(आत्मगतम् ।) एतदपि मया कर्तव्यमासीत् । अहो ! अकरुणाः खल्वीश्वराः । (एदं पि मए कत्तव्वं आसी । अहो ! अकरुणा खु इस्सरा ।)

चेटी—आर्ये ! मेदानीमन्यच्चिन्तयित्वा । एष जामाता मणिभूम्यां स्नायति । शीघ्रं तावद् गुम्फत्वार्या । (अय्ये ! मा दाणिं अण्णं चिंतिअ । एसो जामादुओ मणिभूमीए ण्हाअदि । सिग्घं दाव गुम्हदु अय्या ।)

वासवदत्ता—(आत्मगतम् ।) न शक्नोम्यन्यच्चिन्तयितुम् । (प्रकाशम् ।) हला ! किं दृष्टो जामाता ? (ण सक्कणोमि अण्णं चिंतेदुं । हळा ! किं दिट्ठो जामादुओ ?)

चेटी—आम् । दृष्टो भर्तृदारिकायाः स्नेहेनास्माकं कौतूहलेन च । (आम्, दिट्ठो भट्टिदारिआए सिणेहेन अम्हाअं कोदूहळेण अ ।)

वासवदत्ता—कीदृशो जामाता ? (कीदिसो जामादुओ ?)

चन्द्रलेखेव । न मंडितश्चासौ भद्रकश्च अमण्डितभद्रकस्तम् । प्रियङ्गुः फलिनी तस्यास्तन्मूलस्थ इति यावत् । शिलापट्टकस्तस्मिन् । कः कालः गत इति शेषः । कौतुकमालां मंगलमालां च दूर्वायुक्तां मधूकपुष्पमालाम् । कर्तव्यमासीत् । नियति-

---

१ णीहारगदा पडिवदचन्द० (निहारगता प्रतिपच्चन्द्र०) २ णिउणा आवन्तिआ त्ति । ३ गि० किल. ४ होइ. ५ अलं दाणिं अणुचि०. ६ कहं ण.

चेटी—आर्ये ! भणामि तावद् । नेदृशो दृष्टपूर्वः । (अय्ये ! भणामि दाव णं ईरिसो दिट्ठपुरुवो ।)

वासवदत्ता—हला ! भण भण किं दर्शनीयः ? (हळा ! भणाहि भणाहि किं दंसणीओ ?)

चेटी—शक्यं भणितुं शरचापहीनः कामदेव इति । (सक्कं भणिदुं सरचावहीणो कामदेवो त्ति ।)

वासवदत्ता—भवत्वेतावत् । (होदु एत्तअ ।)

चेटी—किंनिमित्तं वारयसि ? (किंणिमित्तं वारेसि ?)

वासवदत्ता—अयुक्तं परपुरुषसंकीर्तनं श्रोतुम् । (अजुत्तं परपुरुसंकित्तणं सोदुं ।)

चेटी—तेन हि गुम्फत्वार्या शीघ्रम् । (तेण हि गुम्हदु अय्या सिग्घं ।)

वासवदत्ता—इयं गुम्फामि । आनय तावत् । (इअं गुम्हामि आणेहि दाव ।)

चेटी—गृह्णात्वार्या । (गण्हदु अय्या ।)

वासवदत्ता[3]—(वर्जयित्वा विलोक्य ।) इदं तावदौषधं किं नाम ? (इमं दाव ओसहं किं णाम ?)

चेटी—अविधवाकरणं नाम । (अविहवाकरणं णाम ।)

वासवदत्ता—(आत्मगतम् ।) इदं बहुशो गुम्फितव्यं मम च पद्मावत्याश्च । (प्रकाशम् ।) इदं तावदौषधं किं नाम ? (इदं बहुसो गुम्हिदव्वं मम अ पदुमावदीए अ । इदं दाव ओसहं किं णाम ?)

चेटी—सपत्नीमर्दनं नाम । (सवत्तिमद्दणं णाम ।)

वासवदत्ता—इदं न गुम्फितव्यम् । (इदं ण गुम्हिदव्वं ।)

विहितमित्याशयः । ईश्वरा इष्टानिष्टकरणे समर्था देवाः । **चेटी**—मा अलमर्थे । इदानीमस्मिन्मङ्गलकाले । अन्यत्स्वबन्धुवियोगदुःखादिकम् । भवत्वेतावदलमतःपरं तद्वर्णनेन । वर्जयित्वा पुष्पभाजनमावर्ज्य । पुष्पेभ्योऽन्यद्गुम्फनीयं दृष्ट्वा पृच्छति इदं तावदोषधं किमिति । अविधवा क्रियते अनेनेति । बहुशो गुम्फितव्यं स्वस्याप्यवैधव्यस्येष्टत्वात् । समानः पतिर्यस्याः सा सपत्नी । सपत्नी मर्द्यते विनाश्यतेऽनेनेति

---

१ दाव ईदिसो जामादुओ अदिट्ठपुरुवो. २ सअं हि भअवं (स्वयं हि भगवान्); स सर. ३ वास०–(आत्मगतम् ।) इयं गुम्फामि मन्दभागा (इअं गुम्हामि मन्दभाआ) (आवर्ज्य वि० प्रकाशम् ।)

चेटी—कस्मात् ? (कीसं[1] ?)

वासवदत्ता—उपरता तस्य भार्या तन्निष्प्रयोजनमिति । (उवरदा तस्स भय्या । तं णिप्पओअणं त्ति ।)

(प्रविश्य अपरा ।)

चेटी—त्वरतां त्वरतामार्या । एष जामाता अविधवाभिरभ्यन्तरचतुःशालं प्रवेश्यते । [तुवरदु तुवरदु अय्या । एसो जामादुओ अविहवाहिं अब्भंतरचउस्सालं पवेसीअदि ।]

वासवदत्ता—अयि ! वदामि गृहाणैतत् । [अइ ! वदामि गण्ह एदं]

चेटी—शोभनम् । आर्ये ! गच्छामि तावदहम् । [सोहणं[3] । अय्ये ! गच्छामि दाव अहं ।]

(उभे निष्क्रान्ते ।)

वासवदत्ता—गतैषा । अहो ! अत्याहितम् । आर्यपुत्रोऽपि नाम परकीयः संवृत्तः । अहमपि शय्यायां मम दुःखं विनोदयामि यदि निद्रां लभे । [गदा ऐसा । अहो ! अच्चाहिदं । अय्यउत्तो वि णाम परकेरओ संवुत्तो । अहंवि सय्याए मम दुक्खं विणोदेमि जद्दि णिद्दं ळभामि ।]

(निष्क्रान्ता ।)

इति तृतीयोऽङ्कः ।

अथ चतुर्थोऽङ्कः ।

(ततः प्रविशति विदूषकः ।)

विदूषकः—(सहर्षम् ।) भोः ! दिष्टया तत्रभवतो वत्सराजस्याभिप्रेत-विवाहमङ्गलरमणीयः कालो दृष्टः । भोः ! को नामैतज्जानाति तादृशे

सपत्नीमर्दनम् । अविधवाभिः सुवासिनीभिः । सुवासिनीभिरेव वरो विवाहचतुष्कं प्रापयितव्य इति आचारः । अविदेति विषादे ।

अथ जातविवाहस्यापि नायकस्य स्मृत्युपस्थापितैर्वासवदत्तायां सैवानुरक्तिः पद्मावत्यां च दाक्षिण्यानुवृत्तिः तथा जानत्या जाताश्वासाया वासवदत्ताया सपत्नी-सम्पन्नत्वे सत्त्वावष्टम्भेन वर्तनमित्यादिवृत्तान्तं प्रपञ्चयितुं चतुर्थाङ्कमारभते कविः । **विदूषकः**—अस्य लक्षणं सुधाकरे—'विकृताङ्गवयोवेषैर्हास्यकारी विदूषकः ।' इति ।

---

१ किंणिमित्तम्. २ हअं तुवरामि । भद्दे गह्न. ३ हला वासो आणेदव्वे (वास आनेतव्यं) । गच्छामि. ४ एसा जाव दाणिं भाअधेओणिवुत्तं दुक्खं विणोदेमि । अहो इ. ५ अविदा.

वयमनर्थसलिलावर्ते प्रक्षिप्ताः पुनरुन्मङ्क्ष्याम इति । इदानीं प्रासादेषूष्यते अन्तःपुरदीर्घिकासु स्नायते प्रकृतिमधुरसुकुमाराणि मोदकखाद्यानि खाद्यन्त इत्यनप्सरस्संवास उत्तरकुरुवासो मयानुभूयते । एकः खलु महान् दोषः ममाहारः सुष्ठु न परिणमति सुप्रच्छदनायां शय्यायां निद्रां न लभे यथा वातशोणितमभित इव वर्तत इति पश्यामि । भोः सुखं नाममपरि-भूतमकल्यवर्तं च । [भो दिट्ठिआ तत्तहोदो वच्छराअस्स अभिप्पेदविवाह-मंगळरमणिज्जो काळो दिट्ठो । भो को णाम एदं जाणादि तादिसे वयं अणत्थस-ळिळावत्ते पक्खित्ता उण उम्मज्जिस्सामो त्ति । इदाणिं पासादेसु वसीअदि अंदेउर-दिग्घिआसु ण्हाईअदि पकिदिमउरसुउमाराणि मोदअखज्जआणि खज्जीअंति त्ति अणच्छरसंवासो उत्तरकुरुवासो मए अणुभवीअदि । एको खु महंतो दोसो मम आहारो सुट्ठु ण परिणमदि सुप्पच्छदणाए सय्याए णिद्दं ण ळभामि जह वादसोणिदं अभिदो विअ वत्तदि त्ति पेक्खामि । भो सुहं णामअपरिभूदं अकळ्ळवत्तं च ।]

(ततः प्रविशति चेटी ।)

चेटी—कुत्र न खलु गत आर्यवसन्तकः ? [परिक्रम्यावलोक्य ।] अहो एष आर्यवसन्तकः । [उपगम्य ।] आर्य वसन्तक ! कः कालस्त्वामन्विष्यामि । [कहिं णु खु गदो अय्यवसंतओ । अम्हो एसो अय्यवसंतओ । अय्य वसंतअ ! को काळो तुमं अण्णेसामि ?]

विदूषकः—(दृष्ट्वा) किंनिमित्तं भद्रे ! मामन्विष्यसि ? [किंणिमित्तं भद्दे ! मं अण्णेससि ?]

चेटी—अस्माकं भट्टिनी भणति अपि स्नातो जामातेति । [अम्हाणं भट्टिणी भणादि ' अवि ण्हादो जामादुओ ' त्ति ।]

अस्य प्राकृतं पाठ्यम् । तदुक्तं–' विदूषकविटादीनां पाठ्यं नु प्राकृतं भवेत् । ' इति । अभिप्रेतमिष्टं यद्विवाहमङ्गलं तेन रमणीयः । अनर्थ एव सलिलावर्तोऽम्भसां भ्रमः तस्मिन् । अविद्यमानोप्सरसां संवासो यस्मिंस्तादृशः । उत्तरकुरवो नाम देवभूमिः । अप्सरःसंवासरहितं स्वर्गसुखमित्यर्थः । परिणमति जीर्यति । शोभनं प्रच्छदनं प्रच्छदपटो यस्यां सा सुप्रच्छदना । वातेन सम्पृक्तं रक्तं वातरक्तं तदाख्यो रोगः । तदुक्तं—' वातरक्तं तथाष्टधा । वाताधिक्येन पित्ताच्च कफाद्दोषत्रयेण च । रक्ताधिक्येन दोषाणां द्वन्द्वेन त्रिविधः स्मृतः ॥ ' (शा. सं.) अभितः वर्तते समीपस्थमिति पश्यामि । आमयेन रोगेण परिभूतं ग्रस्तम् । कल्यस्य निरामयस्य वर्तः वर्तनमशनमिति यावत् । कल्यवर्तः । नास्ति कल्यवर्तः यस्मिंस्तदकल्यवर्तम् । यद्वा कल्ये प्रातः

विदूषकः—किंनिमित्तं भवती पृच्छति ? [किंणिमित्तं[1] भोदि पुच्छदि ?]।

चेटी—किमन्यत् ? सुमनोवर्णकमानयामीति । [किमण्णं ? सुमणाव-ण्णअं आणेमि त्ति ।]

विदूषकः—स्नातस्तत्रभवान् । सर्वमानयतु भवती वर्जयित्वा भोजनम् । [ण्हादो तत्तभवं । सव्वं आणेदु भोदी वज्जिअ भोअणं ।]

चेटी—किंनिमित्तं वारयसि भोजनम् ? [किंणिमित्तं वारेसि भोअणं ?]

विदूषकः—अधन्यस्य मम कोकिलानामक्षिपरिवर्त इव कुक्षिपरिवर्तः संवृत्तः । [अधण्णस्स मम कोइळाणं अक्खिपरिवट्टो विअ कुक्खिपरिवट्टो संवुत्तो ।]

चेटी—ईदृश एव भव । [ईदिसो एव्व होहि ।]

विदूषकः—गच्छतु भवती । यावदहमपि तत्रभवतः सकाशं गच्छामि । [गच्छदु भोदी । जाव अहं वि तत्तहोदो सआसं गच्छामि ।]

(निष्क्रान्तौ ।)

प्रवेशकः ।

(ततः प्रविशति सपरिवारा पद्मावती आवन्तिकावेषधारिणी वासवदत्ता च ।)

चेटी—किंनिमित्तं भर्तृदारिका प्रमदवनमागता ? [किंणिमित्तं भट्टिदारिआ पमदवणं आअदा ।]

पद्मावती—हला ! ते तावच्छेफालिकागुल्मकाः पश्यामि कुसुमिता वा न वेति । [हळा ! ताणि दाव सेहालिआगुम्हआणि पेक्खामि कुसुमिदाणि वा ण वेत्ति ।]

चेटी—भर्तृदारिके ! ते कुसुमिता नाम प्रवालान्तरितैरिव मौक्तिकलम्ब-कैराचिताः कुसुमैः । [भट्टिदारिए ! ताणि कुसुमिदाणि णाम पवाळंतरिदेहिं विअ मोत्तिआलंबएहिं आइदाणि कुसुमेहिं ।]

वर्तः अशनं कल्यवर्तः प्रातराशः । तद्रहितम् । सुमनसः पुष्पाणि वर्णकमङ्गरागश्चैतेषां समाहारः सुमनोवर्णकम् । 'गात्रानुलेपनी वर्तिर्वर्णकं स्याद्विलेपनम् ।' इत्यमरः । सुमनोभिः सहितं वर्णकमिति वा । अधन्यस्य भाग्यरहितस्य परिवर्तः परिवृत्तिः । कुक्षिपरिवर्तः उदरविकृतिः । जठराग्निमान्द्यमिति यावत् । ईदृश एव भवेति विदूषकस्यौदरिकत्वं जानत्याः परिहासोक्तिः । शेफालिकानां निर्गुंडीणां गुल्मकाः गुल्माः । प्रवालान्तरितैः विद्रुमव्यवहितैः । मौक्तिकलम्बकैः लम्बमानै मुक्ताहारैः ।

---

१ भोदी (भवती) २ सुमनावर्ण०. ३ आणेदुं (आनेतुं). ४ मौक्तिका० ।

पद्मावती—हला ! यद्येवं किमिदानीं विलम्बसे ? [हळा ! जदि एव्वं किं दाणिं विळंबेसि ?]

चेटी—तेन ह्यस्मिन् शिलापट्टके मुहूर्तकमुपविशतु भर्तृदारिका । यावदहमपि कुसुमावचयं करोमि । [तेण हि इमस्सिं सिळावट्टए मुहुत्तअं उपविसदु भट्टिदारिआ । जाव अहं वि कुसुमावचअं करेमि ।]

पद्मावती—आर्ये ! किमत्रोपविशावः ? [अय्ये ! किं एत्थ उपविसामो ?]

वासवदत्ता—एवं भवतु । [एव्वं होदु]

(उभे उपविशतः ।)

चेटी—(तथा कृत्वा ।) पश्यतु पश्यतु भर्तृदारिका अर्धमनःशिलापट्टकैरिव शेफालिकाकुसुमैः पूरितं मेऽञ्जलिम् । [पेक्खदु पेक्खदु भट्टिदारिआ अद्धमणसिळावट्टएहिं विअ सेहालिआकुसुमेहिं पूरिअं मे अंजलिं ।]

पद्मावती—(दृष्ट्वा) अहो ! विचित्रता कुसुमानाम् । पश्यतु पश्यत्वार्या । [अहो ! विइत्तदा कुसुमाणं । पेक्खदु पेक्खदु अय्या ।]

वासवदत्ता—अहो दर्शनीयता कुसुमानाम् । [अहो दंसणीअदा कुसुमाणं ।]

चेटी—भर्तृदारिके ! किं भूयोऽवचेष्यामि ? [भट्टिदारिए ! किं भूयो अवइणुस्सं ।]

पद्मावती—हला ! मा मा भूयोऽवाचित्य । [हळा ! मा मा भूयो अवइणिअ ।]

वासवदत्ता—हला ! किंनिमित्तं वारयसि ? [हळा ! किंणिमित्तं वारेसि ?]

पद्मावती—आर्यपुत्रेण इहागत्येमां कुसुमसमृद्धिं दृष्ट्वा संमानिता वयम् । [अय्यउत्तो इह आअच्छिअ इमं कुसुमसमिद्धिं पेक्खिअ सम्माणिदा भवेअं ।]

वासवदत्ता—हला ! प्रियस्ते भर्ता । [हळा ! पिओ दे भत्ता ।]

पद्मावती—आर्ये ! न जानामि । आर्यपुत्रेण विरहितोत्कण्ठिता भवामि । [अय्ये ! ण आणामि । अय्यउत्तेण विरहिदा उक्कंठिदा होमि ।]

मनःशब्दवाच्या शिला मनःशिला । शाकपार्थिवादिः । धातुविशेषः । तस्याः पट्टः । अर्धमेकदेशो मनःशिलापट्टो येषां तैरिति विग्रहः । 'अद्धा पाठः प्रामादिकः ।' इति गणपतिशास्त्रिणः । कुसुमसमृद्धिं शेफालिकागुल्मानां पुष्पाढ्यत्वम् । वासवदत्ता–संमानिता भवेयमिति श्रुत्वा पृच्छति प्रियस्ते भर्तेति । उत्कण्ठिता पर्युत्सुका ।

---

१ जइ अय्यउत्तो इह दाव ..पेक्खेद यद्यार्यपुत्र इह तावदा० प्रेक्षेत.)

वासवदत्ता—[आत्मगतम् ।] दुष्करं खल्वहं करोमि । इयमपि नामैवं मन्त्रयते । [दुक्करं खु अहं करेमि । इअं वि णाम एव्वं मंतेदि ।]

चेटी—अभिजातं खलु भर्तृदारिकया मन्त्रितं प्रियो मे भर्तेति । [अभिजादं खु भट्टिदारिआए मंतिदं 'पिओ मे भत्त'त्ति ।]

पद्मावती—एकः खलु मे संदेहः । [एक्को खु मे संदेहो ।]

वासवदत्ता—किं किम् ? [किं किं ?]

पद्मावती—यथा ममार्यपुत्रस्तथैवार्याया वासवदत्ताया इति । [जह मम अय्यउत्तो तह एव्व अय्याए वासवदत्ताए त्ति ।]

वासवदत्ता—अतोऽप्यधिकम् । [अदो वि अहिअं ।]

पद्मावती—कथं त्वं जानासि ? [कहं तुवं जाणासि ?]

वासवदत्ता—(आत्मगतम् ।) हम् । आर्यपुत्रपक्षपातेनातिक्रान्तः समुदाचारः । एवं तावद् भणिष्यामि । यद्यल्पः स्नेहः सा स्वजनं न परित्यजति ! [हं । अय्यउत्तपक्खवादेण अदिक्कंदो समुदाआरो । एव्वं दाव भणिस्सं । (प्रकाशम् ।) जइ अप्पो सिणेहो सा सजणं ण परित्तजदि ।]

पद्मावती—भवितव्यम् । [होदव्वं ।]

चेटी—भर्तृदारिके ! साधु भर्तारं भण अहमपि वीणां शिक्षिष्य इति । [भट्टिदारिए ! साहु भट्टारं भणाहि अहं पि वीणं सिक्खिस्सामित्ति ।]

पद्मावती—उक्तो मयार्यपुत्रः । [उत्तो मए अय्यउत्तो ।]

वासवदत्ता—ततः किं भणितम् ? [तदो किं भणिदं ?]

पद्मावती—अभणित्वा किंचिद् दीर्घं निःश्वस्य तूष्णीकः संवृत्तः । [अभणिअ किंचि दिग्घं णिस्ससिअ तुण्हीओ संवुत्तो ।]

वासवदत्ता—ततस्त्वं किमिव तर्कयसि ? [तदो तुवं किं विअ तक्केसि ?]

पद्मावती—तर्कयाम्यार्याया वासवदत्ताया गुणान् स्मृत्वा दक्षिणतया

वास०—दुष्करं खल्विति अहमपि अत्यन्तं पर्याकुला भवामि । अभिजातं अभिजात्यानुरूपं न तु साक्षात् । यथा मम प्रिय इति शेषः । स्वजनं मातापित्रादिकम् । न त्यजति न पर्यत्यक्ष्यत् । यस्मात्परित्यक्तस्तस्मादधिकतरं प्रियः । भवितव्यमनल्पेन स्नेहेनेत्यर्थः । दक्षिणतया दाक्षिण्येन ।

---

१ एत्तओ. २ सिणेहेण . ... आरो । भाद एवं ... ३ जुज्जइ (युज्यते). ४ किंति.

ममाग्रतो न रोदितीति । [तक्केमि अय्याए वासवदत्ताए गुणाणि सुमरिअ दक्खिण्णदाए मम अग्गदो ण रोदिदि त्ति ।]

वासवदत्ता—[आत्मगतम् ।] धन्या खल्वस्मि यद्येवं सत्यं भवेत् । [धञ्ञा खु म्हि जदि एव्वं सच्चं भवे ।]

(ततः प्रविशति राजा विदूषकश्च ।)

विदूषकः—ही ही । प्रचितपतितबन्धुजीवकुसुमविरलवातरमणीयं प्रमदवनम् । इतस्तावद् भवान् । [ही ही । पचिअपडिअबंधुजीवकुसुमविरळवादरमणिज्जं पमदवणं । इदो दाव भवं ।]

राजा—वयस्य वसन्तक ! अयमयमागच्छामि ।

कामेनोज्जयिनीं गते मयि तदा कामप्यवस्थां गते
दृष्ट्वा स्वैरमवन्तिराजतनयां पञ्चेषवः पातिताः ।
तैरद्यापि सशल्यमेव हृदयं भूयश्च विद्धा वयं
पञ्चेषुर्मदनो यदा कथमयं षष्ठः शरः पातितः ॥ १ ॥

विदूषकः—कुत्र नु खलु गता तत्रभवती पद्मावती ? लतामण्डपं गता भवेद् उताहो असनकुसुमसंचितं व्याघ्रचर्मावगुण्ठितमिव पर्वततिलकं नाम शिलापट्टकं गता भवेद् अथवा अधिककटुकगन्धसप्तच्छदवनं प्रविष्टा भवेद् अथवालिखितमृगपक्षिसकुलं दारुपर्वतकं गता भवेत् । (ऊर्ध्वमवलोक्य ।) ही ही । शरत्कालनिर्मलेऽन्तरिक्षे प्रसादितबलदेवबाहुदर्शनीयां सारसपङ्क्तिं

मन्मनःखेदपरिजिहीर्षयेति यावत् । हीहीति विस्मये । **प्रचितेति** । प्रचितानि संहृतानि च तानि पतितानि बन्धुजीवकुसुमानि तैः विरलेन सौम्येन वातेन च रमणीयम् । नवविवर्धितेति पाठे नवानि विवर्धितानि इत्यादि । **कामेनेति** । उज्जयिनीं गते । प्रद्योतेन राज्ञा युक्त्या गृहीते सतीति शेषः । तदा स्वैरं विश्रब्धमवन्तिराजतनयां दृष्ट्वा कामप्यनिर्वचनीयामवस्थां गते मयि कामेन पञ्च अपि इषवः पातिताः । तेन अद्यापि हृदयं सशल्यमेव । न च तेऽद्याप्युद्धृता इति यावत् । भूयः पुनश्च वयं विद्धाः । यदा यदि मदनः पंचेषवो यस्य स पञ्चेषुस्तदा तर्हि अयं षष्ठः शरः कथं पातितः ? अहो आश्चर्यमिदमिति भावः । शार्दूलवि॰ वृत्तम् ॥ १ ॥ असनकुसुमैः सर्जकपुष्पैः । संचितमाच्छादितम् । अतो व्याघ्रचर्मणावगुण्ठितमिव । अधिककटुकः गन्धः यस्य । सप्तपर्णवृक्षः । आलिखिता मृगपक्षिणस्तैः व्याप्तम् । दारुनिर्मितः पर्वतः दारुपर्वतकः । °निर्मले

---

१ दक्खिण्णदाए (दाक्षिण्यतया). २ पात. ३ णवविवड्ढिअबन्धु॰ णिरळसंपात (नवविवर्धित ...संपात) ४ इदो इदो.

यावत् समाहितं गच्छन्तीं पश्यतु तावद् भवान् । (कहिं णु खु गदा तत्तहोदी पदुमावदी ? ळदामंडवं गदा भवे उदाहो असणकुसुमसञ्चिदं वग्घचम्मावगुंठिदं विअ पव्वदतिळअं णाम सिळापट्टअं गदा भवे आदु अधिअकडुअगंधसत्तच्छदवणं पविट्ठा भवे अहव आळिहिदमिअपक्खिसंकुळं दारुपव्वदअं गदा भवे । ही ही सरअकाळणिम्मळे अंतरिक्खे पसादिअबळदेवबाहुदंसणीअं सारसपंतिं जाव समाहिदं गच्छंतिं पेक्खदु दाव भवं ।)

राजा—वयस्य ! पश्याम्येनाम् ।

ऋज्वायतां च विरलां च नतोन्नतां च
सप्तर्षिवंशकुटिलां च निवर्तनेषु ।
निर्मुच्यमानभुजगोदरनिर्मलस्य
सीमामिवाम्बरतलस्य विभज्यमानाम् ॥ २ ॥

चेटी—पश्यतु पश्यतु भर्तृदारिका एतां कोकनदमालापाण्डुररमणीयां सारसपङ्क्तिं यावत् समाहितं गच्छन्तीम् । अहो भर्ता । (पेक्खदु पेक्खदु मट्टिदारिआ[2] एदं कोकणदमाळापंडररमणीअं सारसपंतिं जाव समाहिदं गच्छंति । अम्मो भट्टा ।)

पद्मावती—हम् । आर्यपुत्रः । आर्ये ! तव कारणादार्यपुत्रदर्शनं परिहरामि । तदिमं तावन्माधवीलतामण्डपं प्रविशामः । (हं[3] । अय्यउत्तो । अय्ये ! तव कारणादो अय्यउत्तदंसणं परिहरामि । ता इमं दाव माहवीळदामंडवं पविसामो ।)

वासवदत्ता—एवं भवतु । (एव्वं होदु ।)

निरभ्रत्वात् । प्रसादितौ धवलौ । बलदेवबाहू तद्वद्दर्शनीयाम् । धावल्या-दैर्घ्याच्च । यावत्साकल्येन । समाहितं सुसंघटितं यथा तथा । **ऋज्वायतामिति** । ऋजुः अजिह्मा च सा आयता दीर्घा च ताम् । विरलामसंहताम् । नता नीचा च सा पुनः उन्नता च तां नतोन्नताम् । तथा च निवर्तनेषु परावर्तनेषु सप्तर्षिवंशमिव सप्तर्षिसार्थमिव कुटिलां वक्राम् । अथ च निर्मुच्यमानं निर्मोकान्निष्पतद्भुजगोदरमिव निर्मलस्य अम्बरतलस्य विभज्यमानां पृथक् क्रियमाणां सीमामिव स्थिताम् । उपमोत्प्रेक्षाभ्यां संसृष्टा स्वभावोक्तिरलंकारः । वसन्ततिलका वृत्तम् ॥ २ ॥ कोक-नदानां कमलानाम् । कोकनदशब्दोऽत्र कमलसामान्यपरः । न तु रक्तोत्पलपरः । कोकनदमालावत्पाण्डुरा चासौ रमणीया च । तव कारणात्त्वं परपुरुषदर्शनं परिहर-

---

१ दंसणीआ पन्ती समाहिदा गच्छदि । २ एसा ... रमणिज्जसारसपन्ती ... हिदा गच्छदि ३ हला.

(तथा कुर्वन्ति ।)

विदूषकः—तत्रभवती पद्मावतीहागत्य निर्गता भवेत् । (तत्तहोदी पदुमावदी इह आअच्छिअ णिग्गदा भवे ।)

राजा—कथं भवान् जानाति ?

विदूषकः—इमानवचितकुसुमान् शेफालिकागुच्छकान् प्रेक्षतां तावद् भवान् । (इमाणि अवइदकुसुमाणि सेफालिआगुच्छआणि पेक्खदु दाव भवं ।)

राजा—अहो ! विचित्रता कुसुमस्य वसन्तक ।

वासवदत्ता—(आत्मगतम् ।) वसन्तकसंकीर्तनेनाहं पुनर्जानामि उज्जयिन्यां वर्त इति । [वसंतअसंकित्तणेण अहं पुण जाणामि उज्जइणीए वत्तामि त्ति ।]

राजा—वसन्तक ! अस्मिन्नेवासीनौ शिलातले पद्मावतीं प्रतीक्षिष्यावहे ।

विदूषकः—भोस्तथा । (उपविश्योत्थाय ।) ही ही शरत्कालतीक्ष्णो दु:सह आतपः । तदिमं तावन्माधवीमण्डपं प्रविशावः । (भो तह । ही ही सरअकाळतिक्खो दुस्सहो आदवो । ता इमं दाव माहवीमंडवं पविसामो ।)

राजा—बाढम् । गच्छाग्रतः ।

विदूषकः—एवं भवतु । [एव्वं होदु ।]

(उभौ परिक्रामतः ।)

पद्मावती—सर्वमाकुलं कर्तुकाम आर्यवसन्तकः । किमिदानीं कुर्मः ? [सव्वं आउळं कत्तुकामोअय्यवसंतओ । किं दाणिं करेम्ह ?]

चेटी—भर्तृदारिके ! एतां मधुकरपरिनिलीनामवलम्बलतामवधूय भर्तारं वारयिष्यामि । [भट्टिदारिए ! ऍदं महुअरपरिणिळीणं ओळंबळदं ओधूय भट्टारं वारइस्सं ।]

पद्मावती—एवं कुरु । [एव्वं करेहि ।]

सीति तवोपरोधपरिहारार्थम् । अवचितकुसुमान् अवचितानि कुसुमानि येषां तान् । वसन्तकसंकीर्तनेन वसन्तक इति नाम्नः संकीर्तनेन । तीक्ष्णस्तीव्रः । सर्वं राजदर्शनपरिहारार्थं कृतां योजनाम् । आकुलं व्यर्थमित्यर्थः । मधुकराः परिनिलीना निभृतं स्थिता यस्यां तां मधुकरपरिनिलीनाम् । अवलम्बलतां मुख्यां द्वारावस्थिता-

---

१ आणि अ. २ एव्वं करेमि । एदं इ०.

(चेटी तथा करोति ।)

विदूषकः—अविधा अविधा तिष्ठतु तिष्ठतु तावद् भवान् । [अविहा अविहा चिट्ठदु चिट्ठदु दाव भवं ।]

राजा—किमर्थम् ?

विदूषकः—दास्याःपुत्रैर्मधुकरैः पीडितोऽस्मि । [दासीएपुत्तेहिं महुअरेहिं पीडिदो म्हि]

राजा—मा मा भवानेवम् । मधुकरसंत्रासः परिहार्यः । पश्य

मधुमदकला मधुकरा मदनार्ताभिः प्रियाभिरुपगूढाः ।
पादन्यासविषण्णा वयमिव कान्तावियुक्ताः स्युः ॥ ३ ॥

तस्मादिहैवासिष्यावहे ।

विदूषकः—एवं भवतु (एव्वं होदु ।)

(उभावुपविशतः ।)

राजा—(अवलोक्य ।)

पादाक्रान्तानि पुष्पाणि सोष्म चेदं शिलातलम् ।
नूनं काचिदिहासीना मां दृष्ट्वा सहसा गता ॥*

चेटी—भर्तृदारिके ! रुद्धाः खलु स्मो वयम् । [भट्टिदारिए रुद्धा खु म्ह वयं ।]

पद्मावती—दिष्ट्योपविष्ट आर्यपुत्रः । [दिट्ठिआ उववि्ट्ठो अय्यउत्तो ।]

वासवदत्ता—(आत्मगतम् ।) दिष्ट्या प्रकृतिस्थशरीर आर्यपुत्रः । [दिट्ठिआ पकिदित्थसरीरो अय्यउत्तो ।]

माधारभूतां लताम् । अविहा अविहेति संभ्रमे । दास्याःपुत्रैरित्याक्रोशवचनेन क्रोधः सूचितः । **मधुमदेति** । मधुनो मदः मधुमदस्तेन कला अव्यक्तमधुरनादाः । यद्वा कला मूकाः । 'जडो मूकः कलोऽप्यवाक्' इति यादवः। मदनार्ताभिः कामपीडिताभिः प्रियाभिः । उपगूढा आश्लिष्टाः मधुकराः आवयोः पादन्यासेन पादसंक्रमेण विषण्णाः खिन्नाः सन्तः वयमिवाहमिव । कान्ताभिर्वियुक्ताः स्युर्भवेयुः ॥ ३ ॥ **पादेति**—पादेनाक्रान्तानि मर्दितानि कुसुमानि तत्र पतितानि शेफालिकापुष्पाणि । इदं शिलातलं च सोष्म उष्मणा सहितम् । अतो नूनं ध्रुवमिहासीना काचिन्मां दृष्ट्वा सहसा सद्यो गता ॥ रुद्धाः प्रतिबद्धनिर्गमाः । प्रकृतिस्थं यथापूर्वं शरीरं यस्य । साश्रुपातेति

---

१ भो तह (तथा). *अयं ग्रन्थः श्रीमद्भिः गणपतिशास्त्रिभिः रामचन्द्रप्रणीते नाट्यदर्पणे–यथा भासकृते स्वप्नवासवदत्ते शेफालिकामण्डपशिलातलमवलोक्य वत्सराजः —इत्युपन्यासपूर्वमनुमानोदाहरणत्वेनोदाहृतः । इत्यत्रैव योग्यतया निवेशितः ।

चेटी—भर्तृदारिके ! साश्रुपाता खल्वार्याया दृष्टिः । [भट्टिदारिए ! सस्सुपादा खु अय्याए दिट्ठी ।]

वासवदत्ता—एषा खलु मधुकराणामविनयात् काशकुसुमरेणुना पतितेन सोदका मे दृष्टिः । [एसा खु महुअराणं अविणआदो कासकुसुमरेणुणा पडिदेण सोदआ मे दिट्ठी ।]

पद्मावती—युज्यते । [जुज्जई ।]

विदूषकः—भो ! शून्यं खल्विदं प्रमदवनम् । प्रष्टव्यं किंचिदस्ति । पृच्छामि भवन्तम् । [भो ! सुण्णं खु इदं पमदवणं । पुच्छिदव्वं किंचि अत्थि । पुच्छामि भवंतं ।]

राजा—छन्दतः ।

विदूषकः—का भवतः प्रिया तदानीं तत्रभवती वासवदत्ता इदानीं पद्मावती वा ? [का भवदो पिआ तदाणिं तत्तहोदी वासवदत्ता इदाणिं पदुमावदी वा ?]

राजा—किमिदानीं भवान् महति बहुमानसङ्कटे मां न्यस्यति ?

पद्मावती—हला ! यादृशे सङ्कटे निक्षिप्त आर्यपुत्रः । [हळा ! जादिसे संकडे निक्खित्तो अय्यउत्तो ।]

वासवदत्ता—(आत्मगतम् ।) अहं च मन्दभागा । [अहं अ मंदभाआ ।]

विदूषकः—स्वैरं स्वैरं भणतु भवान् । एकोपरता अपरासंनिहिता । [सेरं सेरं भणादु भवं । एक्का उवरदा अवरा असण्णिहिदा ।]

राजा—वयस्य ! न खलु न खलु ब्रूयाम् । भवांस्तु मुखरः ।

पद्मावती—एतावता भणितमार्यपुत्रेण । [एत्तएण भणिदं अय्यउत्तेण ।]

विदूषकः—भोः ! सत्येन शपामि कस्मा अपि नाख्यास्ये । एषा संदष्टा मे जिह्वा । [भो ! सच्चेणं[1] सवामि कस्स वि ण आचक्खिस्सं । एसा संदट्ठा मे जीहा ।

भर्तारं प्रकृतिस्थं दृष्ट्वा वासवदत्ताया आनन्दाश्रुपूर्णे नयने जाते । तद्दृष्टवत्याश्चेट्या इयमुक्तिः । तदानीं जीवन्त्यां वासवदत्तायामित्यर्थः । **बहुमानसंकटे**—बहुमानः तारतम्येन प्रियतरत्वकथनरूपः स एव संकटं तस्मिन् । यादृशे संकटे नियुक्तस्तादृक्पश्येति शेषः । स्वैरं विश्रब्धम् । यतः एकेति । मुखरः वाचालः । अयन्त्रितजिह्वः । वासवदत्तेति ब्रूयां चेत्पद्मावतीं कथयेदिति भावः । एतावता मुखर इति वचनेन । संदष्टा दन्तपीडनेन नियन्त्रितेति यावत् । पुरोभागिता वैयात्यं धार्ष्ट्यं

---

१ सच्चेण वि.

राजा—नोत्सहे सखे ! वक्तुम् ।

पद्मावती—अहो ! अस्य पुरोभागिता । एतावता हृदयं न जानाति । [अहो ! इमस्स पुरोभाइदा । एत्तिएण हिॲअं ण जाणादि ।]

विदूषकः—किं न भणति मम ? अनाख्यायास्माच्छिलापट्टकान्न शक्यमेकपदमपि गन्तुम् । एष रुद्धोऽत्रभवान् । [किं णं भणादि मम ? अणाचक्खिअ इमादो सिळावट्टआदो ण सक्कं एक्कपदं वि गमिदुं । एसो रुद्धो अत्तभवं ।]

राजा—किं बलात्कारेण ?

विदूषकः—आम् ! बलात्कारेण । [आम् ! बळक्कारेण ।]

राजा—तेन हि पश्यामस्तावत् ।

विदूषकः—प्रसीदतु प्रसीदतु भवान् । वयस्यभावेन शापितोऽसि यदि सत्यं न भणासि । [पसीददु पसीददु भवं । वअस्सभावेण साविदो सि जइ सच्चं ण भणासि ।]

राजा—का गतिः ? श्रूयताम्

पद्मावती बहुमता मम यद्यपि रूपशीलमाधुर्यैः ।
वासवदत्ताबद्धं न तु तावन्मे मनो हरति ॥ ४ ॥

वासवदत्ता—(आत्मगतम् ।) भवतु भवतु । दत्तं वेतनमस्य परिखेदस्य । अहो अज्ञातवासोऽप्यत्र बहुगुणः संपद्यते । [भोदु भोदु । दिण्णं वेदणं इमस्स परिखेदस्य । अहो अञ्ञादवासं पि एत्थ बहुगुणं संपज्जइ ।]

चेटी—भर्तृदारिके ! अदाक्षिण्यः खलु भर्ता । [भट्टिदारिए अदक्खिञ्ञो खु भट्टा ।]

पद्मावती—हला ! मा मैवम् । सदाक्षिण्य एवार्यपुत्रः य इदानीमप्यार्याया वासवदत्ताया गुणान् स्मरति । [हळा ! मा मा एव्वं । सदक्खिञ्ञो एव्व अय्यउत्तो जो इदाणिं वि अय्याए वासवदत्ताए गुणानि सुमरदि ।]

वा । एतावता यदुक्तं तावता । बलात्कारेण स्वशक्त्या । स्वसामर्थ्यं जानन्मृदूक्त्याह प्रसीदत्विति । **पद्मावतीति** । रूपं च शीलं च माधुर्यं वचसो रम्यत्वं च तैः । वासवदत्तायामाबद्धं वासवदत्तयात्मनिबद्धं वा । वासवदत्तागुणैः समधिकं समाकृष्टं मे मनोऽतस्सैव प्रेयसीति भावः ॥ ४ ॥ **वासव०**—भर्तुरात्मन्यनुरागप्रकर्षपरं वचनं श्रुत्वाह दत्त-

---

१ हिअअं जाणीअदि (हृदयं ज्ञायते). २ कथं ण. ३ जडमणाचक्खिअं (यद्यनाख्येयं). ४ कथम्.

वासवदत्ता—भद्रे ! अभिजनस्य सदृशं मन्त्रितम् । [भद्दे ! अभिजणस्स सदिसं मंतिदं ।]

राजा—उक्तं मया । भवानिदानीं कथयतु । का भवतः प्रिया तदा वासवदत्ता इदानीं पद्मावती वा ?

पद्मावती—आर्यपुत्रोऽपि वसन्तकः सवृत्तः । [अय्यउत्तो पि वसंतओ संवुत्तो ।]

विदूषकः—किं मे विप्रलपितेन ? उभे अपि तत्रभवत्यौ मे बहुमते । [किं मे विप्पळविदेण ? उभओ वि तत्तहोदीओ मे बहुमदाओ ।]

राजा—वैधेय[1] ! मामेवं बलाच्छ्रुत्वा किमिदानीं नाभिभाषसे ?

विदूषकः—किं मामपि बलात्कारेण ? [किं मं पि बळक्कारेण ?]

राजा—अथ किम् ? बलात्कारेण ।

विदूषकः—तेन हि न शक्यं श्रोतुम् । [तेण हि ण शक्कं सोदुं ।]

राजा—प्रसीदतु प्रसीदतु महाब्राह्मणः । स्वैरं स्वैरमभिधीयताम् ।

विदूषकः—इदानीं शृणोतु भवान् । तत्रभवती वासवदत्ता मे बहुमता । तत्रभवती पद्मावती तरुणी दर्शनीया अकोपना अनहंकारा मधुरवाक् सदाक्षिण्या । अयं चापरो महान् गुणः स्निग्धेन भोजनेन मां प्रत्युद्गच्छति कुत्र नु खलु गत आर्य वसन्तक इति ! [इदाणिं सुणादु भवं । तत्तहोदी वासवदत्ता[2] मे बहुमदा । तत्तहोदी पदुमावदी तरुणी दंसणीआ अकोवणा अणहक्कारा महुररवाआ सदक्खिञ्ञा । अअं च अवरो महंतो[3] गुणो सिणिद्धेण भोअणेण मं पच्चुग्गच्छइ[4] कहिं णु खु गदो अय्यवसंतओ ' त्ति !]

वासवदत्ता—भवतु भवतु वसन्तक ! स्मरेदानीमेतत् । [भोदु भोदु वसंतअ ! सुमरेहि दाणिं एदं ।]

मिति । वेतनं मूल्यं । मम खेदः परिमार्जित इत्यर्थः । बहुगुणः बहुफलः । अदाक्षिण्यः नास्ति दाक्षिण्यं यस्य । स्वभर्तृदारिकायाः परितोषार्थमिदम् । **पद्मावती**–मा मैवमित्यादिना तस्या मनऔदार्यं मत्सराभावश्च सूचितः । विप्रलपितेन निरर्थकजल्पनेन । वैधेय मूर्ख ! न त्वया सत्यं कथितमिति भावः । महान् गुणः पद्मावत्या इत्यर्थः । विदूषकस्य भोजनप्रियत्वादिदम् । अपि हेति परिहासार्थम् ।

---

१ मूर्ख. २ दत्ता वि. ३ विसेसो मह०. ४ च्छइ वासवदत्ता.

राजा—भवतु भवतु वसन्तक ! सर्वमेतत् कथयिष्ये देव्यै वासवदत्तायै ।

विदूषकः—अविधा वासवदत्ता । कुत्र वासवदत्ता ? चिरात् खलूपरता वासवदत्ता । [अविहा वासवदत्ता । कहिं वासवदत्ता ? चिरा खु उवरदा वासवदत्ता ।]

राजा—(सविषादम् ।) एवम् । उपरता वासवदत्ता । वयस्य !

अनेन परिहासेन व्याक्षिप्तं मे मनस्त्वया ।
ततो वाणी तथैवेयं पूर्वाभ्यासेन निस्सृता ॥ ५ ॥

पद्मावती—रमणीयः खलु कथायोगो नृशंसेन विसंवादितः । [रमणीओ खु कहाजोओ णिसंसेण विसंवादिओ ।]

वासवदत्ता—(आत्मगतम् ।) भवतु भवतु विश्वस्तास्मि । अहो ! प्रियं नाम ईदृशं वचनमप्रत्यक्षं श्रूयते । [भोदु भोदु विस्सत्थम्हि । अहो ! पिअं णाम ईदिसं वअणं अप्पच्चक्खं सुणीअदि ।]

विदूषकः—धारयतु धारयतु भवान् । अनतिक्रमणीयो हि विधिः । ईदृशमिदानीमेतत् । [धारेदु धारेदु भवं । अणदिक्कमणीओ हि विही । ईदिसं दाणिं एदं ।]

राजा—वयस्य ! न जानाति भवानवस्थाम् । कुतः ?

दुःखं त्यक्तुं बद्धमूलोऽनुरागः
स्मृत्वा स्मृत्वा याति दुःखं नवत्वम् ।

अनेनेति । अनेन परिहासेन नर्मभाषितेन मे मनस्त्वया व्याक्षिप्तं परमार्थाद्दूरं नीतम् । वासवदत्तापरं कृतामिति यावत् । ततः मनसः पर्याकुलत्वात्पूर्वाभ्यासेनेयं वाणी तथैव जीवन्त्यां वासवदत्तायां यथा तथा निस्सृता ॥ ५ ॥ कथायोग आलापानुबन्धः । रमणीयः स्वभर्तुरात्मनश्च वासवदत्तापरस्यालापस्य मनोहारित्वात्तथा । नृशंसेन क्रूरेण । परसुखासहिष्णुनेति यावत् । विसंवादितोऽन्यथात्वं प्रापितः । विश्वस्तास्मि सपत्नीपरिग्रहे आर्यपुत्रो मयि तथैवानुरक्त इति दृढं जानामीत्यर्थः । अप्रत्यक्षमतो न चाटूक्तिरियमिति भावः । **विदूषकः** । स्ववयस्यं विक्लवं दृष्ट्वाह धारयत्विति । धारयतु धारयतु आत्मानं धैर्यमवलम्ब्य स्थीयतामित्यर्थः । अनतिक्रमणीयोऽनुल्लङ्घनीयः । विधिः सर्वत्र प्रभवतीति भावः । **दुःखमिति** । बद्धं मूलं येन स बद्धमूलः, चिरपरिचयरूढ इत्यर्थः । अनुरागः अत्र वासवदत्ताविषयकः । तथा च स्मृत्वा पुनः पुनः स्मृतिविषयीकृत्य तानि तानि वासवदत्ताप्रणयचेष्टितानीति शेषः । दुःखं नवत्वं

---

१ एतन्नास्ति क्वचित्. २ त्यक्तम्.

यात्रा त्वेषा यद् विमुच्येह[1] बाष्पं
प्राप्तानृण्या याति बुद्धिः प्रसादम् ॥ ६ ॥

विदूषकः—अश्रुपातक्लिन्नं खलु तत्रभवतो मुखम् । यावन्मुखोदकमानयामि । (निष्क्रान्तः ।) [अस्सुपादकिलिण्णं खु तत्तहोदो मुहं । जाव मुहोदअं आणेमि ।]

पद्मावती—आर्ये ! बाष्पाकुलपटान्तरितमार्यपुत्रस्य मुखम् । यावनिष्क्रामामः । [अय्ये ! बप्फाउळपडंतरिदं अय्यउत्तस्स मुहं । जाव णिक्कमम्ह ।]

वासवदत्ता—एवं भवतु । अथवा तिष्ठ त्वम् । उत्कण्ठितं[2] भर्तारमुज्झित्वायुक्तं निर्गमनम् । अहमेव गमिष्यामि । [एव्वं होदु । अहव चिट्ठ तुवं । उक्कंठिदं उत्तारं उज्झिअ अजुत्तं णिग्गमणं । अहं एव्व गमिस्सं ।]

चेटी—सुष्ठ्वार्या भणाति । उपसर्पतु तावद् भर्तृदारिका । [सुट्ठु अय्या भणादि । उवसप्पदु दाव भट्टिदारिआ ।]

पद्मावती—किं नु खलु प्रविशामि ? [किं णु खु पविसामि ?]

वासवदत्ता—हला ! प्रविश । [हळा ! पविस ।] (इत्युक्त्वा निष्क्रान्ता ।)

(प्रविश्य ।)

विदूषकः—(नलिनीपत्रेण जलं गृहीत्वा ।) एषा तत्रभवती पद्मावती । [एसा तत्तहोदी पदुमावदी ।]

पद्मावती—आर्य वसन्तक ! किमेतत् ? [अय्य वसंतअ ! किं एदं ?]

विदूषकः—एतदिदम् । इदमेतत् । [ऐदं[3] इदं । इदं एदं ।]

याति नवीभवति । एवं सत्यपि बाष्पमोचनेन कोर्थ इति चेत् यात्रा लोकरीतिस्तु एषा यदिह लोके बाष्पमश्रुजलमित्यर्थः । विमुच्य विसृज्य । बाष्पमोक्षेण दुःखं प्रदर्श्य आनृण्यमृणाभावं प्राप्ता बुद्धिः प्रसादं याति । कृतकार्यत्वात्प्रसन्ना भवति । विमुच्येतेति पाठे एषा लोकयात्रा यद् बाष्पं विमुच्येत मोक्तव्यं विरहिणेति शेषः । एवं प्राप्तानृण्येत्यादि । दुःखितैः बाष्पमोचनेन दुःखनिर्वापणं कर्तव्यम् । यतः । शोकक्षोभं च हृदयं प्रलापैरेव धार्यते । इति भावः । शालिनी वृत्तम् ॥६॥ क्लिन्नमार्द्रम् । मुखोदकं मुखाय मुखप्रक्षालनार्थमुदकम् । बाष्पाकुलं बाष्पव्याप्तमत एव पटान्तरितमिव । बाष्पाणां पटलेनान्तरितं बाष्पपटलान्तरितमिति साधीयान्पाठः। अतो गच्छामश्चेदार्यपुत्रो न पश्येत् । विदूषकस्तु जलानयनार्थे निर्गत एव । उत्कण्ठितं जातोत्कलिकम् । इदमेतदिति अकस्मात्पद्मावतीं

---

१ विमुच्येत. २ न युक्तमिदानीमुत्कण्ठितमार्यमेकाकिनं विसृज्य गन्तुम् [ण युक्तं दाणिं उक्कण्ठिअं अय्यं एआइणं विसज्जि अगन्तुं]. ३ भोदि इदं । पद्मा०—किं एदं णाम । विदू०—भोदि एदं इदं इ०.

पद्मावती—भणतु भणत्वार्यो भणतु । [भणादु भणादु अय्यो भणादु ।]

विदूषकः—भवति ! वातनीतेन काशकुसुमरेणुना क्षितिपतितेन साश्रु[1]पातं खलु तत्रभवतो मुखम । तद् गृह्णातु भवतीदं मुखोदकम् । [भोदि ! वादणीदेण कासकुसुमरेणुणा अक्खिणिपडिदेण सस्सुपादं खु तत्तहोदो मुहं । ता गण्हदु होदी दं मुहोदअं ।

पद्मावती—(आत्मगतम् ।) अहो सदाक्षिण्यस्य जनस्य परिजनोऽपि सदाक्षिण्य एव भवति । (उपेत्य ।) जयत्वार्यपुत्रः । [अहो सदक्खिञ्ञस्स जणस्स परिजणो वि सदक्खिञ्ञो एव्व होदि ।]

राजा—अये ! पद्मावती । (अपवार्य ।) वसन्तक ! किमिदम् ?

विदूषकः—(कर्णे ।) एवमिव । [एव्वं विअ ।]

राजा—साधु वसन्तक ! साधु । (आचम्य ।) पद्मावति ! आस्यताम् ।

पद्मावती—यदार्यपुत्र आज्ञापयति । (उपविशति ।) [जं अय्यउत्तो आणवेदि ।]

राजा—पद्मावति !

शरच्छशाङ्कगौरेण वाताविद्धेन भामिनि ! ।
काशपुष्पलवेनेदं साश्रुपातं मुखं मम ॥ ७ ॥

(आत्मगतम् ।)

इयं बाला नवोद्वाहा सत्यं श्रुत्वा व्यथां व्रजेत् ।
कामं धीरस्वभावेयं स्त्रीस्वभावस्तु कातरः ॥ ८ ॥

विदूषकः—उचितं तत्रभवतो मगधराजस्यापराह्णकाले भवन्तमग्रतः

दृष्टवतो विदूषकस्य संभ्रमोक्तिः । प्रत्युत्पन्नमतिराह वातनीतेनेति । दाक्षिण्यं परचित्तानुवर्तित्वम् । किमिदं पद्मावत्या कथमयं वृत्तान्तो ज्ञातः ? **विदू०**—कर्णे एवमिव एवं मया सत्यं गोपायता कथितमित्यर्थः । आचम्य मुखं प्रक्षाल्य । विदूषकोक्तमेव समर्थयति—**शरच्छशाङ्केति** । भामिनि ! शरच्चन्द्रवद्गौरेण वातेनाविद्ध आक्षिप्तः वाताविद्धस्तेन काशपुष्पाणां लवेन रेणुना मम मुखं साश्रुपातं जातम् ॥ ७ ॥ **इयमिति** । इयं पद्मावती बाला अप्रौढा । नवोद्वाहा नवः अचिरान्निर्वृत्तः उद्वाहः परिणयो यस्याः सा तथोक्ता । सत्यं वासवदत्तास्मृतिजन्योऽश्रुपात इति श्रुत्वा यथा व्रजेत् । इयं कामं धीरस्वभावा प्रकृत्या धीरा । तु तथापि सामान्यतः स्त्रीस्वभावः कातरः ॥ ८ ॥ **इमं विषयमाक्षेप्तुकामो विदूषक आह उचितमिति** । **अह्नः** अपरमपराह्णः । **एकदेशिसमासः** ।

---

१ अश्रुपातक्लिन्नं (अस्सुपादकिलिण्णं) ।

कृत्वा सुहृज्जनदर्शनम् । सत्कारो हि नाम सत्कारेण प्रतीष्टः प्रीतिमुत्पादयति । तदुत्तिष्ठतु तावद् भवान् । [उइदं तत्तहोदो मअधराअस्स अवरण्हकाले भवंतं अग्गदो करिअ सुहिज्जणदंसणं । सक्कारो हि णाम सक्कारेण पडिच्छिदो पीदिं उप्पादेदि । ता उट्ठेदु दाव भवं ।]

राजा—(उत्थाय ।) बाढम् । प्रथमः कल्पः ।

गुणानां वा विशालानां सत्काराणां च नित्यशः ।
कर्तारः सुलभा लोके विज्ञातारस्तु दुर्लभाः ॥ ९ ॥

(निष्क्रान्ताः सर्वे ।)

इति चतुर्थोऽङ्कः ।

अथ पञ्चमोऽङ्कः ।

(ततः प्रविशति पद्मिनिका ।)

पद्मिनिका—मधुकरिके मधुकरिके ! आगच्छ तावच्छीघ्रम् । [महुअरिए महुअरिए ! आअच्छ दाव सिग्घं ।]

(प्रविश्य ।)

मधुकरिका—हला ! इयमस्मि । किं क्रियताम् ? [हळा ! इअम्हि किं करीअदु ?]

पद्मिनिका—हला ! किं न जानासि त्वं भर्तृदारिका पद्मावती शीर्षवेदनया दुःखितेति ? [हळा ! किं ण जाणासि तुवं भट्टिदारिआ पदुमावदी सीसवेदणाए दुक्खाविदेत्ति ?]

मधुकरिका—हा धिक् । [हद्धि ।]

पद्मिनिका—हला ! गच्छ शीघ्रमार्यामावन्तिकां शब्दापय । केवलं भर्तृदारिकायाः शीर्षवेदनामेव निवेदय । ततः स्वयमेवागमिष्यति । [हळा ! गच्छ सिग्घं अय्यं आवंतिअं सद्दावेहि । केवळं भट्टिदारिआए सीसवेदणं एव्व णिवेदेहि । तदो सअं एव्व आगमिस्सदि ।]

तस्य काले । अग्रतः कृत्वा पुरोधाय । प्रतीष्टः स्वीकृतः । **गुणानामिति** । विशालानां महतां गुणानां सत्कार्यकारित्वादीनां सत्काराणां कर्तारः नित्यशः सुलभाः । तेषां विज्ञातारः गुणग्राहिणः सत्कारबहुमानिनश्च दुर्लभाः ॥ १० ॥ इति चतुर्थोऽङ्कः ।

शब्दापयाकारय । निवेदय केवलम् । न तु त्वमाहूता पद्मावत्येति ब्रूहीत्यर्थः ।

मधुकरिका—हला ! किं सा करिष्यति ? [हळा ! किं सा करिस्सदि ?]

पद्मिनिका—सा खल्विदानीं मधुराभिः कथाभिर्भर्तृदारिकायाः शीर्षवेदनां विनोदयति । [सा हु दाणिं महुराहि कहाहि भट्टिदारिआए सीसवेदणं विणोदेदि ।]

मधुकरिका—युज्यते । कुत्र शयनीयं रचितं भर्तृदारिकायाः ? [जुज्जइ । कहिं सअणीयं रइदं भट्टिदारिआए ?]

पद्मिनिका—समुद्रगृहके किल शय्यास्तीर्णा । गच्छेदानीं त्वम् । अहमपि भर्त्रे निवेदनार्थमार्यत्रसन्तकमन्विष्यामि । [समुद्दगिहके किळ सेज्जात्थिण्णा । गच्छ दाणिं तुवं । अहं वि भट्टिणो णिवेदणत्थं अय्यवसंतअं अण्णेसामि ।]

मधुकरिका—एवं भवतु । (निष्क्रान्ता ।) [एव्वं होदु ।]

पद्मिनिका—कुत्रेदानीमार्यवसन्तकं पेश्यामि ? [कहिं दाणिं अय्यवसंतअं पेक्खामि ?]

(ततः प्रविशति विदूषकः ।)

विदूषकः—अद्य खलु देवीवियोगविधुरहृदयस्य तत्रभवतो वत्सराजस्य पद्मावतीपाणिग्रहणसमीरितस्यात्यन्तसुखावहे मङ्गलोत्सवे मदनाग्निदाहोऽधिकतरं वर्धते । (पद्मिनिकां विलोक्य ।) अयि ! पद्मिनिका । पद्मिनिके किमिह वर्तते ? [अज्ज खुं देवीविओअविहुरहिअअस्स तत्तहोदो वच्छराअस्स पदुमावदीपाणिग्गहणसमीरिअस्स अच्चंतसुहावहे मंगळोसवे मदणग्गिदाहो अहिअदरं वड्ढइ । अयि ! पदुमिणिआ । पदुमिणिए ! किं इह वत्तदि ?]

पद्मिनिका—आर्य वसन्तक ! किं न जानासि त्वं भर्तृदारिका पद्मावती शीर्षवेदनया दुःखितेति ? [अय्य वसंतअ ! किं ण जाणासि तुवं भट्टिदारिआ पदुमावदी सीसवेदणाए दुक्खाविदेत्ति ?]

विनोदयति अपनेष्यति। शय्यास्तीर्णा तत्र सागत्य स्वप्स्यतीति । देव्या वासवदत्ताया वियोगेन विधुरः विक्लवस्तस्य । विगता धूर्यस्येति विधुरः । 'ऋक्पूरब्धूःपथामानक्षे' इत्यच् । पद्मावत्याः पाणिग्रहणेन समीरितः । संधुक्षितः । समीरितस्येति पाठे प्रेरितस्य । अत्यन्तं सुखमावहतीति तथा अत्यन्तसुखकरे । दुःखमस्याः संजातमिति दुःखिता पीडि-

१ करेहि कुरु. २ प्रेक्षे. ३ वि (अपि). ४ विहुरस्स (विधुरस्य). ५ समीरिदो (समीरितः).

विदूषकः—भवति ! सत्यं न जानामि । [भोदि ! सच्चं ण जाणामि ।]

पद्मिनिका—तेन हि भर्त्रे निवेदयैनाम् । यावदहमपि शीर्षानुलेपनं त्वरयामि । [तेण हि भट्टिणो णिवेदेहि णं । जाव अहं वि सीस्साणुळेवणं तुवारेमि ।]

विदूषकः—कुत्र शयनीयं रचितं पद्मावत्याः ? [कहिं सअणीअं रइदं पदुमावदीए ?]

पद्मिनिका—समुद्रगृहके किल शय्यास्तीर्णा । [समुद्दगिहके किळ सेज्जात्थिण्णा ।]

विदूषकः—गच्छतु भवती । यावदहमपि तत्रभवते निवेदयिष्यामि । [गच्छदु भोदी । जाव अहं वि तत्तहोदो णिवेदइस्सं ।]

(निष्क्रान्तौ ।)

प्रवेशकः ।

(ततः प्रविशति राजा ।)

राजा—

> **श्लाघ्यामवन्तिनृपतेः सदृशीं तनूजां**
> **कालक्रमेण पुनरागतदारभारः ।**
> **लावाणके हुतवहेन हृताङ्गयष्टिं**
> **तां पद्मिनीं हिमहतामिव चिन्तयामि ॥ १ ॥**

(प्रविश्य ।)

विदूषकः—त्वरतां त्वरतां तावद् भवान् । (तुवरदु तुवरदु दाव भवं ।)

राजा—किमर्थम् ?

ता । शीर्षानुलेपनं शिरोवेदनापनयनार्थमनुलेपनम् । त्वरयामि त्वरितं सम्पाद्यागमिष्यामीत्यर्थः । **श्लाघ्यामिति** । कालक्रमेण वासवदत्तोपरमादनन्तरं गच्छता कालेन पुनः आगतो दाराणां भार्याया भारो यस्य तादृशोऽहम् । अनेन पत्नीपरिग्रहो मम भार एव न तु सुखहेतुरिति सूचितम् । श्लाघ्यां प्रशस्यामवन्तिनृपतेः प्रद्योतस्य सदृशीं तुल्यगुणरूपां तनूजां कन्यां लावाणके तदाख्यग्रामे हुतवहेनाग्निना हृता अङ्गं शरीरं यष्टिरिव तनुत्वादङ्गयष्टिर्यस्याः तथोक्तां तामविस्मरणीयां वासवदत्तां हिमेन तुषारेण हतां दग्धां पद्मिनीं नलिनीमिव चिन्तयामि । उपमा । वसन्ततिलका वृत्तम् ॥ १ ॥

---

१ सिग्घं भ० णिवेदेहि । जाव.

विदूषकः—तत्रभवती पद्मावती शीर्षवेदनया दुःखिता । (तत्तहोदी पदुमावदी सीसवेदणाए दुक्खाविदा ।)

राजा—कैवमाह ?

विदूषकः—पद्मिनिकया कथितम् । (पदुमिणिआए कहिदं ।)

राजा—भोः कष्टम् !

रूपश्रिया समुदितां गुणतश्च युक्तां
लब्ध्वा प्रियां मम तु मन्द इवाद्य शोकः ।
पूर्वाभिघातसरुजोऽप्यनुभूतदुःखः
पद्मावतीमपि तथैव समर्थयामि ॥ २ ॥

अथ कस्मिन् प्रदेशे वर्तते पद्मावती ?

विदूषकः—समुद्रगृहके किल शय्यास्तीर्णा । (समुद्दगिहके किळ सेज्जात्थिण्णा ।)

राजा—तेन हि तस्य मार्गमादेशय ।

विदूषकः—एत्वेतु भवान् । (एदु एदु भवं ।) (उभौ परिक्रामतः ।)

विदूषकः—इदं समुद्रगृहकम् । प्रविशतु भवान् । (इदं समुद्दगिहकं । पविसदुं भवं ।)

राजा—पूर्वं प्रविश ।

विदूषकः—भोः ! तथा । (प्रविश्य ।) अविधा तिष्ठतु तिष्ठतु तावद्भवान् । (भो ! तह अविहा चिट्ठदु चिट्ठदु दाव भवं ।)

राजा—किमर्थम् ?

विदूषकः—एष खलु दीपप्रभासूचितरूपो वसुधातले परिवर्तमानोऽयं काकोदरः । (एसो खु दीवप्पभासूइदरूवो वसुधातळे परिवत्तमाणो अअंकाओदरो ।)

रूपश्रियेति । रूपश्रिया सौन्दर्यसम्पत्त्या समुदितां युक्तां गुणतश्च गुणैश्च युक्तामुपेतां प्रियां पद्मावतीं प्राप्य लब्ध्वा पूर्वः यः अभिघातः वासवदत्तानिधनरूपस्तेन । रुजा सहिता सरुक्, तस्य सरुजः अपि, मम शोकस्तु अद्य मन्द इव किंचिदधरीभूत आसीत् । तथापि अनुभूतं दुःखं वासवदत्ताविनाशोत्पन्नं येन तथाभूतोऽहं पद्मावतीमपि तदस्वास्थ्यवार्ताश्रवणात् तथैव समर्थयामि । पद्मावत्यपि मम दुर्दैवाद्विनश्येत् किमिति मन्ये । वसन्ततिलका वृत्तम् ॥२॥ पाठान्तरे दीपप्रभया अवसूचितं रूपं यस्य । काकस्येव

---

१ शदु दाव (तावत्). २ प्पभावसूचि०.

राजा—(प्रविश्यावलोक्य सस्मितम् ।) अहो ! सर्पव्यक्तिर्वैधेयस्य ।

ऋज्वायतां हि मुखतोरणलोलमालां
भ्रष्टां क्षितौ त्वमवगच्छसि मूर्ख ! सर्पम् ।
मन्दानिलेन निशि या परिवर्तमाना
किंचित् करोति भुजगस्य विचेष्टितानि ॥ ३ ॥

विदूषकः—(निरूप्य ।) सुष्ठु भवान् भणति । न खल्वयं काकोदरः । (प्रविश्यावलोक्य ।) तत्रभवती पद्मावतीहागत्य निर्गता भवेत् । (सुट्ठु भवं भणादि । ण हु अअं काओजरो । तत्तहोदी पदुमावदी इह आअच्छिअ णिग्गदा भवे ।)

राजा—वयस्य ! अनागतया भवितव्यम् ।

विदूषकः—कथं भवान् जानाति ? (कहं भवं जाणादि ?)

राजा—किमत्र ज्ञेयम् ? पश्य

शय्या नावनता तथास्तृतसमा न व्याकुलप्रच्छदा
न क्लिष्टं हि शिरोपधानममलं शीर्षाभिघातौषधैः ।
रोगे दृष्टिविलोभनं जनयितुं शोभा न काचित् कृता
प्राणी प्राप्य रुजा पुनर्न शयनं शीघ्रं स्वयं मुञ्चति ॥ ४ ॥

विदूषकः—तेन ह्यस्यां शय्यायां मुहूर्तकमुपविश्य तत्रभवतीं प्रति-

---

उदरं यस्य स काकोदरः सर्पः । सर्पव्यक्तिः सर्प इति भासः । **ऋज्वायतेति** । हे मूर्ख ! ऋजुः सरला चासौ आयता दीर्घा च तामृज्वायतां क्षितौ भ्रष्टां पतितां मुखतोरणे समुद्रगृहस्य बहिर्निर्गमद्वारे स्थिता लोला माला तां सर्पमवगच्छसि सर्प इति मन्यसे । तत्र हेतुमाह-या मन्दानिलेन परिवर्तमाना चलन्ती भुजगस्य विचेष्टितानि किंचित्करोति । वायुवशाचलिता भुजग इव भासते इत्यर्थः । वसन्ततिलका वृत्तम् ॥ ३ ॥ **शय्येति** तथा यथापूर्वमास्तृतमास्तरणं यस्याः सा तथास्तृता चासौ समा च तथास्तृतसमा शय्या न अवनता शरीरभारेणेति यावत् । यद्वा तथा इति पृथक्पदम् । व्याकुलः अङ्गपरिवर्तनेनासंस्थितः प्रच्छदपटो यस्यास्तथा न । तथा च अमलं शिरोपधानं शिरस्योपबर्हम् । अकारान्तो शिरशब्दः क्वचिदुपलभ्यते । तदुक्तम्-'शिरोवाची शिरोदन्तो रजोवाची रजस्तथा ।' इति । शीर्षाभिघातौषधैः शीर्षाभिघातः शिरोरोगस्तस्यौषधैः । 'ओषधेरजातौ' इति स्वार्थेऽण् । न क्लिष्टं दूषितम् । तथा च रोगे सति दृष्टेः विलोभनं दृष्टेरन्यत्राकृष्टया पीडाऽसंवेदनार्थं काचित् शोभा न कृता । अत्रार्थान्तरं न्यस्यति । प्राणी रुजा रोगपीडया शयनं प्राप्य । रुजमिति पाठे रुजं प्राप्य शयनमिति योजनीयम् । स्वयं शीघ्रं न मुञ्चति । चिरं शयनमधिशयान एव तिष्ठति ॥ शार्दूलविक्रीडितं

---

१ च. २ रुजम्.

पालयतु भवान् । (तेण हि इमस्सिं सय्याए मुहुत्तअं उववि‌सिअ तत्तहोदिं पडिवाळेदु भवं ।)

राजा—बाढम् । (उपविश्य) वयस्य ! निद्रा मां बाधते । कथ्यतां काचित् कथा ।

विदूषकः—अहं कथयिष्यामि । हों इति करोत्वत्रभवान् (अहं कहइस्सं । हों त्ति करेदु अत्तभवं ।)

राजा—बाढम् ।

विदूषकः—अस्ति नगर्युज्जयिनी नाम । तत्राधिकरमणीयान्युदकस्नानानि वर्तन्ते किल । (अत्थि णअरी उज्जइणी णाम । तहिं अहिअरमणीआणि उदअ[1]ण्हाणाणि वत्तंति किळ ।)

राजा—कथमुज्जयिनी नाम ?

विदूषकः—यद्यनभिप्रेतैषा कथा अन्यां कथयिष्यामि ? (जइ अणभिप्पेदा एसा कहा अण्णं कहइस्सं ?)

राजा—वयस्य ! न खलु नाभिप्रेतैषा कथा । किं तु

स्मराम्यवन्त्याधिपतेः सुतायाः
प्रस्थानकाले स्वजनं स्मरन्त्याः ।
बाष्पं प्रवृत्तं[2] नयनान्तलग्नं
स्नेहान्ममैवोरसि पातयन्त्याः ॥ ५ ॥

अपि च ।

बहुशोऽप्युपदेशेषु यया मामीक्षमाणया ।
हस्तेन स्रस्तकोणेन कृतमाकाशवादितम् ॥ ६ ॥

वृत्तम् ॥ ४ ॥ हों इति कथयितुर्वाक्यावसाने श्रोत्रा क्रियमाणः श्रुतमित्यर्थसूचनार्थः ध्वनिविशेषः । उदकस्नानानि अवगाहक्षमा जलप्रदेशाः । **स्मरामीति** । प्रस्थानकाले उज्जयिनीं विहाय मया सह कौशाम्बीं प्रति प्रयाणसमये स्वजनं मातापित्रादिकं स्मरन्त्याः प्रवृत्तम् । प्रवृद्धमिति पाठान्तरम् । नयनान्तलग्नं बाष्पं स्नेहान्ममैवोरसि पातयन्त्याः । अवन्त्या आ समन्तादधिपतिराधिपतिः तस्य सुतायाः वासवदत्तायाः स्मरामि । यद्वा अवन्त्या हेतुभूतया अधिपतिः । गवा स्वामीतिवत् । 'अधीगर्थदयेशां कर्मणि' इति कर्मणि शेषे षष्ठी । इन्द्रवज्रोपेन्द्रवज्रामिश्रा उपजातिश्छन्दः ॥५॥ **बहुश इति** । यया मामीक्षमाणया मदवलोकनैकपरया उपदेशेषु वीणावादनशिक्षणेषु बहुशोऽनेक-

१ उदअन्हानानि (उदयह्नानानि). २ प्रवृद्धं.

विदूषकः—भवतु अन्यां कथयिष्यामि। अस्ति नगरं ब्रह्मदत्तं नाम। तत्र किल राजा काम्पिल्यो नाम। [भोदु अण्णं कहइस्सं। अत्थि णअरं बम्हदत्तं णाम। तहिं किळ राआ कंपिळ्ळो णाम।]

राजा—किमिति किमिति?

विदूषकः—(पुनस्तदेव पठति।)

राजा—मूर्ख! राजा ब्रह्मदत्तः नगरं काम्पिल्यमित्यभिधीयताम्।

विदूषकः—किं राजा ब्रह्मदत्तः नगरं काम्पिल्यम्? [किं राआ बम्हदत्तो णअरं कपिळ्ळं?]

राजा—एवमेतत्।

विदूषकः—तेन हि मुहूर्तकं प्रतिपालयतु भवान् यावदोष्ठगतं करिष्यामि। राजा ब्रह्मदत्तः नगरं काम्पिल्यम्। (इति बहुशस्तदेव पठित्वा।) इदानीं शृणोतु भवान्। अयि! सुप्तोऽत्रभवान्। अतिशीतलेयं वेला। आत्मनः प्रावारकं गृहीत्वागमिष्यामि। [तेण हि मुहुत्तअं पडिवाळेदु भवं जाव ओट्ठगअं करिस्सं। राआ बम्हदत्तो णअरं कंपिळ्ळं। इदार्णि सुणादु भवं। अयि! सुत्तो अत्तभवं। अदिसीदळा इअं वेळा। अत्तणो पावरअं गण्हिअ आअमिस्सं।] (निष्क्रान्तः।)

(ततः प्रविशति वासवदत्ता आवन्तिकावेषेण चेटी च।)

चेटी—एत्वेत्वार्या। दृढं खलु भर्तृदारिका शीर्षवेदनया दुःखिता। (एदु एदु अय्या। दिढं खु भट्टिदारिआ सीसवेदणाए दुक्खाविदा।)

वासवदत्ता—हा धिक्! कुत्र शयनीयं रचितं पद्मावत्याः? [हद्धि! कहिं सअणीअं रइदं पदुमावदीए?]

चेटी—समुद्रगृहके किल शय्यास्तीर्णा। [समुद्दगिहके किळ सेज्जात्थिण्णा।]

वारं स्रस्तः कोणो वीणावादनसाधनं यस्मात्तेन हस्तेन मद्गतचित्ततया स्रस्तमपि कोणमजानत्या आकाशवादितं कृतं तस्याः स्मरामीति पूर्वेण सम्बन्धः ॥६॥ नगरं ब्रह्मदत्तमित्यादि। विदूषकस्य स्मृतिवैकल्यं सुप्रथितमेव। वस्तुतस्त्वयं राजनगरयोः नामव्युत्क्रमः परिहासाय। ओष्ठगतमभ्यासेन सुपठितमिति यावत्। प्रावारकमावरणवस्त्रम्। **चेटी** च–इयं मधुकरिकाख्या चेटी पद्मिनिकाख्यया चेट्यावन्तिकानयनाय प्राक्प्रहिता।

---

१ इह लहुअदरं एदु (इह लघुकतरमेतु) २ रिआ पदुमावदी.

वासवदत्ता—तेन ह्यग्रतो याहि । [तेण हि अग्गदो याहि ।]

(उभे परिक्रामतः ।)

चेटी—इदं समुद्रगृहकम् । प्रविशत्वार्या । यावदहमपि शीर्षानुलेपनं त्वरयामि । (इदं समुद्दगिहकं । पविसदु अय्या । जाव अहं वि सीसाणुलेवणं तुवारेमि ।) (निष्क्रान्ता ।)

वासवदत्ता—अहो अकरुणाः खल्वीश्वरा मे । विरहपर्युत्सुकस्यार्यपुत्रस्य विश्रमस्थानभूतेयमपि नाम पद्मावत्यवस्था जाता । यावत् प्रविशामि (प्रविश्यावलोक्य ।) अहो ! परिजनस्य प्रमादः । अवस्थां पद्मावतीं केवलं दीपसहायां कृत्वा परित्यजति । इयं पद्मावत्यवसुप्ता । यावदुपविशामि । अथवान्यासनपरिग्रहेणाल्प इव स्नेहः प्रतिभाति । तदस्यां शय्यायामुपविशामि । (उपविश्य ।) किं नु खल्वेतया सहोपविशन्त्या अद्य प्रह्लादितमिव मे हृदयम् । दिष्ट्याविच्छिन्नसुखनिःश्वासा । निवृत्तरोगया भवितव्यम् । अथवैकदेशसंविभागतया शयनीयस्य सूचयति मामालिङ्गेति । यावच्छयिष्ये । [अहो ! अकरुणा खु इस्सरा मे[1] । विरहपय्युस्सुअस्स अय्यउत्तस्स विस्समत्थाणभूदा इअं पि णाम पदुमावदी अस्सत्था जादा । जाव पविसामि । अहो ! परिजणस्स पमादो । अस्सत्थं पदुमावदिं केवळं दीवसहाअं करिअ परित्तजदि[2] । इअं पदुमावदी ओसुत्ता । जाव उवविसामि । अहव अञ्जासणपरिग्गहेण अप्पो विअ सिणेहो पडिभादि । ता इमस्सिं सय्याए उवविसामि[3] । किं णु खु एदाए सह उववसंतीए अज्ज पह्ळादिदं विअ मे हिअअं । दिट्ठिआ अविच्छिण्णसुहणिस्सासा । णिव्वुत्तरोआए होदव्वं । अहव एअदेससंविभाअदाए सअणीअस्स[4] सूएदि मं आळिंगेहि त्ति । जाव सइस्सं ।] (शयनं नाटयति ।)

राजा—(स्वप्नायते ।) हा वासवदत्ते !

प्रमादोऽनवधानता । अस्वस्थां सरुजाम् । दीप एव सहायो यस्याः तां तथोक्ताम् । अन्यदासनमन्यासनं तस्य परिग्रहेण स्वीकरणेन । प्रह्लादितं प्रमुदितं । अविच्छिन्नः संततः सुखः निःश्वासो यस्याः । एकदेशस्य संविभागः तस्य भावः एकदेशसंविभागता तया । शयनस्यैकदेशे सुप्ताऽतोऽन्यस्मिन्मया तन्निकटमेव शयितव्यमित्याशयोऽस्याः इति ।

---

१ मम वि. २ विसज्जिअ णिग्गदो (विसृज्य निर्गतः) ३ मुहुत्तं उव. ४ णीअस्स आआरेण (आकारेण).

वासवदत्ता—(सहसोत्थाय ।) हम् । आर्यपुत्रः न खलु पद्मावती । किं नु खलु दृष्टास्मि ? महान् खल्वार्ययौगन्धरायणस्य प्रतिज्ञाभारो मम दर्शनेन निष्फलः संवृत्तः । [हं । अय्यउत्तो ण हु पदुमावदी । किं णु खु दिट्ठम्हि महंतो खु अय्यजोअंधराअणस्स पडिण्णाहारो मम दंसणेण णिप्फळो संवुत्तो[1] ।]

राजा—हा अवन्तिराजपुत्रि[2] !

वासवदत्ता—दिष्टया स्वप्नायते खल्वार्यपुत्रः । नात्र कश्चिज्जनः । यावन्मुहूर्तकं स्थित्वा दृष्टिं हृदयं च तोषयामि । [दिट्ठिआ सिविणाअदि खु अय्यउत्तो । ण[3] एत्थ कोच्चि जणो । जाव मुहुत्तअं चिट्ठिअ दिट्ठिं हिअअं च तोसेमि ।]

राजा—हा प्रिये ! हा प्रियशिष्ये ! देहि मे प्रतिवचनम् ।

वासवदत्ता—आलपामि भर्तः ! आलपामि । [आळवामि भट्टा ! आळवामि ।]

राजा—किं कुपितासि ?

वासवदत्ता—न हि न हि, दुःखितास्मि । (ण हि ण हि, दुक्खिदम्हि ।)

राजा—यद्यकुपिता किमर्थं नालंकृतासि ?

वासवदत्ता—इतः परं किम् ? [इदो वरं किं ?]

राजा—किं विरचिकां स्मरसि ?

वासवदत्ता—(सरोषम् ।) आ अपेहि । इहापि विरचिका । [आ अवेहि । इहावि विरचिआ ।]

राजा—तेन हि विरचिकार्थं[4] भवतीं प्रसादयामि । (हस्तौ प्रसारयति ।)

प्रतिज्ञाभारः—विजयलाभेन प्रतिष्ठिते स्वामिनि एतामुपनेष्यामीत्येवंरूपः । अहं दृष्टा स्यां चेद्वत्सराजः मां जीवन्तीं जानीयात्तथा सति सर्वमेव तन्त्रमाकुलीभवेदित्याशयः । स्वप्नायते न तु मां दृष्ट्वा प्रत्यभिज्ञयाह्वयतीत्यर्थः । **विरचिकां** स्मरसि । तेन हि विरचिकार्थं भवतीं प्रसादयामि इति स्वप्नायमानस्य राज्ञो वाक्यम् । विरचिका (ता) नाम काचिदन्तःपुरपरिचारका वत्सराजेन पूर्वसंगता । तां कदाचिद्राजा गुप्तं भेजे । तज्ज्ञात्वा कुपितां वासवदत्तां पादपतनेन प्रसादयामास ।

---

१ अस्मात्परं–मन्दभाआए मए किं किदं (मन्दभागया मया किं कृतम् ।) इत्यधिकम्. २ पुत्रि वासवदत्ते. ३ ण खु एत्थ कोवि जणो । भोदु (भवतु) मुहु०. ४ विरचिताम्.

वासवदत्ता—चिरं स्थितास्मि । कोऽपि मां पश्येत् । तद् गमिष्यामि । अथवा शय्याप्रलम्बितमार्यपुत्रस्य हस्तं शयनीय आरोप्य गमिष्यामि । [चिरं ठिदम्हि । को वि मं पेक्खे । ता गमिस्सं । अहव सय्यापळंबिअं अय्यउत्तस्स हत्थं सअणीए आरोविअ गमिस्सं ।] (तथा कृत्वा निष्क्रान्ता ।)

राजा—(सहसोत्थाय ।) वासवदत्ते ! तिष्ठ तिष्ठ । हा धिक् !

निष्क्रामन् संभ्रमेणाहं द्वारपक्षेण ताडितः ।
ततो व्यक्तं न जानामि भूतार्थोऽयं मनोरथः ॥ ७ ॥

(प्रविश्य ।)

विदूषकः—अयि ! प्रतिबुद्धोऽत्रभवान् । [अइ ! पडिबुद्धो अत्तभवं ।]

राजा—वयस्य ! प्रियमावेदये । धरते खलु वासवदत्ता ।

विदूषकः—अविधा वासवदत्ता । कुत्र वासवदत्ता ? चिरात् खलूपरता वासवदत्ता । [अविहा वासवदत्ता । कहिं वासवदत्ता ? चिरा खु उवरदा वासवदत्ता ।]

राजा—वयस्य ! मा मैवम् ।

शय्यायामवसुप्तं मां बोधयित्वा सखे ! गता ।
दग्धेति ब्रुवता पूर्वं वञ्चितोऽस्मि रुमण्वता ॥ ८ ॥

विदूषकः—अविधा असंभावनीयमेतत् । आः ! उदकस्नानसंकीर्तनेन तत्रभवतीं चिन्तयता सा स्वप्ने दृष्टा भवेत् । [अविहा असंभावणीअं एदं । आ ! उदण्हाणसंकित्तणेण तत्तहोदिं चिंतअंतेण सा सिविणे दिट्ठा भवे ।]

राजा—एवं मया स्वप्नो दृष्टः ।

शय्याप्रलम्बितं—शय्याप्रान्तादधोलम्बमानम् । **निष्क्रामन्निति** । अहं संभ्रमेण त्वरया वासवदत्ता स्यान्न वेति परीक्षणार्थं निष्क्रामन्द्वारपक्षेण द्वारपार्श्वेन ताडितः प्रतिहत इत्यर्थः । ततस्तस्मात्कारणात् । अयं मनोरथः गता स्त्री वासवदत्तै-वेत्येवंरूपः भूतार्थः सत्यो न वेति व्यक्तं न जानामीत्यर्थः ॥ ७ ॥ धरते जीवति । ध्रियते इत्येव साधु । उपरता मृता । **शय्यायामिति** । शय्यायामवसुप्तं निद्रां गतं मां बोधयित्वा गता । दग्धेति पूर्वं ब्रुवता रुमण्वता वञ्चितोऽस्मि प्रतारितोऽस्मि ॥८॥ उदकस्नानसंकीर्तनेन अस्ति नगर्युज्जयिनी नामेत्यत्र ४५ पृष्ठे ।

---

१ इह कोवि जणो मं पेक्खे । ण जुत्तं चिट्ठिदुं (युक्तं स्थातुम्) । अहवा. २ मा दार्णि अणत्थं विचिन्तिअ । उदअज्जाणसंकित्तणेण तत्तहोदिं विचिन्तिअ तत्तहोदि विव (मेदानीमनर्थं विचिन्त्य । उदयस्नानसंकीर्तनेन ... ... तत्रभवतीव) सिविणे. ३ एदं ण.

यदि तावदयं स्वप्नो धन्यमप्रतिबोधनम् ।
अथायं विभ्रमो वा स्याद्विभ्रमो ह्यस्तु मे चिरम् ॥ ९ ॥

विदूषकः—भो वयस्य ! एतस्मिन् नगरेऽवन्तिसुन्दरी नाम यक्षिणी प्रतिवसति । सा त्वया दृष्टा भवेत् । [भो[1] वअस्स ! एदस्सिं णअरे अवंतिसुन्दरी णाम जक्खिणी पडिवसदि । सा तुए दिट्ठा भवे ।]

राजा—न न;

स्वप्नस्यान्ते विबुद्धेन नेत्रविप्रोषिताञ्जनम् ।
चारित्रमपि रक्षन्त्या दृष्टं दीर्घालकं मुखम् ॥ १० ॥

अपि च वयस्य ! पश्य पश्य;

योऽयं संत्रस्तया देव्या तया बाहुर्निपीडितः ।
स्वप्नेऽप्युत्पन्नसंस्पर्शो रोमहर्षं न मुञ्चति ॥ ११ ॥

विदूषकः—मेदानीं भवाननर्थं चिन्तयित्वा । एत्वेतु भवान् । चतुःशालं प्रविशावः । [मा दाणिं भवं अणत्थं चिंतिअ । एदु एदु भवं । चउस्सालं पविसामो ।]

(प्रविश्य ।)

काञ्चुकीयः—जयत्वार्यपुत्रः[3] । अस्माकं महाराजो दर्शको भवन्तमाह—एष खलु भवतोऽमात्यो रुमण्वान् महता बलसमुदयेनोपयातः खल्वारुणि-

यदि तावदिति । यदि तावदयं स्वप्नः । स्वप्नेऽनुभूतः वासवदत्तासंगम इति यावत् । तर्हि तस्मादप्रतिबोधनमजागरः धन्यमभीष्टतमम् । अथेति पक्षान्तरे । अयं विभ्रमो मनसो भ्रान्तिर्वा मे चिराद्विभ्रमोऽस्तु । हि यस्मात्तथा सति चिरं वासवदत्तासमागमः स्यादिति भावः ॥ ९ ॥ **स्वप्नस्येति** । स्वप्नस्य निद्राया अन्ते विबुद्धेन चारित्रं रक्षन्त्या अपि परपुरुषदर्शनपरिहारार्थं झटित्यपक्रामन्त्या अपीत्यर्थः । नेत्राभ्यां विप्रोषितं निर्गतमञ्जनं यस्मिन् तथाभूतं दीर्घालकमबद्धवेणिकं प्रोषितभर्तृत्वान्मुखं दृष्टम् । अतो वासवदत्तैव सा, न तु यक्षिणीति निश्चयः ॥ १० ॥ **योऽयमिति** । यः अयं बाहुः संत्रस्तया भीतया देव्या निपीडितो दृढं धृतः सोऽयं स्वप्नेऽपि उत्पन्नः संस्पर्शो यस्य तथा सन्नपि रोम्णां हर्षं रोमहर्षं सात्विकभावान्यतमं न मुञ्चति रोमाञ्चित एव तिष्ठति । तं पश्येति सम्बन्धः ॥ ११ ॥ **आर्यपुत्रः**—स्वराजदारिकाया भर्तेति कृत्वायं काञ्चुकीयस्योपचारः । आरुणिं तव शत्रुम् । पादाभ्यामततीति पदातिः ।

१ मा दाणिं भवं अदिमत्तं सन्तप्पिअ । इमस्सिं राअउळे (मेदानीं भवानतिमात्रं सन्तप्य । अस्मिन्राजकुले). २ अत्ताणं ओभसिअं कादुं (आत्मानमवहसितं कर्तुम् ।). ३ जयतु जयत्वा० ४ समुदायेन.

मभिघातयितुम् । तथा[1] हस्त्यश्वरथपदातीनि मामकानि विजयाङ्गानि संनद्धानि । तदुत्तिष्ठतु भवान् ! । अपि च,

भिन्नास्ते रिपवो भवद्गुणरताः पौराः समाश्वासिताः
पार्ष्णी यापि[2] भवत्प्रयाणसमये तस्या विधानं कृतम् ।
यद्यत् साध्यमरिप्रमाथजननं तत्तन्मयानुष्ठितं
तीर्णा चापि बलैर्नदी त्रिपथगा वत्साश्च हस्ते तव ॥ १२ ॥

राजा—(उत्थाय ।) बाढम् । अयमिदानीम्,

उपेत्य नागेन्द्रतुरंगतीर्णे तमारुणिं दारुणकर्मदक्षम् ।
विकीर्णबाणोग्रतरङ्गभङ्गे महार्णवाभे युधि नाशयामि ॥ १३ ॥

(निष्क्रान्ताः सर्वे ।)

इति पञ्चमोऽङ्कः ।

'पादस्य पदाज्यातिगोपहतेषु' इति पादस्य पद इत्यदन्त आदेशः । अज्यतिभ्यां पादे च । इति इणु । सन्नद्धानि सज्जानि । 'सन्नद्धो वर्मितः सज्जः' इत्यमरः । **भिन्ना** इति । ते रिपवः भिन्नाः विनाशितप्रायाः । यद्वा भेदं गताः । अस्मन्नयेनासंहताः कृताः । भवद्गुणेषु रताः भवद्गुणैस्त्वय्यनुरक्ता इत्यर्थः । पौराः समाश्वासिताः । भवतः प्रयाणसमये अभियानकाले या पार्ष्णी सैन्यपृष्ठम् । पार्ष्णिशब्दात्स्त्रीलिङ्गात् 'कृदिकारादक्तिनः' इति ङीषु । तस्याः विधानं कृतं तद्रक्षणोपायो विरचितः । अत्र कामन्दकः—'पुरश्च पश्चाच्च यदा समर्थस्तदाभियायान्महते फलाय । पुरः प्रसर्पन्नविशुद्धपृष्ठः प्राप्नोति तीव्रं खलु पार्ष्णिभेदम् ॥' इति । अरेः शत्रोः प्रमाथो विनाशस्तस्य जननं कारकं यद्यत्साध्यं करणीयं तत्तन्मयानुष्ठितम् । बलैरस्माकं सैन्यैः त्रिपथगा नदी गङ्गापि तीर्णा । वत्साश्च तव हस्ते स्थिता मन्तव्याः । शार्दूलविक्रीडितं वृत्तम् ॥ १२ ॥ **उपेत्येति** । नागेन्द्राश्च तुरङ्गाश्च नागेन्द्रतुरङ्गाः तीर्णाः कृतसंचारा यस्मिन् । 'कीर्णे' इति पाठे कीर्णा यस्मिन् । नागेन्द्रतुरङ्गमिति सेनाङ्गत्वात्समाहारद्वंद्वो वा । विकीर्णा बाणा बाणावल्य इत्यर्थः । उग्रास्तरङ्गभङ्गा यस्मिंस्तादृशे । अर्णवस्य सागरस्येव आभा यस्य । अर्णवेन सदृशे वा । युधि संग्रामे । युच्छब्दस्य स्त्रीलिङ्गत्वेऽप्यत्र प्रयोगवशात्पुल्लिंगता बोध्या । दारुणकर्मणि दक्षं चतुरमारुणिमुपेत्य नाशयामि । उपमालंकारः । उपेन्द्रवज्रा छन्दः ॥ १३ ॥

इति पञ्चमोऽङ्कः ॥

---

१ तथा च. २ चापि.

अथ षष्ठोऽङ्कः ।

(ततः प्रविशति काञ्चुकीयः ।)

काञ्चुकीयः—क इह भोः ! काञ्चनतोरणद्वारमशून्यं कुरुते ?

(प्रविश्य ।)

प्रतीहारी—आर्य ! अहं विजया । किं क्रियताम् ? [अय्य ! अहं विजआ । किं करीअदु ?]

काञ्चुकीयः—भवति ! निवेद्यतां निवेद्यतां वत्सराज्यलाभप्रवृद्धोदयायोदयनाय एव खलु महासेनस्य सकाशाद् रैभ्यसगोत्रः काञ्चुकीयः प्राप्तः तत्रभवत्या चाङ्गारवत्या प्रेषितार्या वसुन्धरा नाम वासवदत्ताधात्री च प्रतीहारमुपस्थिताविति ।

प्रतीहारी—आर्य ! अदेशकालः प्रतीहारस्य । [अय्य ! अदेशकाळो पडिहारस्य ।]

काञ्चुकीयः—कथमदेशकालो नाम ?

प्रतीहारी—श्रृणोत्वार्यः । अद्य भर्तुः सूर्यामुखप्रासादगतेन केनापि वीणा वादिता । तां च श्रुत्वा भर्त्रा भणितं घोषवत्याः शब्द इव श्रूयत इति ।

अथ पञ्चमाङ्कावसाने सूचिते संग्रामे लब्धजयस्य उदयनस्य राज्यप्राप्त्यनन्तरं प्रथमाङ्के यौगन्धरायणेन सूचितस्यार्थजातस्य यथायथं विप्रकीर्णस्यैकत्रोपसंग्रहार्थं षष्ठाङ्कं प्रारभते । तत्रादौ नायकस्य पुना राज्यप्राप्तिं तदनन्तरं यथाकथंचिद् दृष्टया घोषवत्या कृतं पर्याकुलत्वं च दर्शयितुं काञ्चुकीयप्रवेशं प्रस्तौति **ततः प्रविशतीति** । **काञ्चनेति** । काञ्चनस्य तोरणं बहिर्द्वारं राजकुलस्येत्यर्थात् । तस्य द्वारम् । अशून्यं सनाथं कुरुते । तत्र वर्तते इत्यर्थः । वत्सदेशराज्यलाभेन प्रवृद्ध उदयो यस्य तस्मै । समानं गोत्रं यस्य स सगोत्रः । रैभ्यस्य सगोत्रः । अङ्गारवती महासेनपत्नी वासवदत्ताजननी । देशयुक्तः कालः देशकालः । अप्रशस्तः देशकालः अदेशकालः । प्रतीहार्या निवेदनस्यायोग्योऽयं कालो देशश्चेति भावः । सूर्यामुखप्रासादः सूर्याभिमुखप्रासादः । सूर्या विवाहदेवता सा मङ्गलार्थं दारुशिलाद्युत्कीर्णा मुखे यस्य स सूर्यामुखः प्रासादः । इति गणपतिशास्त्रिणः । तं गतेन । घोषवत्याः तदाख्याया वीणाया वासुकिभ्रात्रा वसुनेमिनोदयनाय

---

१ काञ्चनरत्न० २ विजये ... महाराजाय वत्स०.

[सुणादु अय्यो । अज्ज भट्टिणो सुँय्यामुहप्पासादगणेण केण वि वीणा वादिदा । तं च सुणिअ भट्टिणा भणिअं घोसवदीए सद्दो विअ सुणीअदि त्ति ।]

काञ्चुकीयः—ततस्ततः ?

प्रतीहारी—ततस्तत्र गत्वा पृष्टः कुतोऽस्या वीणाया आगम इति । तेन भणितमस्माभिर्नर्मदातीरे कूर्चगुल्मलग्ना दृष्टा । यदि प्रयोजनमनया उपनीयतां भर्त्रा इति । तां चोपनीतामङ्के कृत्वा मोहं गतो भर्ता । ततो मोहप्रत्यागतेन बाष्पपर्याकुलेन मुखेन भर्त्रा भणितं दृष्टासि 'घोषवति ! सा खलु न दृश्यते ' इति । आर्य ! ईदृशोऽनवसरः । कथं निवेदयामि ?

[तदो तहिं गच्छिअ पुच्छिदो कुदो इमाए वीणाए आगमो त्ति । तेण भणिअं अम्हेहिं णम्मदातीरे कुय्यगुम्मळग्गा दिट्ठा । जइ प्पओअणं इमाँए उवणीअदु भट्टिणा त्ति । तं च उवणीदं अंके करिअ मोहं गदो भट्टा । तदो मोहप्पच्चागदेण बप्फपय्यौउळेण मुहेण भट्टिणा भणिअं दिट्ठासि 'घोषवदि ! सा हु ण दिस्सदि' त्ति । अय्य ! इदिसो अणवसरो । कहं णिवेदेमि ?]

काञ्चुकीयः—भवति ! निवेद्यताम् । इदमपि तदाश्रयमेव ।

प्रतीहारी—आर्य ! इयं निवेदयामि । एष भर्ता सूर्यामुखप्रासादादवतरति । तदिहैव निवेदयिष्यामि । [अय्य ! इअं णिवेदेमि । एसो भट्टा सुँय्यामुहप्पासादादो ओदरइ । ता इह एव्व णिवेदइस्सं ।]

काञ्चुकीयः—भवति ! तथा ।

(उभौ निष्क्रान्तौ ।)

मिश्रविष्कम्भकः ।

दत्तायाः । कूर्चगुल्मलग्ना कूर्चानां दर्भाणां गुल्मे स्तम्बे लग्ना संसक्ता । उपनीयतां गृह्यतामित्यर्थः । ' उपनीयतां भर्त्रे ' इति पाठः न सम्यक्सङ्गच्छते । मोहात्प्रत्यागतः मोहप्रत्यागतः लब्धसंज्ञः । बाष्पैः पर्याकुलेन व्याप्तेन । सा मम प्रिया वासवदत्ता । अनवसरः अकालः । तदाश्रयं वासवदत्तासम्बद्धम् । मिश्रविष्कम्भकः । एतल्लक्षणम्—'वृत्तवर्तिष्यमाणानां कथांशानां निदर्शकः । संक्षिप्तार्थस्तु विष्कम्भो मध्यपात्रप्रयोजितः । एकानेककृतः शुद्धो संकीर्णो नीचमध्यमैः ॥ ' इति । अत्र काञ्चुकीयो मध्यमपात्रम् ।

---

१ सय्या. २ इमाए वीणाए. ३ भट्टिणो (भर्त्रे). ४ पय्याउलोच्छूणमुहेण (कुलोच्छूनमुखेन). ५ निवेद्यतां निवे०. ६ सय्या.

(ततः प्रविशति राजा विदूषकश्च ।)

राजा—

श्रुतिसुखनिनदे ! कथं नु देव्याः स्तनयुगले जघनस्थले च सुप्ता ।
विहगगणरजोविकीर्णदण्डा प्रतिभयमध्युषितास्यरण्यवासम् ॥ १ ॥

अपि च । अस्निग्धासि घोषवति ! या तपस्विन्या न स्मरसि ।

श्रोणीसमुद्वहनपार्श्वनिपीडितानि
खेदस्तनान्तरसुखान्युपगूहितानि ।
उद्दिश्य मां च विरहे परिदेवितानि
वाद्यान्तरेषु कथितानि च सस्मितानि ॥ २ ॥

विदूषकः—अलमिदानीं भवानतिमात्रं संतप्य । [अळं दाणिं भवं अदिमत्तं संतप्पिअ ।]

राजा—वयस्य ! मा मैवम्,

चिरप्रसुप्तः कामो मे वीणया प्रतिबोधितः ।
तां तु देवीं न पश्यामि यस्या घोषवती प्रिया ॥ ३ ॥

वसन्तक ! शिल्पिजनसकाशान्नवयोगां[1] घोषवतीं कृत्वा शीघ्रमानय ।

विदूषकः—यद् भवानाज्ञापयति । [जं भवं आणवेदि ।] (वीणां गृहीत्वा निष्क्रान्तः ।)

राजा घोषवतीमुद्दिश्याह—**श्रुतिसुखेति** । हे श्रुतिसुखः कर्णमधुरः निनदो यस्याः सा तत्सम्बुद्धिः, घोषवति ! देव्या वासवदत्तायाः स्तनयुगे जघनस्थले च सुप्ता सुखस्थितेत्यर्थः । त्वं विहगगणस्य पक्षिसमूहस्य रजसा धूल्या विकीर्णो व्याप्तो दण्डो यस्यास्तादृशी प्रतिभयं भयङ्करमरण्यवासमध्युषितासि । 'उपान्वध्याङ्वस' इति द्वितीया । पुष्पिताग्रा वृत्तम् ॥ १ ॥ अस्निग्धा निःस्नेहा येत्यादि श्लोकान्वयि । या त्वं तपस्विन्या अनुकम्प्याया वासवदत्तायाः श्रोण्यां कट्यां वादनकाले समुद्वहनं तेन पार्श्वस्य निपीडितानि । यद्वा श्रोणीव श्रोणी वीणाया ककुभाख्यमधोङ्गं तस्या उद्वहनानि धारणानि पार्श्वनिपीडितानि वीणादण्डघर्षणानि । खेदे वादनश्रमे सति खेदेन वा स्तनान्तरे कुचान्तराले सुखानि उपगूहितान्यालिङ्गनानि । विरहे मामुद्दिश्य मत्सम्बन्धेन परिदेवितानि विलापान् । वाद्यान्तरेषु वादनविषयान्तरेषु सस्मितानि कथितानि भाषणानि न स्मरसीत्यन्वयः । वसन्ततिलकं वृत्तम् ॥ २ ॥ **चिरप्रसुप्त** इति । चिरं प्रसुप्तः शयितः । निलीनः स्थित इत्यर्थः । मम कामः वीणया प्रतिबोधितः, उत्तेजित इति यावत् । यस्या इयं घोषवती प्रिया तां देवीं तु न पश्यामि ॥ ३ ॥ शिल्पं कलाऽस्यास्तीति शिल्पी ।

---

१ सकाशं गत्वा नव०.

(प्रविश्य ।)

प्रतीहारी—जयतु भर्ता । एष खलु महासेनस्य सकाशाद् रैभ्यसगोत्रः काञ्चुकीयो देव्याङ्गारवत्या प्रेषितार्या वसुन्धरा नाम वासवदत्ताधात्री च प्रतिहारमुपस्थितौ । [जेदु भट्टा । एसो खु महासेणस्स सआसादो रब्भसगोत्तो कंचुईओ देवीए अंगारवदीए पेसिदा अय्या वसुंधरा णाम वासवदत्ताधत्ती अ पडिहारं उवट्ठिदा ।]

राजा—तेन हि पद्मावती तावदाहूयताम् ।

प्रतीहारी—यद् भर्ताज्ञापयाति । [जं भट्टा आणवेदि ।] (निष्क्रान्ता ।)

राजा—किं नु खलु शीघ्रमिदानीमयं वृत्तान्तो महासेनेन विदितः ?

(ततः प्रविशति पद्मावती प्रतीहारी च ।)

प्रतीहारी—एत्वेतु भर्तृदारिका । (एदु एदु भट्टिदारिआ ।)

पद्मावती—जयत्वार्यपुत्रः । [जेदु अय्यउत्तो ।]

राजा—पद्मावति ! किं श्रुतं महासेनस्य सकाशाद् रैभ्यसगोत्रः काञ्चुकीयः प्राप्तस्तत्रभवत्या चाङ्गारवत्या प्रेषितार्या वसुन्धरा नाम वासवदत्ताधात्री च प्रतिहारमुपस्थिताविति ?

पद्मावती—आर्यपुत्र ! प्रियं मे ज्ञातिकुलस्य कुशलवृत्तान्तं श्रोतुम् । [अय्यउत्त ! पिअं मे ञादिकुळस्स कुसलवुत्तंतं सोदुं ।]

राजा—अनुरूपमेतद् भवत्याभिहितं 'वासवदत्तास्वजनो मे स्वजनः' इति । पद्मावति ! आस्यताम् । किमिदानीं नास्यते ?

पद्मावती—आर्यपुत्र ! किं मया सहोपविष्ट एतं जनं प्रेक्षिष्यते ? [अय्यउत्त ! किं मए सह उवविट्ठो एदं जणं पेक्खिस्सदि ?]

राजा—कोऽत्र दोषः ?

पद्मावती—आर्यपुत्रस्यापरः परिग्रह इत्युदासीनमिव भवति । [अय्यउत्तस्स अवरो परिग्गहो त्ति उदासीणं विअ होदि ।]

शिल्पी वीणावाद्यकारः । तत्सकाशाद् घोषवतीं नवो योगो घटना दूषितभागापनयनेन नवावयवसम्पादनेन नवीकरणं यस्यास्ताम् । समानं गोत्रमस्य सगोत्रः । ज्योतिर्जन-पदेत्यादिना सः । रैभ्यस्य सगोत्रः । अङ्गारवती वासवदत्तामाता । अयं वृत्तान्तः मम पद्मावतीपरिग्रहस्य वार्ता । ज्ञातिकुलस्य स्वजनकुलस्य । प्रेक्षिष्यते भवानिति शेषः । परिग्रहः भार्या । अहं द्वितीयभार्या । अतो ममैकत्रोपवेशनं न रुचिकरं भवेदित्यर्थः ।

---

१ अहो शीघ्र०. २ स्ससि (द्रक्ष्यसि.) ३ ण सिलाहणीयं (न श्लाघनीयं).

राजा—कलत्रदर्शनार्हं जनं कलत्रदर्शनात् परिहरतीति बहुदोषमुत्पादयति । तस्मादास्यताम् ।

पद्मावती—यदार्यपुत्र आज्ञापयति । (उपविश्य ।) आर्यपुत्र ! तातो वाम्बा वा किं नु खलु भणिष्यतीत्याविग्नेव संवृत्ता । [जं अय्यउत्तो आणवेदि । अय्यउत्त ! तादो वा अंबा वा किं णु खु भणिस्सदि त्ति आविग्गा विअ संवुत्ता ।]

राजा—पद्मावति ! एवमेतत्,

> **किं वक्ष्यतीति हृदयं परिशङ्कितं मे**
> **कन्या मयाप्यपहृता न च रक्षिता सा ।**
> **भाग्यैश्चलैर्महदवाप्तगुणोपघातः**
> **पुत्रः पितुर्जनितरोष इवास्मि भीतः ॥ ४ ॥**

पद्मावती—ननु किं शक्यं रक्षितुं प्राप्तकाले ? [णं किं सक्कं रक्खिदुं पत्तकाळे ?]

प्रतीहारी—एष काञ्चुकीयो धात्री च प्रतिहारमुपस्थितौ । [एसो कंचुईओ धत्ती अ पडिहारं उवट्ठिदा ।]

राजा—शीघ्रं प्रवेश्यताम् ।

प्रतीहारी—यद् भर्ताज्ञापयति । [जं भट्टा आणवेदि ।] (निष्क्रान्ता ।)

(ततः प्रविशति काञ्चुकीयो धात्री प्रतिहारी च ।)

कलेन मधुरवचनेन त्रायते इति कलत्रं भार्या । कलत्रदर्शनस्यार्हमुचितम् । कलत्रदर्शनात्परिहरति तस्य कलत्रदर्शनं निरुणद्धि । इत्येतं महान्तं निन्दारूपं जनयति । तातः महासेनः अम्बाङ्गारवती । वासवदत्तापितरौ आत्मन एवेत्याचारानुरोधादियमुक्तिः । किं नु खलु भणिष्यति कञ्चुकिद्वारेण धात्रीमुखेन चेति शेषः । प्रियमप्रियं वेति आविग्ना पर्याकुला ।

किमिति । प्रद्योतः किं वक्ष्यति प्रहितजनद्वारेत्यर्थात् । इति मे हृदयं परिशङ्कितं जातशङ्कं वर्तते । यतस्तस्य कन्या मयापहृतापि न रक्षिता न सम्यक्पालिता । यतोऽग्निदग्धा । सम्यक्पालने कन्यापहरणमक्षमिष्यतेति भावः । चलैः चञ्चलैः भाग्यैः । दैवस्यास्थिरतयेति यावत् । न तु स्वदोषैः । महद्यथा स्यात्तथा अवाप्तः गुणानामुपघातः सदाचारभ्रंशः येन सोऽहम् जनितः उत्पादितो रोषो येन स पुत्रः पितुरिव भीतोऽस्मि । वसन्ततिलका वृत्तम् ॥ ४ ॥ ननु इति जिज्ञासायां । प्राप्तकाले विनाशकाले प्राप्ते किं रक्षितुं शक्यं ? न किमपीति, न खेदः कार्य इत्यर्थः ।

---

१ सत्यमेतत्. २ न (ण).

काञ्चुकीयः—भोः !

संबन्धिराज्यमिदमेत्य महान् प्रहर्षः
स्मृत्वा पुनर्नृपसुतानिधनं विषादः ।
किं नाम दैव ! भवता न कृतं यदि स्याद्
राज्यं परैरपहृतं कुशलं च देव्याः ॥ ५ ॥

प्रतीहारी—एष भर्ता । उपसर्पत्वार्यः । [एसो भट्टा । उवसप्पदु अय्यो ।]

काञ्चुकीयः—(उपेत्य ।) जयत्वार्यपुत्रः ।

धात्री—जयतु भर्ता । [जेदु भट्टा ।]

राजा—(सबहुमानम् ।) आर्य !

पृथिव्यां राजवंशानामुदयास्तमयप्रभुः ।
अपि राजा स कुशली मया काङ्क्षितबान्धवः ॥ ६ ॥

काञ्चुकीयः—अथ किम् ? कुशली महासेनः ? इहापि सर्वगतं कुशलं पृच्छति ।

राजा—(आसनादुत्थाय ।) किमाज्ञापयति महासेनः ?

काञ्चुकीयः—सदृशमेतद् वैदेहीपुत्रस्य । नन्वासनस्थेनैव भवता श्रोतव्यो महासेनस्य संदेशः ।

राजा—यदाज्ञापयति महासेनः । (उपविशति ।)

काञ्चुकीयः—दिष्ट्या परैरपहृतं राज्यं पुनः प्रत्यानीतमिति । कुतः ?

सम्बन्धीति । इदं सम्बन्धिनः बन्धोरुदयनस्य राज्यमेत्य मम महान्प्रहर्ष आविर्भवति । पुनः नृपसुताया अस्माक नृपतेः सुताया वासवदत्ताया निधनं स्मृत्वा महान् विषादः प्रादुर्भवति । हे दैव विधे ! भवता किं नाम कृतं भवेद्यदि परैरपहृतं राज्यं स्यात्तथा च देव्या वासवदत्तायाश्च कुशलं स्यात् । वासवदत्ता कथमप्यग्निदाहान्निर्मुक्ता कुशलिनी स्यादित्यर्थः । सर्वमेव कृतं भवेदित्यर्थः । वसन्ततिलका वृत्तम् ॥ ५ ॥ **काञ्चु०**—आर्यपुत्रेति भर्तृदारिकेतिवत्तद्देशोचितः नृपं प्रत्युपचारः । **पृथिव्यामिति** । पृथिव्यां मह्यां । स्थितानाम् । वंशे भवा वंश्याः । 'दिगादिभ्यो यत्' इति यत्प्रत्ययः । राज्ञां वंश्या राजवंश्याः, तेषामुदय उत्कर्षोऽस्तमयो विनाशश्च तयोः प्रभुस्तत्करणशक्तः । अनेन तस्य सार्वभौमत्वं दर्शितम् । तथा मया कांक्षितश्चासौ बान्धवश्च स राजा महासेनः कुशली अपि कुशली किम् ! ॥६॥ सर्वे गतं सर्वगतं सर्वसम्बन्धि । वैदेहीपुत्रस्य वैदेही विदेहराजतनया उदयनस्य माता ।

कातरा येऽप्यशक्ता वा नोत्साहस्तेषु जायते ।
प्रायेण हि नरेन्द्रश्रीः सोत्साहैरेव भुज्यते ॥ ७ ॥

राजा—आर्य ! सर्वमेतन्महासेनस्य प्रभावः । कुतः ?

अहमवजितः पूर्वं तावत् सुतैः सह लालितो
दृढमपहृता कन्या भूयो मया न च रक्षिता ।
निधनमपि च श्रुत्वा तस्यास्तथैव मयि स्वता
ननु यदुचितान् वत्सान् प्राप्तुं नृपोऽत्र हि कारणम् ॥ ८ ॥

काञ्चुकीयः—एष महासेनस्य संदेशः । देव्याः संदेशमिहात्रभवती[1] कथयिष्यति ।

राजा—हा अम्ब !

षोडशान्तःपुरज्येष्ठा पुण्या नगरदेवता ।
मम प्रवासदुःखार्ता माता कुशलिनी ननु ? ॥ ९ ॥

धात्री—अरोगा भट्टिनी भर्तारं सर्वगतं कुशलं पृच्छति । [अरोआ भट्टिणी भट्टारं सव्वगदं कुसळं पुच्छदि ।]

राजा—सर्वगतं कुशलमिति । अम्ब ! ईदृशं कुशलम् ?

कातरा इति । ये नृपाः कातरा भीरवोऽशक्ता दुर्बला वा तेषु उत्साहः अध्यवसायः न जायते । ते कस्मिन्नपि कर्मणि उत्साहेन न प्रवर्तन्ते इत्यर्थः । हि प्रायेण नरेन्द्रश्रीः राज्यलक्ष्मीः । यद्वा हे नरेन्द्र श्रीः इति पदच्छेदः । सोत्साहैः धैर्यशक्तिसहकृतोत्साहसम्पन्नैरेव भुज्यते । अप्रस्तुतप्रशंसालंकारः ॥७॥ **अहमिति ।** पूर्वं तावदहमवजितोऽपि सुतैः सह लालितः । सुतनिर्विशेषं प्रेम्णा पालितः । न तु शत्रुवत्पीडितः । मया तस्य कन्या दृढं कठोरं यथा तथा अपहृता न तु सावधानतया रक्षिता । अपायादिति शेषः । तस्या निधनं श्रुत्वा मृत्युवार्तां लब्ध्वापि । विद्वेषकारणे सत्यपि । तथैव पूर्ववदेव मयि स्वता आत्मीयत्वबुद्धिः । ननु उचितान् मम विषयभूतान् वत्सान् वत्सदेशं प्राप्तुं यदशक्यमिति शेषः । यद्वा वत्सान्प्राप्तुं यदुपकारकमभूत्तत्र । हि निश्चयेन नृपः महासेनः कारणम् । मुख्यतो महासेनप्रभावादेव मया राज्यं लब्धमिति भावः । हरिणी वृत्तम् । 'नसभरसला गः षड्वेदैर्हयैर्हरिणी मता ।' इति लक्षणम् ॥ ८ ॥ **षोडशेति ।** षोडशानामन्तःपुराणामवरोधस्त्रीणां ज्येष्ठा प्रधानभूता । पुण्या नगरदेवता पुरदेवतावत्स्थिता । मम प्रवासदुःखेनार्ता पीडिता माता श्वश्रूः अङ्गारवती कुशलिनी क्षेमवती ननु किम् ? नन्विति प्रश्ने ॥ ९ ॥ अरोगा अविद्यमानो रोगो यस्याः

---

१ तत्रभवत्याः.

धात्री—मेदानीं भर्तातिमात्रं संतप्तुम् । [मा दाणिं भट्टा अदिमत्तं संतप्पिदुं ।]

काञ्चुकीयः—धारयत्वार्यपुत्रः । उपरताप्यनुपरता महासेनपुत्री एवमनुकम्प्यमानार्यपुत्रेण । अथवा,

कः कं शक्तो रक्षितुं मृत्युकाले रज्जुच्छेदे के घटं धारयन्ति ।
एवं लोकस्तुल्यधर्मो वनानां काले काले छिद्यते रुह्यते च ॥ १० ॥

राजा—आर्य ! मा मैवम् ;

महासेनस्य दुहिता शिष्या देवी च मे प्रिया ।
कथं सा न मया शक्या स्मर्तुं देहान्तरेष्वपि ॥ ११ ॥

धात्री—आह भट्टिनी–' उपरता वासवदत्ता । मम वा महासेनस्य वा यादृशौ गोपालकपालकौ तादृश एव त्वं प्रथममेवाभिप्रेतो जामातेति । एतन्निमित्तमुज्जायिनीमानीतः । अनग्निसाक्षिकं वीणाव्यपदेशेन दत्ता । आत्मनश्चपलतयानिर्वृत्तविवाहमङ्गल एव गतः । अथ चावाभ्यां तव च वासवदत्तायाश्च प्रतिकृतिं चित्रफलकायामालिख्य विवाहो निर्वृत्तः । एषा चित्रफलका तव सकाशं प्रेषिता । एतां दृष्ट्वा निर्वृतो भव । ' [आह भट्टिणी–

सा तथोक्ता । अनामया । ईदृशं कुशलं यद्वासवदत्ताविरहितोऽस्मि । मा संतप्तुमलं सन्तापेन । धारयतु धैर्यावष्टम्भेन चित्तं स्थिरीकरोतु । **कः कमिति** । कः अप्रमत्तोऽपि मृत्युकाले उपस्थिते कं रक्षितुं समर्थः ? न कोऽपीत्यर्थः । रज्जोः छेदे रज्जुच्छेदे सति । रज्जौ छिन्नायां रज्जुबद्धं घटं के धारयन्ति ? न कोऽपीत्यर्थः । एवं दैवायत्तत्वात् लोकः वनानां वृक्षाणां तुल्यः धर्मः यस्य स तुल्यधर्मः समानधर्मा । अत्र अनिजकरणं समासान्तरविधेरनित्यत्वात् । यद्वा तुल्यधर्मेति पठनीयम् । काले काले छिद्यते लूयते नश्यति च । रुह्यते रोहति जायते च । दृष्टान्तालङ्कारः । शालिनीवृत्तम् । लक्षणमुक्तम् ॥ १० ॥ **महासेनस्येति** । महासेनदुहिता ततो मे शिष्या प्रिया देवी च । सा मया देहान्तरेषु अन्येषु जन्मसु किमुतैतस्मिन् स्मर्तुं कथं न शक्या ? सर्वदा स्मर्यैतैव ॥ ११ ॥ गोपालकपालकौ तस्याः सुतौ । अभिप्रेतो मनसेष्टः । एतन्निमित्तं जामातृकरणार्थम् । अग्निः साक्षी साक्षाद्द्रष्टा यस्मिन्कर्मणि तदग्निसाक्षिकं, तन्न भवतीत्यनग्निसाक्षिकम् । यथाविधि विवाहमकृत्वेत्यर्थः । वीणाव्यपदेशेन वीणावादनशिक्षामिषेण । आत्मनः चपलतया अधीरतया । अग्निसाक्षिकविवाहकरणावधिमप्रतिपाल्यैव । अथ च युवयोर्गमनानन्तरम् । प्रतिकृतिं चित्रम् । चित्रफलकेति स्त्रीलिङ्गप्रयोगः कवेर्निरङ्कुशत्वात् । निर्वृत आश्वस्त-

---

१ सन्तपिअ । इदिसं दाणिं एदं (सन्तप्य । ईदृशमिदानीमेतत्) । २ मार्य०

'उवरदा वासवदत्ता। मम वा महासेणस्स वा जादिसा गोवाळअपाळआ तादिसो एव्व तुमं पुढमं एव्व अभिप्पेदो जामादुअत्ति। एदण्णिमित्तं उज्जइणिं आणीदो। अणग्गिसक्खिअं वीणाववदेसेण दिण्णा। अत्तणो चवळदाए अणिव्वुत्तविवाहमंगळो एव्व गदो। अंह अ अम्हेहिं तव अ वासवदत्ताए अ पडिकिदिं चित्तफळआए आळिहिअ विवाहो णिव्वुत्तो। एसा चित्तफळआ तव सआसं पेसिदा। एदं पेक्खिअ णिव्वुदो होहि।']

राजा—अहो! अतिस्निग्धमनुरूपं चाभिहितं तत्रभवत्या।

वाक्यमेतत् प्रियतरं राज्यलाभशतादपि।
अपराद्धेष्वपि स्नेहो यदस्मासु न विस्मृतः॥ १२॥

पद्मावती—आर्यपुत्र! चित्रगतं गुरुजनं दृष्ट्वाभिवादयितुमिच्छामि। [अय्यउत्त! चित्तगदं गुरुअणं पेक्खिअ अभिवादेदुं इच्छामि।]

धात्री—पश्यतु पश्यतु भर्तृदारिका। [पेक्खदु पेक्खदु भट्टिदारिआ।] (चित्रफलकां दर्शयति।)

पद्मावती—(दृष्ट्वा आत्मगतम्।) हम्। अतिसदृशी खल्वियमार्याया आवन्तिकायाः। (प्रकाशम्।) आर्यपुत्र! सदृशी खल्वियमार्यायाः। (हं, अदिसदिसी खु इअं अय्याए आवंतिआए। अय्यउत्त! सदिसी खु इयं अय्याए।)

राजा—न सदृशी सैवेति मन्ये। भोः! कष्टम्,

अस्य स्निग्धस्य वर्णस्य विपत्तिर्दारुणा कथम्।
इदं च मुखमाधुर्यं कथं दूषितमग्निना?॥ १३॥

पद्मावती—आर्यपुत्रस्य प्रतिकृतिं दृष्ट्वा जानामीयमार्यया सदृशी न वेति। [अय्यउत्तस्स पडिकिदिं पेक्खिअ जाणामि इअं अय्याए सदिसी ण वेत्ति।]

धात्री—पश्यतु पश्यतु भर्तृदारिका। [पेक्खदु पेक्खदु भट्टिदारिआ।]

चित्तः। प्रतिकृतिविलोकनेनात्मानं विनोदयेति यावत्। अनुरूपं स्वमहानुभावतासदृशम्। **वाक्यमिति**। एतद्वाक्यम्। राज्यानां लाभास्तेषां शतं राज्यलाभशतं तस्मादपि प्रियतरम्। यद्यस्मादपराद्धेषु कृतापराधेष्वप्यस्मासु स्नेहः पुत्रवात्सल्यं न विस्मृतम् ॥ १२॥ गुरुजनं वासवदत्तां प्रथमपत्नीम्। सदृशी खल्वियमार्याया वासवदत्ताया इति प्रश्नः। न सदृशी केवलमिति शेषः। **अस्येति**। अस्यालेख्यप्रतीयमानस्य। स्निग्धस्य नयनप्रीतिकरस्य। दारुणाग्निदाहाद्विपत्तिर्नाशः कथम्! जातेति शेषः। इदं च मुखमाधुर्यं मुखसौन्दर्यमग्निना कथं दूषितम्! इत्यहो दैवदुर्विपाकः कोऽपि ॥१३॥ आर्यपुत्रस्य प्रतिकृतिं प्रेक्ष्य यदि आर्यपुत्रस्य प्रतिकृतिरार्यपुत्रेण संवदेत्तर्हि आर्याया

---

१ जूषितं. २ पेक्खिदुमिच्छामी.

पद्मावती—(दृष्ट्वा ।) आर्यपुत्रस्य प्रतिकृत्याः सदृशतया जानामीयमार्यया सदृशीति । [अय्यउत्तस्स पडिकिदीए सदिसदाए जाणामि इअं अय्याए सदिसि त्ति ।

राजा—देवि ! चित्रदर्शनात् प्रभृति प्रहृष्टोद्विग्नामिव त्वां पश्यामि । किमिदम् ?

पद्मावती—आर्यपुत्र ! अस्याः प्रतिकृत्याः सदृशीहैव प्रतिवसति । [अय्यउत्त ! इमाए पडिकिदीए सदिसी इह एव्व पडिवसदि ।]

राजा—किं[2] वासवदत्तायाः ?

पद्मावती—आम् । [आम् ।]

राजा—तेन हि शीघ्रमानीयताम्[3] ।

पद्मावती—आर्यपुत्र ! मम कन्याभावे केनापि ब्राह्मणेन मम भगिनिकेति न्यासो निक्षिप्तः । प्रोषितभर्तृका परपुरुषदर्शनं परिहरति । तदार्या पश्यतु सदृशी न वेति । [अय्यउत्त ! मम कण्णाभावे केण वि बम्हणेन मम भइणिअत्ति ण्णासो णिक्खित्तो । पोसिदभत्तुआ परपुरुसदंसणं परिहरदि । तो अय्या पेक्खदु सदिसी ण वत्ति ।]

राजा—

> **यदि विप्रस्य भगिनी व्यक्तमन्या भविष्यति ।**
> **परस्परगता लोके दृश्यते रूपतुल्यता ॥ १४ ॥**

(प्रविश्य ।)

प्रतीहारी—जयतु भर्ता । एष उज्जयिनीयो ब्राह्मणो भट्टिन्या हस्ते मम भगिनिकेति न्यासो निक्षिप्तः तं प्रतिग्रहीतुं प्रतिहारमुपस्थितः । [जेदु भट्टा । एसो उज्जइणीओ बम्हणो भट्टिणीए हत्थे मम भइणिअत्ति ण्णासो णिक्खित्तो तं पडिग्गहिदुं पडिहारं उवट्ठिदो ।]

अपि तथेति प्रतीतिर्जायेतेति भावः । प्रहृष्टा जातहर्षा चासौ उद्विग्ना खिन्ना च । आत्मन्यत्यन्तस्निग्धावन्तिकैव वासवदत्ता सा च जीवतीति हर्षः । वासवदत्तालाभे आर्यपुत्रो मयि तथा न स्निह्येदिति विषादः । भगिनिकेति कथयित्वा न्यासो न्यस्तो न्यासत्वेन मयि निक्षिप्ता । **यदीति** । यदि सा विप्रस्य भगिनी तर्हि व्यक्तं स्पष्टमन्या भविष्यति, न तु वासवदत्ता । यतः लोके परस्परं गता परस्परगता रूपतुल्यता समानरूपता दृश्यते । लोके रूपसंवाद उपलभ्यते इत्यर्थः ॥ १४ ॥

---

१ ०उत्तपडिकिदिसादिसाभाए (आर्यपुत्रप्रतिकृतिसदृशाभायाः). २ न किं. ३ प्रवेश्यताम्. ४ ता अय्यं मए सह आअदं पेक्खि आजाणादु अय्यउत्तो [आर्यां मया सहागतां दृष्ट्वा जानात्वार्यपुत्रः]।

राजा—पद्मावति ! किं नु स ब्राह्मणः ?

पद्मावती—भवितव्यम् । [होदव्वं ।]

राजा—शीघ्रं प्रवेश्यतामभ्यन्तरसमुदाचारेण स ब्राह्मणः ।

प्रतीहारी—यद् भर्ताज्ञापयति । [जं भट्टा आणवेदि ।] (निष्क्रान्ता ।)

राजा—पद्मावति ! त्वमपि तामानय ।

पद्मावती—यदार्यपुत्र आज्ञापयति । [जं अय्यपुत्तो आणवेदि ।] (निष्क्रान्ता ।)

(ततः प्रविशति यौगन्धरायणः प्रतीहारी च ।)

यौगन्धरायणः—(आत्मगतम् ।) भोः !

प्रच्छाद्य राजमहिषीं नृपतेर्हितार्थे
कामं मया कृतमिदं हितमित्यवेक्ष्य ।
सिद्धेऽपि नाम मम कर्मणि पार्थिवोऽसौ
किं वक्ष्यतीति हृदयं परिशङ्कितं मे ॥ १५ ॥

प्रतीहारी—एष भर्ता । उपसर्पत्वार्यः । [ऐसो भट्टा । उपसप्पदु अय्यो ।]

यौगन्धरायणः—(उपसृत्य ।) जयतु भवान् जयतु ।

राजा—श्रुतपूर्व इव स्वरः । भो ब्राह्मण ! किं भवतः स्वसा पद्मावत्या हस्ते न्यास इति निक्षिप्ता ?

यौगन्धरायणः—अथ किम् ?

राजा—तेन हि त्वर्यतां त्वर्यतामस्य भगिनिका ।

प्रतीहारी—यद् भर्ताज्ञापयति । [जं भट्टा आणवेदि ।] (निष्क्रान्ता ।)

(ततः प्रविशति पद्मावती आवन्तिका प्रतीहारी च ।)

पद्मावती—एत्वेत्वार्या । प्रियं ते निवेदयामि । [एदु एदु अय्या । पिअं दे णिवेदेमि ।]

अभ्यन्तरसमुदाचारेण अभ्यन्तरमन्तर्गृहं तस्य समुचितेनाचारेण । अर्घ्यपाद्यादिदानेन सत्कृत्येत्यर्थः । **प्रच्छाद्येति** । राजमहिषीं वासवदत्तां नृपतेरुदयनस्यैव हिताय राज्यप्राप्तिपद्मावतीविवाहादीष्टसिद्धये । प्रच्छाद्य वह्निना दग्धेति प्रवादं संचार्यापवाद्य गुप्तं स्थापयित्वा मया इदं हितमित्यवेक्ष्य कामं स्वच्छन्दं कृतम् । मम कर्मणि उद्दिष्टकार्ये सिद्धेऽपि नामासौ पार्थिवः किं वक्ष्यतीति मे हृदयं परिशङ्कितं शङ्कापर्याकुलं वर्तते । वसन्ततिलकम् ॥ १५ ॥

---

१ ब्राह्मणवेषः यौग०. २ अस्मात्प्राक् एदु एदु अय्यौ. ३ भोः श्रुत०.

आवन्तिका—किं किम् ?

पद्मावती—भ्राता ते आगतः । [भादा दे आअदो ।]

आवन्तिका—दिष्टयेदानीमपि स्मराति । [दिट्ठिआ इदाणिं पि सुमरदि ।]

पद्मावती—(उपसृत्य ।) जयत्वार्यपुत्रः । एष न्यासः । [जेदु अय्यउत्तो । एसो णासो ।]

राजा—निर्यातय पद्मावति ! अथवा साक्षिमन्न्यासो निर्यातयितव्यः । इहात्रभवान् रैभ्यः अत्रभवती चाधिकरणं भविष्यतः ।

पद्मावती—आर्य ! नीयतामिदानीमार्या । [अय्यं ! णीअदां दाणिं अय्या ।]

धात्री—(अवन्तिकां निर्वर्ण्य ।) अम्मो ! भर्तृदारिका वासवदत्ता । [अम्मो ! भट्टिदारिआ वासवदत्ता ।]

राजा—कथं महासेनपुत्री ? देवि ! प्रविश त्वमभ्यन्तरं पद्मावत्या सह ।

यौगन्धरायणः—न खलु न खलु प्रवेष्टव्यम् । मम भगिनी खल्वेषा[3] ।

राजा—किं भवानाह—महासेनपुत्री खल्वेषा ?

यौगन्धरायणः—भो राजन् !

> **भारतानां कुले जातो विनीतो ज्ञानवाञ्छुचिः ।**
> **तन्नार्हसि बलाद्धर्तुं राजधर्मस्य देशिकः ॥ १६ ॥**

राजा—भवतु पश्यामस्तावद्रूपसादृश्यम् । संक्षिप्यतां यवनिका ।

यौगन्धरायणः—जयतु स्वामी ।

वासवदत्ता—जयत्वार्यपुत्रः । (जेदु अय्यउत्तो ।)

राजा—अये ! असौ यौगन्धरायणः । इयं महासेनपुत्री ।

इदानीमपि इयतः कालादनन्तरम् । निर्यातय प्रत्यर्पय । साक्षिमत्साक्षिसमक्षम् । अधिकरणं न्यायपरिषत् । **भारतानामिति** । भारतानां भरतवंशीयानां कुले जातः विनीतः सम्यक्शिक्षितः । ज्ञानवान् शुचिः शुद्धान्तःकरणो राजधर्मस्य प्रजासम्यक्परिपालनरूपस्य देशिकः त्वं तां बलाद्धर्तुं नार्हसि ॥ १६ ॥ संक्षिप्यतामपनीयताम् ।

---

१ पेक्खदु. २ अम्ब इअं दाणिं अय्या. ३ एषा । भोः.

किं नु सत्यमिदं स्वप्नः सा भूयो दृश्यते मया ।
अनयाप्येवमेवाहं दृष्टया वञ्चितस्तदा ॥ १७ ॥

यौगन्धरायणः—स्वामिन् ! देव्यपनयेन कृतापराधः **खल्वहम्** । तत् क्षन्तुमर्हति स्वामी । (इति पादयोः पतति ।)

राजा—(उत्थाप्य ।) यौगन्धरायणो भवान् ननु ।

मिथ्योन्मादैश्च युद्धैश्च शास्त्रदृष्टैश्च मन्त्रितैः ।
भवद्यत्नैः खलु वयं मज्जमानाः समुद्धृताः ॥ १८ ॥

यौगन्धरायणः—स्वामिभाग्यानामनुगन्तारो वयम् ।

पद्मावती—अहो ! आर्या खल्वियम् । आर्ये ! सखीजनसमुदाचारेणाजानत्यातिक्रान्तः समुदाचारः । तच्छीर्षेण प्रसादयामि । [अम्महे ! अय्या खु इअं । अय्ये ! सहीजणसमुदाआरेण अजाणंतीए अदिक्कंदो समुदाआरो । ता सीसेण पसादेमि ।]

वासवदत्ता—(पद्मावतीमुत्थाप्य ।) उत्तिष्ठोत्तिष्ठाविधवे ! उत्तिष्ठ । अर्थिस्वं नाम शरीरमपराध्यति । [उट्ठेहि उट्ठेहि अविहवे ! उट्ठेहि । अत्थिसअं णाम सरीरं अवरज्झइ ।]

पद्मावती—अनुगृहीतास्मि । [अणुग्गहिदम्हि ।]

राजा—वयस्य यौगन्धरायण ! देव्यपनये का कृता ते बुद्धिः

यौगन्धरायणः—कौशाम्बीमात्रं परिपालयामीति ।

किं न्विति । इदं सत्यं यथार्थं किन्नु । अथवा स्वप्नोऽयं यत्सा महासेनपुत्री मया भूयः पुनरपि दृश्यते । अनयाप्येवमेव दृष्टयाहं तदा समुद्रगृहे सुप्तः वञ्चितः । मद्धस्तं झटित्याकृष्य गमनादिति भावः ॥ १७ ॥ **मिथ्येति** । मिथ्या अवास्तवा उन्मादास्तैः कपटोन्मादचेष्टितैरित्यर्थः । युद्धैः शास्त्रदृष्टैर्नीतिशास्त्रोपस्कृतैर्मन्त्रितैः मन्त्रणैः । भवद्यत्नैश्चापदि मज्जमाना वयं समुद्धृताः खलु ॥ १८ ॥ अनुगन्तार आपदि मुखे च स्वामिनमनुवर्तमाना इत्यर्थः । सखीजनवत्समुदाचारेण । सख्यामिव माननीयायामपि त्वय्याचरितमित्यर्थः । अर्थिनः यौगन्धरायणस्य स्वं । नामेति अलीके । तथा व्यपदिष्टं शरीरं ममेत्यर्थः । अपराध्यति । न तु भवती मम वास्तवं स्वरूपमजानती । यद्वा अपराध्यतीति प्रश्नकाकुः । अर्थिनः स्वभूतं शरीरं सर्वथार्थिपराधीनं तदाज्ञापूरणैकप्रवणं शरीरमपराध्यति । नैवेत्यर्थः। का कृता बुद्धिः कस्ते हेतुः? कौशाम्बी वत्सराजधानी। कौशाम्बी एव कौशाम्बीमात्रम् । न त्वखिलं वत्सराज्यं शत्रुहस्तगतत्वात् ।

---

१ अम्मो.

राजा—अथ पद्मावत्या हस्ते किं न्यासकारणम् ?

यौगन्धरायणः—पुष्पकभद्रादिभिरादेशिकैरादिष्टा स्वामिनो देवी भविष्यतीति ।

राजा—इदमपि रुमण्वता ज्ञातम् ।

यौगन्धरायणः—स्वामिन् ! सर्वैरेव ज्ञातम् ।

राजा—अहो ! शठः खलु रुमण्वान् ।

यौगन्धरायणः—स्वामिन् ! देव्याः कुशलनिवेदनार्थमद्यैव प्रतिनिवर्ततामत्रभवान् रैभ्योऽत्रभवती च ।

राजा—न न । सर्व एव वयं यास्यामो देव्या पद्मावत्या सह ।

यौगन्धरायणः—यदाज्ञापयति स्वामी ।

भरतवाक्यम् ।

इमां सागरपर्यन्तां हिमवद्विन्ध्यकुण्डलाम् ।
महीमेकातपत्राङ्कां राजसिंहः प्रशास्तु नः ॥ १९ ॥

(निष्क्रान्ताः सर्वे ।)

इति षष्ठोऽङ्कः ।

इति स्वप्नवासवदत्तमवसितम् ।

अतो देव्यपनयनेन सिद्धे पद्मावतीविवाहे तस्या भ्रातुर्दर्शकस्य साहाय्येनाखिलं वत्सराज्यं प्रत्यानीयेत ततो वत्सांस्तव प्रधानामात्य इति परिपालयिष्यामि इति हेतोः इत्यर्थः । परिपालयसीति साधीयान्पाठो भवेत् । सर्वैरेव तव हितैषिभिराप्ततमैः । शठः धूर्तः यो वासवदत्तानिधनशोकविह्वलं मां प्रतिदिनं पश्यन्नपि निश्चितकार्यसिद्ध्यपेक्षया देवीक्षेमवार्तां मां प्रत्यप्रकाशयन्मयि पर्यचरत् । इत्यहो स्वामिकार्यनिष्ठा तस्येति गूढाभिसन्धिः ! **न नेति**–नैतत्पर्याप्तम् । एतादृशेऽभ्युदये सर्वैरेवास्माभिर्गन्तव्यम् । येन महासेनोऽङ्गारवती च संमानितौ वासवदत्ताप्रत्यक्षदर्शनेन च प्रमुदितौ भवेताम् । पद्मावत्याः सान्निध्येन तस्या दाक्षिण्यसपत्नीप्रेमादिगुणसम्पत्तिश्च प्रदर्शिता भवेत् । भरतवाक्यं नटवाक्यम् । नाटकाभिनयसमाप्तौ नटेन देयाशीः । **इमामिति** । नोऽस्माकं राजा सिंह इव राजसिंहः सागराः पर्यन्ताः सीमानो यस्याः सा सागरपर्यन्ता ताम् । हिमवांश्च विन्ध्यश्च हिमवद्विन्ध्यौ कुण्डले यस्याः सा ताम् । एकमेवातपत्रं श्वेतच्छत्रमङ्कः चिह्नं यस्यास्तथाभूताम् । इमां महीं प्रशास्तु । अस्या कृत्स्नाया भुवः स्वामी भूयादित्यर्थः । अनेन प्रशस्तिर्नाम निर्वहणसन्धेश्चरममङ्गमुपक्षिप्तम् । तल्लक्षणमादिभरते–'देवद्विजनृपादीनां प्रशस्तिः स्यात्प्रशंसनम् ।' इति ॥ **इति स्वप्नवासवदत्ताटिप्पणी समाप्ता ।**

---

१ इहात्र० . २ समाप्तम् .

TRANSLATION
OF
SVAPNAVASAVDATTA.

ACT I.

The Nándî (prayer to the deities) being over (*enters the* MANAGER.)

MANAGER—May the arms of Bala (Balaráma) protect thee (the spectator, *i. e.* audience)!—the arms which possess the colour of the newly risen moon, which have full vigour given to them by wine to his beloved), which are full of splendour owing to the presence of Lakṣmî (the goddess of royalty) and which look attractive in (or like) spring.

I thus beg to address you, noble sirs! Ah! What is this, that something like a sound is heard when I am just engaged in addressing (the audience)! Well; I will see (what it is).

(Behind the scenes).

Move away, gentlemen, move away.

MANAGER—Well, I have known it.

All the people in the penance-grove are being impudently (roughly) driven away by the devoted servants of the king of Magadha, accompanying the Princess. (*Exit*).

END OF THE INDUCTION.

(Having entered)

TWO GUARDS—Move away, move away, gentlemen! move away.

(*Then enter* YAUGANDARĀYANA *in the garb of a recluse and* VĀSAVADATTĀ *in the costume of a lady of Avantî*).

YAUGAND—(*Listening*) How, here also people are asked to move away! Why?

Is molestation caused to the self-possessed dwellers of the hermitage, who live satisfied with the fruits of the forest, who deserve respect and who wear bark-garments? Ho, what haughty man is this, a stranger to a modest behaviour, who, elated with (*lit.*, amazed at) evanescent riches converts into a village, by his order, this peaceful penance-grove ? (3)

VĀSAVA.—Noble one, who is this that is driving away ?

YAUGAN.—My lady, he who drives himself away from religious merit.

VĀSAV.—Noble one, I did not mean to ask that. But that (I meant to ask) if even I should be one to be ordered to clear the way.

YAUGAN.—Madam, (even) deities, when not clearly known are insulted.

VĀSAVA.—Noble one, fatigue does not cause so much pain to me as this insult does.

YAUGAN.—This dignity your ladyship has once enjoyed and then given up. So this matter should not be thought over.

Formerly you too had gone (moved about when in your city) in this covetable way; and again you will attain this laudable dignity by the victory of your husband: the cycle of fortune of the world (worldly life) revolving with the course of time, moves like the series of the spokes of a wheel. (4)

THE TWO GUARDS.—Move away, gentle sirs, move away.

(*Enter the* CHAMBERLAIN).

CHAM.—Sambhāṣaka, not indeed, not indeed, should the clearing (of the crowd) be made. Mark,

You should avoid blame being attached to the king; no rough treatment should be accorded to the inmates of the hermitage ; to avoid the insults that are received in a city these high-souled persons come to and reside in a forest. (5)

BOTH.—Be it so, sir. (*Exeunt*).

YAU.—Good ; his look is full of practical knowledge. Dear daughter, let us approach him.

VĀSA.—Noble one, let us do so.

YAU.—(*Approaching,*) Sir, why is this dispersing of the people ?

CHAM.—O hermit.

YAU.—' Hermit ' is an excellent form of address. But not being used to it, it does not well appeal to my mind.

CHAM.—Oh, hear. This is the sister, Padmāvatī by name, of our sovereign, Darśaka, whose name is thus pronounced by the elders. She, having paid a visit to the great Queen, the mother of our king, who is residing in this hermitage, will go to Rājagṛha itself being permitted by her. So it is her intention to take her residence in this hermitage to-day. Your reverences, therefore,

May bring from the forest at will, the holy water, sacrificial sticks, flowers, and *darbhas*, which form the wealth of ascetics. The princess who is a lover of religious rites, will not certainly desire that the sacred duties of ascetics should be obstructed: this is her family vow. (6)

YAU.—*(To himself)*. I see. This then is the daughter of the king of Magadha, Padmāvatī by name, who, as declared by the astrologers, Puspakabhadra and others is to be the queen of my master. Hence,

(Since) hatred or high regard springs from the mind's view-point (looking at a thing), on account of my desire that she should be the wife of my master, greatly do I regard her as my own. (7)

VĀSA.—*(To herself.)* Hearing that she is a princess I come to have even a sisterly affection for her.

(*Enter* PADMĀVATĪ *with her suite and a* MAID)

MAID.— Come, come, princess; here is the hermitage; please enter it.

(*Then enter a female* ASCETIC *seated*).

FEM. ASC.—Welcome to the princess.

VĀSA.—*(To herself.)* This is that princess! Her beauty is, indeed, in keeping with her noble birth.

PADMĀ.—Revered lady, I bow to you.

FEM. ASC.—Live long. Come in, dear child, come in. Penance groves are, indeed, in the case of visitors, their own homes.

PADMĀ.—Well, well; revered lady, I feel at home here. I am beholden to you for these words of high regard.

VĀSA.—Not her form alone, but her speech also is, indeed, charming.

FEM. ASC.—Good woman, does not any king solicit the hand of this sister of the blessed one (king)?

MAID.—There is one, Pradyota by name, king of Ujjayinī. He has been sending messengers (to solicit her) for his son.

VĀSA.—*(To herself.)* Well, well. She has now become mine (my relation).

FEM. ASC.—This form is, indeed, worthy of such high honour. Both the royal families are exalted, we hear.

PADMĀ.—Noble one, did you see the hermits that they might oblige us ? That their desired object may be granted let the hermits be gently requested each to name what he desires.

CHAM.—As your ladyship desires. Ye ascetics that reside in this hermitage, listen, do listen, sirs. Her ladyship, the princess of Magadha here, emboldened by this your confidence in her (shown by your reception) entreats you to name your desired objects to enable you to discharge your religious duties.

Who is in need of a vessel ? Who seeks (desires) a garment. What does he again, that has finished the course of his studies according to his resolve, desire-that he may have to give to his preceptor (as his fee) ? In making this request the daughter of our king, who is a friend of the righteous, wishes that she herself should be favoured: Whatever be the desired object of any body, let him declare that-what should be given and to whom ? (8)

YAU.—Good luck ! I have seen the way (to gain my object). *(Loudly).* You sir, I have an object to seek.

PADMĀ.—Thank God; my visit to the penance-grove has been fruitful.

FEM. ASC.—This hermitage is one in which all the ascetics are quite content. So this one must be a stranger.

CHAM.—Sir, what should be done for you ?

YAU.—Here is my sister. I wish that she, whose husband has gone on a journey, should be taken care of for sometime by her ladyship.

I have nothing to do at all with money, nor with objects of pleasure nor raiments. It is not for livelihood that I have put on this brown garment (become a recluse). This noble-(or, firm-) minded princess, whose observance of religious duties is seen (proved), is able to protect the character of my sister. (9)

VĀSA.—*(To herself)* Ah ! The noble Yaugandharāyaṇa wishes to place me here (in charge of the princess). Well ! He will not take a rash step.

CHAM.—Princess, great (attended with grave responsibility) indeed, is his request. How can we accept it ?

It is easy to give money, easy to relinquish life, and easy to part with penance; (in fact) it will be easy to give every thing else : but it is hard to guard a deposit. (10)

PADMĀ.—Noble one, having first proclaimed 'who desires and what ?' it is improper now to hesitate. So your honour should do what he says.

CHAM.—This is worthily spoken by your ladyship.

MAID.—May the princess live long who thus declares the truth.

FEM. ASC.—Live long, good princess.

CHAM.—My lady, it will be done. *(Approaching)* Sir, her ladyship has undertaken the guardianship of your sister.

YAU.—I am favoured by her ladyship. Dear sister, approach her ladyship.

VÁSA.—*(To herself.)* What help ! Here I go, luckless one.

PADMĀ.—Well, well; she has become mine now.

FEM. ASC.—Since her form is such, she too is a princess, I guess.

MAID.—Your reverence speaks well. I too perceive that she has experienced happiness

YAU.—*(To himself.)* Good heavens ! Half of the burden is lightened (lit. removed). This is all happening as planned with the ministers. So when our master is reinstated and I present her ladyship to him, her ladyship, the princess of Magadha here, will be the object of confidence (his surety). For,

Padmāvatî is to be the crowned queen of our king; this is done through confidence in the words of those the misfortune first predicted by whom was afterwards realised. Surely fate does not go beyond the well tested declarations of the seers. (11)

(Enter a BRAHMACHĀRIN *)*

BRAH.—*(Looking upwards)* It is mid-day. Greatly am I fatigued. In which region then shall I rest myself ? *(Walking on)* Good, I have seen. This must be a penance-grove all round. For,

The deer are roaming about freely and without taking fright, full of confidence engendered by the place as being secure; the trees with their branches loaded with flowers and fruit are all tended with kindness; the herds of cows that form the wealth (of the ascetics) are for the most part brown-coloured; the quarters disclose no fields (of corn); and this smoke (that is seen) is rising from many sources (huts); undoubtedly this is a penance-forest. (12)

I will enter it. (*Having entered.*) Ah, this person is, indeed, unexpected in a hermitage. (*Looking in another direction.*) Or why, there are hermits.

Oh ladies here! There is no harm in going forth?

CHAM.—Freely, freely, you may enter. A hermitage, as is well known, is common to all people.

VĀSAVA.—Hum!

PADMĀ.—Ah, the noble lady avoids the sight of a stranger. Well; it will be easy for me to look after my charge.

CHAM.—Sir, we have entered before you. Accept the hospitality due to a guest.

BRAH.—(*Having performed Āchamana.*). Well, well; my fatigue is gone.

YAU.—Sir, where do you come from? Whither have you to go? Where does the noble one reside?

BRAH.—Hear, sir. I have come from Rājagṛha for acquiring pre-eminence in Vedic lore. I resided at a village named Lāvāṇaka in the Vatsa-territory.

VĀSA.—(*To herself*) Ah! Lāvaṇaka, indeed! My affliction is renewed again, as it were, at the mention of Lāvāṇaka.

YAU.—Now, did you finish the course of your studies?

BRAH.—Not, indeed.

YAU.—If your study is not finished, what is the reason of your coming away?

BRAH.—An exceedingly terrible calamity occurred there.

YAU.—What was it, pray?

BRAH.—A king, Udayana by name. lived there

YAU.—We have heard of the noble Udayana. What of him?

BRAH.—His wife, Vāsavadattā by name, daughter of the king of Avantī, it was said, was deeply loved by him.

YAU.—That was so to be. What next?

BRAH.—Then when the king had gone out a-hunting, she was consumed in the fire that destroyed the village.

VĀSA.—(*To herself.*) False, it is quite false. I live, an unfortunate woman.

YAU.—What then ?

BRAH—Then a minister, Yaugandharāyaṇa by name, wishing to rescue her, fell into the same fire.

YAU.—True that he fell in. What next ?

BRAH.—Then when the king returned and heard the news, he afflicted with the loss of the two, wished to sacrifice his life in the same fire, but was kept off with great efforts by the ministers.

VÁSAVA.—(*To herself.*) I know, I know my husband's tenderness towards me.

YAU.—Then, then ?

BRAH.—Then the king clasped the burnt remains of the decorations she haḍ worn on her person and fell into a swoon.

ALL —Pity !

VÁSAVA.—(*To herself.*) May the noble Yaugandharāyaṇa gain his end now !

MAID.—Princess, her ladyship weeps, to be sure.

PADMÂ.—She must be tender-hearted.

YAU.—Ah, yes ! My sister is kind-hearted by nature. Then then ?

BRAH.—Then very slowly he regained consciousness.

PADMÁ.—Fortunately he lives. My heart became paralysed as it were on hearing that he swooned.

YAU.—Then, then ?

BRAH.—Then that king, with his body reddish with dust owing to his rolling on the ground, suddenly got up and poured many a lament incoherently saying–Alas Vāsavdattā ! Ah daughter of the king of Avantî; O darling ! O my beloved pupil ! To be brief,

Now not even the *Chakravâkas* are like him (in sorrowing); not even others separated from their dearly loved wives; blessed is that woman whom her husband regards like that; though burnt she is, indeed, not burnt owing to the love of her husband. (13)

YAU.—Now sir, did none of the ministers try to compose him ?

BRAH.—There is a minister, Rumanvan by name, who did his best to set right the king.

For he is equal to (like) him in not taking food; he is emaciated owing to continuous weeping; attending to the requirements of the body (such as cleaning it, decorating it, dressing, &c.) with a heavy heart like the king, he assiduously waits upon him day and night; were the king at once to give up his life, he too would cease to exist. (14)

VĀSAVA.—(*To herself.*) Fortunately has my husband been placed in good hands now.

YAU.—(*To himself.*) Oh! a heavy burden (grave responsibility) Rumaṇvan is bearing; for,

The burden (responsible task) I bear allows rest; but in his case it means continuous exertion (worry); for every thing depends on him, on whom depends the king (his life). (15)

(*Aloud*) O! sir, is the king set right (restored to his former peace of mind) now?

BRAH.—That I do not know now. 'Here I joked (*lit.* laughed) with her, here I conversed with her, here I dwelt with her, here I got angry with her, here I slept with her "—as the king was lamenting in this way, the ministers took him with them with a great effort and went away from the village. And when the king had departed, the village, lost its charm like the sky when the stars and the moon have vanished from it.

FEM. ASC.—That king, indeed, must be a possessor of high qualities, who is thus praised even by a stranger.

Maid.—Princess, can some other woman now come to be his (wife)?

PADMÂ.—(*To herself.*) She has spoken as if in consultation with my heart.

BRAH.—I ask leave of you both. I must go now.

BOTH.—You may go and gain your object.

BRAH.—May it be so! (*Exit*)

YAU.—Well, I too wish to depart, permitted by her ladyship.

CHAM.—He says he wishes to go, permitted by your ladyship.

PADMÁ.—Your honour's sister will feel lonely (lit. anxious) without you (in your honour's absence).

YAU.—Being in the hands of worthy persons she will not feel lonely. (*Looking at the* Cham.) I will go now.

CHAM.—May your honour go to see us again.

YAU.—Very well. (*Exit*)

CHAM.—It is now time to enter inside.

PADMĀ.—Venerable lady, I bow to you.

FEM. ASC.--You too be soon united with your husband.

VÂSA.—I thank you (*lit.* I am favoured).

Cham.—Come away then. This way, this way, your ladyships. For now,

The birds have come back to their nests; the hermits have descended into water (for their ablutions) ; the fires being kindled are shining bright; the smoke is moving over the penance grove; and fallen from a great height and with his rays contracted, the sun, too, having turned back his chariot, is slowly making towards the summit of the setting mountain. (16)

(*Exeunt Omens*)

END OF ACT I.

ACT II.

(*Enter a* MAID.)

MAID.—Kunjarikā, O Kunjarikā, where, where, is the princess Padmâvatī? What dost thou say! That the princess has been playing with a ball by the side of the Mādhavī bower. I will then just approach the princess. (*Walking about and looking*). Oh, here is the princess coming hitherwards, playing with her ball, with her face having its pendent ear-rings raised up, bestrewed with drops of perspiration produced by exertion and looking charming owing to exhaustion. I will just approach her. *(Exit)*.

PRAVEŚAKA.

(*Enter* PADMÂVATĪ *playing with her ball, accompanied* by her retinue and VĀSAVADATTÂ).

VÁSA.—Here is your ball, my friend.

PADMÁ.—Lady, let the play stop now; I had so much of it.

VÁSA.—my dear, having long played with the ball, your hands which have their Rāga (redness--pạssion) increased, appear as if not your own (to belong to another—not to be in your power as you cannot play further).

MAID.—Play on, play on, my princess; let the charming time of maidenhood be enjoyed.

PADMÁ.--Revered lady, why are you looking at me steadfastly as if to ridicule me?

VÁSA.--No, no; not at all. My dear, you look more charming to-day. I am surveying your beautiful face as if from all sides (I as if behold your lover's face about you—*i. e.* you look so pretty to-day that your marriage seems to be at hand).

PADMÁ.--Avaunt! Do dot make fun of me now.

VĀSA.--Here I hold my tongue, you, the would-be-daughter-in-law of Mahāsena.

PADMÁ.--Who is this Mahâsena, pray (or I should like to know).

VÁSA.—There is a king of Ujjayinî, Pradyota by name. He bears the name Mahāsena, given him by the vast number of his army.

MAID.—My princess does not desire alliance with that king.

VÁSA.--With whom does she now desire it?

MAID.—There is the king of the Vatsas, Udayana by name. The princess is attracted by (loves him for) his qualities.

VÁSA.--(*To herself.*) She wishes to have my lord for her husband! (*Aloud*) For what reason?

MAID.--Because he is sympathetic.

VÂSA.—(*To herself.*) I know it: I know it. This person (myself) also was infatuated in this way.

MAID.—Princess, if that king happens to be ugly?

VÁSA.—Not indeed, not indeed! He is quite handsome (*lit.* of an engaging appearance.

PADMÁ.—Lady, how do you know it?

VÁSA.—(*To herself.*) In my excess of love for my husband. I have transgressed the bounds of decorum. What shall I do now? Well, I see (know what to do). (*Aloud*) My dear, the people of Ujjayinî say so.

PADMÁ.—That's right. He is not, indeed, rare to (rarely to be seen at) Ujjayinî. That is really called beauty which has a charm for the minds of all.

(*Then enter the* NURSE).

NURSE—Prosperity to the princess! Princess, you are given away.

VÁSA.—Good woman, to whom?

NURSE—To Udayana, king of the Vatsas.

VÁSA.—Now, is it all well with the king?

NURSE—He came here safe; and he has accepted the princess.

VÁsa.—Oh, A great mishap!

NURSE—Where is the mishap in this?

VÁSA.—Not much indeed; only this, that having so publicly grieved (for his wife), he should be indifferent!

NURSE—Lady, the hearts of great men are such as yield to the first onslaught (of grief); but they are easily composed (afterwards).

VÂSA.—Good woman, did he himself solicit her?

NURSE—Not atall, not at all. He had come here on a different errand; and the great king, having marked his exalted birth, his eminent knowledge, his (youthful) age and beauty, himself offered her to him.

VÂSA.—(*To herself.*) Thus it came to pass! My husband is not to blame now.

(*Having entered*)

ANOTHER MAID—Make haste, lady, make haste. To-day, indeed, the constellation in propitious. And our queen says that the nuptial ceremony should be performed just to-day.

VÂSA.—(*To herself.*) The more haste she makes, the more she blindfolds my mind.

NURSE—Come, come princess.

(*Exeunt Omens*)

END OF ACT II.

ACT III.

(Enter VÂSAVADATTÂ *in a pensive mood).*

VÂSA.—Leaving Padmāvati in the quadrangle* of the women's mansion full of the bustle of marriage festivities, I have come here to the Female-garden. I will then first divert the sorrow brought on by fate. *(Walking about)* Oh the great calamity! Even my husband, as he is, now belongs to another. I will sit down. *(Sitting down).* Blessed is the Chakravâka female that does not live when separated (from her mate). I do not, indeed, abandon my life; but in the fond hope that I shall see my husband I live, unfortunate that I am.

(Enter a MAID *with flowers in hand.)*

MAID—Where can the revered Āvantikā have gone? *(Walking about, and looking on.)* Oh, here she is sitting on the stone-slab under the Priyangu creeper, with her heart vacant on account of thought, and wearing a dress decent (*lit.* auspicious) though without ornaments, like the crescent of the moon obscured by mist. I will just approach her. *(Approaching.)* Revered Āvantikā, what a long time I have been looking out for you.

VÂSA.—What for?

MAID.—Our queen says—Her ladyship has sprung from a noble family, affectionate and skilful; let her, therefore, wreathe this wedding-garland.

VÂSA.—For whom am I to wreathe it?

MAID.—For our princess.

VĀSA.—*(To herself.)* Even this was to fall to my lot to do! Oh pitiless, indeed, are the gods!

MAID.—Lady, pray do not think of any other thing now. Here is the son-in-law bathing on the jewel pavement. Your ladyship should wreathe it quickly.

VĀSA.—*(To herself.)* I cannot think of any thing else (but my lord; *(Aloud.)* Friend, did you see the son-in-law?

MAID.—Yes. I saw him, out of love for my princess and our own curiosity to do so.

VĀSA.—And how do you find the son-in-law?

MAID.—Lady, I just say this—one like him was never seen before.

VĀSA.—Friend, say, say—is he handsome?

---

* Or the inner quandrangle being full of the bustle &c., I left Padmā. and have come, &c.

MAID.—It is possible to say—he is the god of love without his bow and arrows.

VÂSA.—Enough of this now ?

MAID.—Why do you prevent me (from saying more) ?

VĀSA.—It is improper to hear the description of another's husband.

MAID.—Then let your ladyship wreathe the garland quickly.

VÂSA.—Here I wreathe it; just bring me the flowers.

MAID.—May your ladyship take these.

VÂSA.—(*Pouring them down and looking.*) What is the name of this herb here ?

MAID.—' Widowhood-warder ' is its name.

VÁSA.—(*To herself.*) This must be woven in plenty; both for me and for Padmāvatī. (*Aloud*) And this herb here-what is its name ?

MAID.—It is called ' The co-wife-destroyer ' !

VÂSA.—This must not be woven.

MAID.—Why not ?

VÂSA.—Because his (first) wife is dead; so it is useless.

(*Entering*).

ANOTHER MAID.—Let your ladyship make haste, let your ladyship make haste; here is the bridegroom being conducted into the inner quadrangle by ladies having their husbands living.

VÁSA.—My girl, I say, take this.

MAID.—Excellent; lady I will go now.

(*Exeunt* BOTH).

VÂSA.—She is gone. Oh the calamity ! Even my husband (now) belongs to another. I will dispel my sorrow by lying on bed if I get sleep (at all). (*Exit*).

END OF ACT III.

AÇT IV.

(*Enter* VIDŪṢAKA).

VIDŪ.—(*Joyfully*) Fortunately have I seen the time charming on account of the coveted marriage-ceremony of his Honour, the king of Vatsa. Oh! Who ever knew that we, who were hurled into the whirlpool of disaster of that kind, should again emerge from it. Now I dwell in palaces, bathe in the pleasure-tanks attached to the inner apartment, eat dainty articles, delicious and soft by nature, and thus I enjoy a residence in paradise (lit, the Uttarakurus) save the company of heavenly nymphs. There is, indeed, one great drawback. The food I eat is not properly digested, and I do not get sleep on a bed having cxcellent coverlets, so that I see as if gout is down upon me on all sides. Oh! It is no real happiness that is overpowered by disease and is without good food.

(*Enter a* MAID.)

MAID.—Where could the noble Vasantaka have gone? (*Walking about and looking on.*) Ah! Here is the noble Vasantaka. (*Approaching.*) Noble Vasantaka, it is such a long time that I have been searching for you.

VIDŪ.—(*Seeing her.*) What for have you been looking for me, good girl?

MAID.—Our queen asks—Has the son-in-law bathed?

VIDŪ.—Why does her ladyship ask that?

MAID.—What else? that I may bring flowers and unguents for him.

VIDŪ.—His Honour has bathed. Your ladyship may bring all except food.

MAID.—Why do you ask me not to bring food?

VIDŪ.—Because unlucky that I am, my stomach has got Parivarta (change upside down derangement) as the cukoos have the Parivarta (change from one side to another) of their eyes.

MAID.—Just be like that!

VIDŪ.—Your ladyship may go. In the meantime I too will go into the presence of his Honour,

(*Exeunt Both*)

PRAVEŚAKA.

(Enter PADMĀVATĪ *with her suit and* VĀSAVADATTĀ *in the costume of* ĀVANTIKĀ *)*

MAID.—Why has my princess come to the Female-garden?

PADMĀ.—Friend, that I may see whether the Sephālikā-clusters have blossomed or not.

MAID.—They have certainly blossomed and are thickset with flowers, as if with pendents of pearls interspersed with coral.

PADMĀ.—If so, why do you delay, now, my dear?

MAID.—Then may the princess sit on this stone-slab for a short while. In the meantime I too will gather the flowers.

PADMĀ.—Lady, shall we sit here?

VĀSA.—Let it be so.

(BOTH *sit down*).

MAID.—*(Having done that, i. e. gathered the flowers.)* May the princess behold, may the princess behold? My *anjali* (cavity formed by the hollowed palms) is filled with the Śephālikā flowers that look like the half cut flakes of red arsenic.

PADMĀ.—Oh the varied hue of the flowers! See, see, revered lady.

VĀSA.—How wonderful is the loveliness of the flowers!

MAID.—Princess, shall I gather the flowers again?

PADMĀ.—Friend, do not, do not, pluck the flowers again.

VĀSA.—Friend, why do you forbid her?

PADMĀ.—Because when my husband will come here and behold this abundance of flowers, I shall feel honoured.

VĀSA.—Do you love your husband, my dear?

PADMĀ.—That I do not know; but separated from my husband I long for him (feel uneasy).

VĀSA.—*(To herself.)* I, indeed, find it hard (a trial); this (princess) also says so.

MAID.—Nobly (decently) indeed, did my princee say 'I love my husband?'.

PADMĀ.—I have one doubt, indeed.

VĀSA.—What is that, what is that?

PADMĀ.—Whether my husband was (as dear) to the revered Vāsavadattā as he is to me.

VĀSA.—More than this.

PADMĀ.—How do you know that?

VĀSA.—*(To herself.)* Ah! Owing to my partiality for my lord I transgressed the bounds of propriety. I will just say this. *(Aloud.)* Had her love been slight she would not have forsaken her relatives.

PADMÂ.—It must have been so.

MAID.—Princess, you can fitly say to your husband—' I, too, would learn to play upon the lute.

PADMÂ.—my husband was requested by me.

VÁSA.—What did he say then?

PADMÁ.—Without saying anything he heaved a long sigh and remained quiet.

VÂSA.—What do you guess may be the reason?

PADMÂ.—I think he remembered the virtues of her ladyship, Vâsavadattâ, but did not weep out of courtesy in my presence.

VÁSA.—(*To herself.*) Blessed, indeed, am I if this be true.

(Then enter the KING *and* VIDŪṢAKA*).*

VIDŪ.—Ho, ho! The Female-garden is lovely (inviting) owing to the gentle breeze blowing (therein) and the fallen Bandhujīva flowers collected in heaps. May your Honour first turn this side.

KING—Friend Vasantaka, here I come.

When I who had gone to Ujjayinī, saw, at will (unchecked), the daughter of the king of Avantī and was reduced to an indescrible state, (all the) five arrows were let fall upon me by Kāma: my heart has to this day their barbs in it; and I am again wounded (with a shaft), when Madana has (is known to have) five arrows only, whence is this sixth arrow dropped on me? (1)

VIDŪ.—Where could her ladyship Padmāvatī have gone? Can she have gone to the arbour of creepers, or repaired to the stone-slab, named Parvata-tilaka (the ornamental mark of the Pleasure-mountain) strewn with the *âsana* flowers and, therefore, looking as if covered with a tiger's skin, or entered the Saptachhada grove with its strong pungent odour, or retired to the wooden-hill, crowded with the painted figures of beasts and birds? (*Looking upwards*) Ho, ho! may your Honour first behold the fight of cranes sailing in a fully even line and looking charming like the extended arms of Baladeva in the clear autumnal sky.

KING.—Friend, I see it,

Now straight and extended, now in a thin line, now sinking down and again rising up, and now crooked like the constellation of the Great Bear in its turnings, as looking and though it were the boundary line that is being marked out (separated) of the sky, and white like the belly of a serpent when being freed from its skin. (2)

MAID.—See, see, my Princess, this flight of cranes moving in a compact mass, charming and white like a garland of Kokanada lotuses. Oh, my lord!

PADMĀ.—Oh, my husband! Revered lady, for your sake, I will avoid the sight of my lord. So we shall just enter the bower of the Mādhavī creeper.

VĀSA.—Let it be so.

(They act accordingly)

VIDŪ.—Her ladyship, Padmāvatī, might have come here and then gone away.

KING.—How do you know it?

VIDŪ.—Your Honour should just see these Śephālikā clusters having flowers plucked off from them.

KING.—Oh the varied appearance of the flowers, Vasantaka!

VĀSA.—*(To herself.)* By his mention of Vasantaka I feel as if I were in Ujjayinī.

KING.—Vasantaka, sitting on this very stone-slab let us wait for Padmāvatī.

VIDŪ.—Oh, we shall do so.

(Sitting and rising.) Ha, ha, the schorching autumnal sun is bearable. Let us just enter this Mādhavî bower.

KING.—Very well; lead the way.

VIDŪ.—Let it be so.

(Both walk about)

PADMĀ.—The noble Vasantaka is going to upset the whole (arrangement). What shall we do now?

MAID.—Princess, I will shake the main (lit. propping) creeper that has bees lurking in it, and keep off the lord.

PADMĀ.—Do so.

MAID.—*(Acts accordingly.)*

VIDŪ.—Help, help! Hold; hold, your Honour.

KING.—What for?

VIDŪ.—I am troubled by these rascally bees.

KING.—You should not say so, you should not. We must avoid frightening the bees. See—

The bees that are humming sweetly through the intoxication of honey and are embraced by their beloveds smitten by passion, will like myself, be separated from their dear mates when disturbed by our steppings. (3)

We shall therefore just sit here.

(BOTH sit down)

KING.—(*Marking the seat*)

The flowers are trodden under feet, and this stone-slab is warm; so some female sitting here must have hurriedly gone away on seeing me.

MAID.—Princess, we have been blocked up.

PADMÂ.—Thank God; my husband has sat down.

VĀSA.—(*To herself.*) Good luck! my husband has his body restored to health.

MAID.—Princess, the eyes of her ladyship are, indeed, filled with tears.

VÁSA.—These my eyes are full of tears owing to the pollen of the Kāśa flowers fallen into them through the rudeness (wanton act) of the bees.

PADMÂ.—That is proper.

VIDû.—Oh, the Pramada-garden is quite lovely. I have something to ask you. Shall I ask you?

KING.—Just as you wish.

VIDŪ.—Who is dearer to you? Her ladyship Vāsavadattā then (when she lived) or Padmāvatî now?

KING.—Why do you put me into this very great difficulty of expressing my high regard?

PADMĀ.—Friend, see into what kind of difficulty my husband is thrown.

VASĀ.—(*To herself.*) and I, too, hapless woman.

VIDŪ.—Freely, freely, may you speak. The one is dead; the other is not near at hand.

KING.—Friend, not indeed, not indeed, shall I tell. You are a babbler.

PADMÂ.—by this much my husband has spoken it out.

VIDŪ.—Oh, I swear by my truth, I will not tell it to any one; here I bite my tongue.

KING.—I cannot bring myself to tell it, friend.

PADMÁ.—Oh his persistence (or forwardness)! He cannot read his heart from this much.

VIDŪ.—What? Your honour does not tell it to me! Without telling it, it is not possible for you to move even a single step from this stone-slab. Here is your Honour held up.

KING.—What, by force?

VIDŪ.—Yes, by force.

KING.—Then let me just see.

VIDÛ.—Be pleased, your Honour, be pleased. I conjure you by my friendship if you will not tell me the truth.

KING.—What help? Hear,

Although Padmāvatī is highly esteemed by me by reason of her personal charms, character and sweetness, still she does not wean my heart set on Vāsavadattà. (4)

VÁSA.—(*To herself.*) Well, well; this my misery has recompense given to it. Oh, my stay in disguise here has had many advantages (lit. borne many fruits).

MAID.—Princess, lord is very unkind (or discourteous).

PADMÀ.—Friend, say not so. My lord is full of kindness, since he remembers even now the virtues of the revered Vāsavadattā.

VÀSA.—Good girl, you have spoken in a manner worthy of your high birth.

KING.—I have told you. You should tell me now—Who is dear to you? Vāsavadattā then or Padmāvatī now.

PADMÀ.—My lord also has become (is acting like) Vasantaka.

VIDÚ.—What is the use of my chattering? Both their ladyships I hold in high esteem.

KING.—Fool, after having heard my answer in this way by force, why do you not speak out now?

VIDÛ—What, (will you have) me too (speak) by force?

KING.—yes, by force.

VIDÛ.—Then you cannot hear it.

KING.—Be pleased, be pleased, great Brāhmaṇa; freely, freely, speak out,

VIDÛ.—Your Honour may hear it now, Her ladyship Vāsavadattā was highly liked by me. Her ladyship Padmávatī, is young, beautiful, not wrathful, free from vanity, of sweet address and courteous. And she possesses this quality above all—' She welcomes me with delicious food, saying—where could the noble Vasantaka have gone'?

VÁSA.—Well, well, Vasantaka; bear these words in your memory now.

KING.—Very good, very good, Vasantaka; I will relate all this to queen Vāsavadattâ.

VIDŪ.—Pity! Vâsavadattā! Where is Vāsavadattā; Vāsavadattā is dead long since.

KING.—(*Sorrowfully.*) Thus it is; dead Vāsavadattā! Friend,

By this joke my mind was drawn far away (from reality), by you; and so by the force of former habit these words escaped me just as they did formerly. (5)

PADMÁ.—A charming narrative (or course conversation) indeed, is married by the heartless fellow.

VÁSA.—*(To herself.)* Well, well; I feel cheered up. Oh, how pleasing it is to hear such words in one's absence (or uttered indirectly).

VIDŪ.—Take courage, take courage, your Honour. (The will of) Fate is intransgressible. Such is this (that has come to pass) now.

KING.—Friend, you do not know the state (I am in). For,

It is difficult to cast off (forget) deep-rooted love; grief revives at each fresh remembrance. It is (in) the course of nature that on shedding tears in this world the mind attains freshness, having a debt paid off (as it were).

VIDŪ.—His honour's face is moistened with the fall of tears: I will just bring water for washing the face with. *(Exit).*

PADMÂ.—Lady, the face of my husband is concealed by the veil of the obstructing tears. In the mean-time we shall depart.

VĀSA.—Be it so. Or rather do you stay. It is not proper to go away leaving your husband affected with tender emotion. I will alone go.

MAID.—The lady speaks well. Let the princess at once go forth.

PADMÂ.—What, shall I go into his presence?

VÁSA.—Do so. *(Exit, having said so).*

(Enter).

VIDÛ.—*(Taking water in a lotus-leaf).* Here is her ladyship, Padmāvatî!

PADMÁ.—Noble Vasantaka, what is this?

VIDÛ.—It is this—This it is.

PADMÂ.—Speak out, speak out–let the noble one speak out.

VIDÚ.—Lady, his Honour's face is full of falling tears owing to the pollen of the Kâśa flowers lying on the ground being wafted therein by the wind. So let your ladyship take this water to him for washing his face.

PADMĀ.— Oh, even the servant of courteous (or clever) man is himself also courteous (or clever) *(Approaching).* Prosperity to my lord? Here is water for washing your face with.

KING.—Ah, Padmāvatī! *(Aside).* Friend, what is this?

VIDÛ.—*(In the ear)* Thus, thus.

KING.—Commendable, friend, commendable. *(Having washed the face).* Padmâvatî, be seated.

PADMÂ.—As my lord commands. *(Sits down).*

KING.—Padmâvatī,

This my face, O charming one, this my face had tears trickling down from it owing to the pollen of the Kāśa flowers, white like the autumnal moon, wafted by the breeze. (7)

(To himself.)

This young girl, newly married, will feel pain on hearing the truth: granted that she is noble-minded, but woman is timid by nature. (7)

VIDÛ.—It is proper that his Honour, the king of Magadha, should see his friends, in the after-noon, giving you the lead. Honour, met with reciprocal honour, begets affection. So let your Honour rise.

KING.—(*Rising.*) Yes, a capital idea.

The conferers of mighty benefits and of high honours are always easily found in this world, but their appreciators are rare. (9)

(Exeunt Omens)

END OF ACT IV.

ACT V.

(*Enter* PADMINIKĀ.)

PADMI.—Madhukarikā, Madhavikā, just come quickly.

(*Entering*)

MADHU.—Here I am, my dear; what is to be done?

PADMI.—Friend, do you not know that princess Padmâvatī is suffering from headache?

MADHU.—Oh, fie upon it!

PADMI.—Friend, go quickly and call the revered Āvantikā; simply tell her just about the headache of the princess; and she will come of her own accord.

MADHU.—Friend, what will she do?

PADMI —She, indeed, will dispel the pain of headache of the princess by telling her sweet stories.

MADHU.—That is right. Where is the bed of the princess arranged?

PADMI.—Her bed is spread out, as I am told, in the Sea-house. Go you now. I too will seek out the noble Vasantaka that he may inform the lord of it.

MADHU.—Let it be so. (*Exit.*)

PADMI.—Where can I see the noble Vasantaka now?

(*Enter* VIDÚṢAKA).

VIDÚ.—To-day, indeed, on this auspicious festive occasion, that has brought great happiness, the burning caused by the fire of love to his Honour, the king of Vatsas, whose heart has been distressed by his separation from his queen and who has been excited by his espousal of Padmāvatî, has increased yet more. (*Seeing* PADMINIKÀ) Oh Padminikā, what is the matter here?

PADMI.—Noble Vasantaka, do you not know that princess Padmāvatî is distressed by headache?

VIDÛ.—My lady, really I do not know it.

PADMI.—Then inform the king of her (suffering). In the meanwhile I too will quickly bring ointment for her head.

VIDÛ.—Where is the bed arranged for Padmâvatī?

PADMI.—The bed is spread in the Sea-house, I am told.

VIDû.—Your ladyship may go; in the meanwhile I will tell this to his Honour.

(*Exeunt* BOTH).

PRAVEŚAKA

(*Enter the* KING.)

KING.—With the burden of wife (married life) come (devolved) upon me again, in course of time, I brood over that laudable (Vāsavadattā), the worthy daughter of Avanti's king, whose tender frame was consumed by the fire at Lâvāṇaka, like a lotus-plant smitten by frost. (1)

(*Entering*)

VIDû.—Make haste, make haste, Your Honour.

KING.—What for.

VIDû.—Her ladyship Padmâvatī has been suffering from headache.

KING.—Who said so?

VIDū.—Padminikā told me.

KING —Oh! alas!

Having obtained a wife, rich in (radiant with) the splendour of beauty and endowed with virtues, I, although yet suffering from the pain of the former blow, felt my grief softened as it were to-day (but) having experienced misery I expect Padmāvatī also to fare similarly (to meet a similar fate). (2)

Now in what place is Padmāvatî?

VIDū —Her bed is placed in the Sea-house.

KING.—Then lead the way just.

VIDū.—Come, come, your Honour.

(BOTH *walk on*)

VIDū.—This is the Sea-house your Honour may enter.

KING.—You enter first.

VIDū.—Oh, I will. (*Entering*). My God! Stay, just stay, your Honour!

KING.—What for?

VIDū.—Here is a snake, rolling on the ground, his form being revealed by the lamp-light.

KING.—(*Entering, and looking at it; with a smile.*) Oh! the fool sees in this a snake!

Fool, you regard the dangling garland of the outer arch, straight and long, fallen on the ground as a snake the garland, which being swayed at night by the gentle breeze, imitates to some extent the movements of a serpent. (3)

VIDū.—(*Marking it closely.*) Your Honour says rightly. This is not indeed, a snake.

(*Entering and looking.*) Her ladyship must have come here and gone away.

KING.—Friend, she could not have come here.

VIDŪ.—How does your Honour know it?

KING.—What is to be known here? See—

The bed evenly spread is not pressed down; its cover is not ruffled; the clean pillow is not soiled with the medicines applied for allying headache; nothing charming is arranged that would engage the eye when there is illness; a person having gone to bed through pain does not leave it again quickly of his own accord. (4)

VIDŪ.—If so, your Honour should sit on this bed for s short while and wait for her ladyship.

KING.—Very well. (*Having sat down*). Friend, sleep overpowers me. Tell some story.

VIDŪ.—I will tell. Your Honour should listen with a 'hum'.

KING.—I will.

VIDŪ.—There is a city, Ujjayinī by name. There are in it, as they say, many bathing places extremely delightful!

KING.—How Ujjayinī, you say!

VIDŪ.—If you do not like this story, I will tell another.

KING.—Friend, not indeed, I do not like this story; but,

I think painfully of the daughter of Avantī's king, remembering her kinsfolk at the time of her departure (with me) and causing to fall through love on my own bosom, the tears that had flowed from her eyes and stuck to their ends. (5)

And of her,

By whom gazing at me, many a time during instruction, the playing (on the lute) was done in the air, with her hand having the bow dropped from it. (6)

VIDŪ.—Well, I will tell another. There is a town Brahmadatta by name. In it lived a king, named Kāmpilya.

KING.—What is it, what is it?

VIDŪ.—(*Repeats the same.*)

KING.—Fool, say—king Brahmadatta, the city Kāmpilya.

VIDŪ.—What? The king Brahmadatta, and the city Kāmpilya?

KING.—So it is.

VIDŪ.—Then your Honour should wait for a short while, in which time I shall make it sit firmly on my lips. (*He repeats several times—*) King Brahamadatta, city Kāmpilya. Now your Honour may hear. Oh! His Honour has fallen asleep. This time is very cold, I will fetch my mantle.

(*Enter* VĀSAVADATTĀ in the disguise of ĀVANTIKĀ and a MAID.)

MAID.—Come, my lady. Very severe, indeed, is the pain of headache that the princess has been suffering from.

VĀSA.—Oh pity ! Where is the bed of Padmāvatī arranged ?

MAID.—In the Sea-house is her bed spread.

VĀSA.—Then lead the way.

(BOTH *walk on*)

MAID.—Here is Sea-house; your ladyship should enter. In the meantime I will quickly bring ointment for the head. *(Exit)*

VĀSA.—Oh, the gods are, indeed, very cruel to me. Even this Padmāvatī, who was the source of solace to my husband, distressed with separation, has been indisposed. I will just enter. *(Entering and looking above.)* Oh the carelessness of the servants ! They have left Padmāvatī, who is ill with only a lamp for her companion. Here is Padmāvatī fast asleep. I will sit down. But if I sit on another seat my affection for her will appear to be slight. So I will sit on this bed. *(Sitting down.)* How comes it that, as I sit beside her to-day, my heart feels enraptured ? Thank God ! Her breathing is easy and continuous (regular). Her pain must have disappeared. Or by her occupying a part of the bed she suggests that I should lie down close to her. *(She acts lying down.)*

KING.—*(Dreams.)* O Vāsavadattā !

VĀSA.—*(Rising suddenly.)* Oh, my husband, and not Padmāvatī, to be sure ? Can it be that I am seen ? Surely the momentous work undertaken by the revered Yaugandharāyaṇa is rendered vain by my being seen.

KING.—O daughter of the king of Avantī !

VĀSA.—Fortunately, my husband is talking in a dream. There is not a single person here. So having stayed here for a short while, I will gratify my sight and heart.

KING.—Ah my beloved ! O my dear pupil ! Give me a reply.

VĀSA.—I will speak, I will speak, my lord.

KING.—Are you angry ?

VĀSA.—Not at all, not at all; I am miserable.

KING.—If you are not angry why have you not put on ornaments?

VĀSA.—What, other than this ?

KING.—What, do you remember Virachikā ?

VĀSA.—*(Angrily)* Avaunt ! Here also Virachikā ?

KING.—In that case I conciliate you with regard to Virachikā. *(Stretches forth his hands.)*

VĀSA.—I have stayed long; some one might see me. So I will go; or I will first replace on the bed the hand of my lord that is hanging down from the couch and then go. *(Does so and departs.)*

KING.—*(Rising up at once.)* Vāsavadattā, stay, stay. Oh pity!

Darting out in haste I was struck by the panel of the door; I, therefore, do not know clearly whether this my desire is a reality. (7)

(Entering)

VIDŪ.—Oh! His Honour has risen from sleep.

KING.—Friend, I have agreeable news to tell you. Vāsavadattā is, forsooth, alive.

VIDŪ.—Tush! Vāsavadattā! Where is Vāsavadattā, Vāsava. is, indeed, long dead.

KING.—Friend, do not, do not say so.

She went away friend, having roused me lying asleep on the bed; I was then deceived by Rumaṇvan when he told me that she was burnt. (8)

VIDŪ.—Pity! This is inconceivable. Ah! By Your Honour thinking of her ladyship at my mention of the bathing-places, she might have been seen in a dream!

KING.—Thus then she was seen by me in a dream!

If at all this was a dream, then it were a blessing not to have awakened from it; or if it be an illusion, let me be under the illusion for a long time. (9)

VIDŪ.—Friend, in this city there dwells a Yakṣiṇī. Avantisundari by name. *She* might have been seen by you.

KING.—No, no.

As I woke up from sleep I saw her face with its flowing (lit. long) tresses and its eyes entirely void of collyrium, though she maintained her (vow of) chastity. (10)

Morever, friend, behold, do behold.

This my arm, which was tightly seized by the agitated queen, does not give up its horripilation though it felt the touch in sleep. (11)

VIDŪ.—Your honour should not think of such vain things. Come, come, my lord; let us enter the inner quadrangle.

(Entering)

THE CHAMBERLAIN—Prosperity to your Honour! Our king, Daraśkā, sends word—Here indeed, has your Honour's war-minister,

Rumaṇvan, come with a large army for extirpating Āruṇi. Similarly the victorious divisions (of my army)--elephants, cavalry and infantry—are equipped for battle, So Your Honour should rise up. Moreover,

Your enemies are divided; the citizens devoted to you owing to your virtues have been cheered up; arrangements have been made for guarding the rear when you will march away; whatever is to be accomplished for causing the complete destruction of the enemy—all that has been accomplished by me; even the three-coursed-river (Ganges) have been crossed by the forces; and Vatsa country is almost in your hands. (11)

KING.—*(Rising)* Excellent! Here now,

Having met that Āruṇī, skilled in doing atrocious deeds, in a battle resembling the ocean crossed over by lordly elephants and horses, and swelling with the fierce waves of the scattered arrows, I will destroy him. (12)

(Exeunt Omens)

END OF ACT V.

ACT VI.

(*Enter* CHAMBERLAIN.)

CHAMB.—Who is here, oh, that attends at the goldarched gate?

(*Entering the Portress.*)

PORTRESS—Sir, it is I, Vijayā. What is to be done?

CHAMB.—Lady, tell, please tell Ụdayana, whose prosperity (power) has increased on account of the acquisition of the kingdom of the Vatsas—Here has come from Mahāsena's presence a Chamberlain, of the family of Raibhya, as also Vâsavadattā's nurse, named the revered Vasundharā sent by queen Angāravatī; and both are waiting at the door.

PORT.—Sir, this is neither the proper place nor the proper time for the announcement.

CHAMB.—How, pray, not the proper place and the time?

PORT.—May Your Honour hear. To-day a lute was played upon by someone residing in the Sûryāmukha palace of our lord. On hearing it my lord said—the sound like that of Ghoṣavatī is heard.

CHAMB.—Then, then?

PORT.—Then my lord having gone there asked—where was the lute got from? He said—It was found by us lying in a clump of reeds on the bank of the Narmadā. If it is wanted my lord may take it. When it was taken to him my lord placed it in his lap and fell into a swoon. Then when he recovered from the swoon, he said, with a face fully covered with tears—Thou art seen, Ghoṣawatī, but she, indeed, is not seen. Sir, thus is the time unsuited; how can I inform him?

CHAMB.—Do inform him, lady; this (our visit) is also in connection with that.

PORT.—Sir, here I inform him. Here is his Highness descending from Súryāmukha palace. So I will inform him just here.

CHAMB.—Lady, do so.

(*Exeunt Both*)

End of the mixed Viskambhaka.

(*Enter the* KING *and* VIDŪṢAKA).

KING.—O thou with a sound gratifying to the ear; how couldst thou, that reposed on the pair of breasts and the lap of the queen, take thy residence, which was dreadful, in a forest, with thy body covered with dust scattered by the flights of birds? (1)

Moreover thou art destitute of affection. O Ghoṣavatī, since thou dost not (sorrowfully) remember—of the poor queen—

The close pressings of thy sides as she bore thee on her hips the happy clasping of thee between her breasts, when fatigued, the lamentations with reference to me when separated from me, and the talking accompanied by smiles in the intervals of music. (2)

VIDû.—Enough of your getting too much worried about it.

KING.—Friend, no; it cannot be so.

My passion that was long dormant has been roused by the lute; but I do not see that queen to whom Ghoṣavatī was dear. (3)

Vasantaka, get the Ghoṣavatī repaired by some artist and bring it back quickly.

VIDū.—As Your Honour commands.

(Exit taking the Vīṇâ with him).

(Entering).

The Portress—Prosperity to the lord ? Here have arrived at the door, a chamberlain, of the family of Raibhya, from Mahāsena, and Vāsavadattā's nurse, named the revered Vasundhará, sent by Queen Angāravatī.

KING.—If so then let Padmāvatī be first called.

PORT.—As my lord commands. *(Exit).*

KING.—Can it be that Mahāsena has now come to know this affair so soon ?

(Enter PADMÂVATĪ *and the* PORTRESS *).*

PORT.—Come, come. my princess.

PADMÂVATÍ—Prosperity to my husband !

KING.—Padmâvatī, did you hear that a chamberlain of the family of Raibhya has come from Mahāsena, as also Vāsavadattà's nurse named the revered Vasundharā, sent by her ladyship Angāravatī and that they are waiting at the door ?

PADMÁ.—Husband, it pleases me to hear about the well-being of my kinsmen.

KING.—This is worthily said by your ladyship, that the relatives of Vāsavadattā are your own relatives. Padmávatī, be seated. Why do you not sit down now ?

PADMÁ —Husband, will Your Honour, seated, with me, see these persons ?

KING.—What is wrong in this ?

PADMĀ.—I am your Honour's second wife; and so it looks something awkward (or, it will be something like being indifferent to the feeling of others).

KING.—(But) the fact that He (I) prevents people fit to see his wife from obtaining a sight of the wife, will lead to serious blame (or, blemish, *viz.*, breach of etiquette). So sit down.

PADMÂ.—As my husband commands *(Sitting down.)* Husband, I have become somewhat uneasy at heart as to what the message of father and mother will be.

KING.—Padmāvatī, so it is,

My heart, too, has become apprehensive as to what he will say. I, on my part, carried away his daughter but did not protect her. Having had a great blow given to my merits (appearing to be utterly destitute of merits) owing to fortune's fickleness I am afraid of him, like a son that has roused the anger of his father. (4)

PADMÂ.—No; what, forsooth, can be saved when its time (of destruction) has arrived.

PORT.—Here are the chamberlain and the nurse waiting at the door.

KING.—Let them come in at once.

PORT.—As the lord commands.

(Exit).

(Enter the CHAMBERLAIN, *the* NURSE *and the* PORTRESS. *)*

CHAMB.—Oh! Great is my joy,

On coming to the kingdom of our kinsman; but again there is sorrow felt when I remember the destruction of our princess. What possibly would not have been done by thee, O fate, had there been the kingdom seized by the enemies (regained) and the queen safe? (5)

PORT.—Here is the lord. Let the noble one approach him.

CHAMB.—*(Going forth)* Prosperity to the lord!

NURSE.—Victory to Your Highness!

KING.—*(With great respect)* Noble one.

Is the king, who has the power to bring about the rise and fall of the offspring of royal races on earth and my coveted relative, all well? (6)

CHAMB.—Just so. Mahāsena is all well; and asks about the well-being of all kinds here.

KING.—*(Rising from his seat.)* What is Mahāsena's message?

CHAMB.—Worthy is this of the son of the princess of Videha. Your Honour should please hear Mahāsena's message, seated on your seat.

KING.—As Mahāsena commands (through you). *(Sits down.)*

CHAMB.—Fortunately is the kingdom regained that was seized by the enemies. For,

No enterprising spirit manifests itself in those, who are timid or weak; generally royal fortune is enjoyed by the energetic alone. (7)

KING.—Noble sir, all this is due to the power of Mahāsena. For,

I was, indeed, first conquered and yet fondled (afterwards) along with his sons; I forcibly carried away his daughter but did not save her (from destruction); and even after hearing of her demise, his regarding me as his own is still the same; or why, that I obtained the Vatsas, over which I used to rule, was owing to that king. (8)

CHAMB.—This is Mahâsena's message; that of the queen, her ladyship here will tell.

KING.—O mother!

Is my mother well—the eldest of the sixteen queens, the holy goodess of the town–who was distressed at my leaving her? (9)

NURSE.—The queen is in good health, and inquires, after your Honour's well being of every kind here.

KING.—Well being of every kind, you say? Mother, of this sort is the well-being!

NURSE.—Enough of grieving very much, my lord.

CHAMB.—Bear up yourself, my lord. Though dead, the daughter of Mahâsena is not dead when thus remembered with tenderness by your lordship. Or rather,

Who is able to protect whom at the time of death? Who can support the pitcher when the rope (attached to it) is cut? Thus man fares equally with (lit. has the same law of life as) trees: each is cut down (dies) when his time comes and grows (is born) again. (10)

KING.—Noble one, do not say so.

Mahāsena's daughter, my pupil and beloved queen—How can I not remember (forget) her even though in different corporeal existences?

NURSE.—My queen sends word to you—Vàsavadattā has ceased to exist. To me and also to Mahāsena, you are just like (as dear as) our Gopālaka and Pālaka, being the son-in-law. as chosen from the first. For this reason you were brought to Ujjayinī. We gave her away to you under the pretext of the lute, without the fire as a witness to the act (actual marriage); owing to your overhastiness you went away without having the auspicious marriage ceremony performed. Thereafter we had the portrait of you and of Vāsavadattā painted on a picture-board and celebrated the wedding. Here is the picture-board sent to you. Be looking at it and comfort yourself.

KING.—Oh, the queen has said what is exceedingly affectionate and befitting her.

This her speech is dearer to me than a hundred acquisitions of a kingdom, since she has not forgotten her affection for us although offenders.

PADMĀ.—Husband, having seen the elderly person (Vāsava.) drawn in the picture I wish to bow to her.

NURSE.– See. see, princess. *(Shows her the picture-board.)*

PADMĀ.—*(Seeing, to herself.)* Hum,—she extremely resembles the revered Āvantikā. *(Aloud)* Husband, is she like the noble lady ?

KING.—Not (only like); but she is the very same, I think. Oh ! how sad ! How could such lovely complexion meet with terrible destruction ! How was this sweetness of face despoiled by fire ? (13)

PADMĀ.—On seeing the portrait of my husband I shall know whether or not she resembles the noble lady.

NURSE —May the princess see it, may the princess see it.

PADMĀ.—*(On seeing.)* From the (exact) resemblance of my husband's portrait I know that this (the lady painted) also resembles the noble lady. (Vāsava.)

KING.—My queen, after you saw the portraits I see that you appear to be greatly delighted and dejected. What can this be ?

PADMĀ.—My husband, one exactly resembling this portrait lives just here.

KING.—What, resembling Vāsavadattā ?

PADMĀ.—Yes.

KING.—If so, bring her here quickly.

PADMĀ.—My husband, while I was a virgin (not married) a certain Brāhmaṇa left her in my charge saying that she was his sister. Being separated from her husband she shuns the sight of other men: so let this lady (nurse) see if she is the same.

KING.—If a Brāhmaṇa's sister, evidently she is another woman· resemblance of form existing between two persons is seen in this world. (14)

(Entering the Portress).

PORT.—Victory to my lord ! Here has a Brāhmaṇa, belonging to Ujjayinī, come to the door to receive back his deposit, a woman, whom he says, he left as his sister in the hands of the queen.

KING.—Padmâvatī, can it be that he is the same Brāhmaṇa ?

PADMĀ.—He may be.

KING.—Let that Brâhmaṇa be ushered in at once, with formalities proper for the inner-apartment.

PORT.—As my lord commands. *(Exit.)*

KING.—Padmāvatī. you too bring her.

PADMÂ.—As my husband commands. *(Exit.)*

(Then enter YAUGANDHARĀYAṆA *and the* PORTRESS *).*

YAU —Oh ! *(To himself.)*

Having concealed the queen for the good of the king I did this of my own will seeing that it was to our advantage; although my enterprise has borne success, still my heart misgives me as to what that monarch will say. (15)

PORT.—Here is the king; your reverence may approach him.—

YAU.—*(Having approached.)* Prosperity to Your Highness, prosperity !

KING.—The voice seems to have been heard before. O Brāhmana, was your sister left as a deposit in the hands of Padmâvatī ?

YAU.—Just so.

KING.—If so, hasten, hasten his sister here.

PORT.—As my lord commands. *(Exit.)*

(Then enter PADMÁVATĪ, ĀVANTIKÂ *and the* PORTRESS *).*

PADMĀ.—Come, come, my lady. I have something pleasant for you.

ĀVAN.—What, what ?

PADMÀ.—Your brother has come.

ÁVAN.—Thank God; he remembers me at least now !

PADMÁ.—*(Having approached.)* Victory to my husband ! Here is the deposit,

KING.—Restore it, Padmāvatî. (But) a deposit ought to be returned in the presence of witnesses. The worthy Raibhya here, and her ladyship will form the court.

PADMÁ.—Sir, take away the revered lady now.

NURSE.—*(Observing* ĀVANTIKĀ *carefully.)* Oh ! Princess Vāsavadattâ !

KING.—How now ! The daughter of Mahāsena ! Queen enter inside with Padmāvatî.

YAU.—Not indeed, not indeed, she should enter in. She is *my* sister.

KING.—What do you say ? She is, to be sure, the daughter of Mahāsena.

YAU.—Oh king!

You are born in the race of Bharata, are well disciplined, learned and pure; it does not, therefore, behove you to take her away by force—you who are to show what are (guide in the matter of) the royal duties. (16)

KING.—Well; let us see the resemblance of form. Let the evil be removed.

YAU.—Prosperity to my master!

VĀSAVA.—Victory to my husband!

KING.—Ah! This is Yaugandharàyaṇa; and this Mahāsena's daughter!

Is it a reality or dream, that she is again seen by me? For by her although seen, I was then deceived. (17)

YAU.—My lord, I have, indeed, committed, a crime by taking away the queen. My lord, therefore, should kindly forgive me. (*With these words falls at his feet.*)

KING.—(*Raising him up*). You are Yaugandharāyaṇa, to be sure.

By false acts of madness, by battles, and by counsels grounded on (supported by) the principles of (political science)—thus indeed by your efforts we were rescued when plunged into adversity. (18)

YAU.—We are followers of our lord's fortunes.

PADMĀ.—Oh! this is the queen. Madam, I, in my ignorance, transgressed the bounds of decorum by treating you as a friend. So I propitiate you with a bow of the head.

VĀSAVA.—(*Raising* PADMĀVATĪ) Rise, rise, oh blessed one, rise. It was my body that was in fault being falsely presented to you as belonging to a suppliant.

PADMĀ.—I am beholden to you.

KING.—Friend Yaugandharāyaṇa, what was your object in deciding to remove the queen?

YAU.—Because I administrated Kauśambî only (and not the whole Vatsa country).

KING.—Now, what was your reason in living her as a deposit in the hands of Padmāvatī?

YAU.—Because it was predicted by the foretellers (astrologers), Pushabhandraka and other, that she was to be the queen of my lord

KING.—Was this too known to Rumaṇvan?

YAU.—My lord, it was know to everyone.

KING.—Oh, what a rogue, indeed, Rumaṇvan was!

Yau.—Lord, let the noble Raibhya and her ladyship here return just to-day and communicate the news of the queen's being safe

King.—No, no; all of us will go along with queen Padmāvatī.

Yau.—As my lord commands

(Bharata Vákya)

May our Rājasimha (lion-like king) rule the earth, having the oceans for her husbands, the Himalaya and Vindhya mountains for her ear-ornaments and marked by one (royal) umbrella !

(Exeunt Omens)

End of Act. VI.

HERE ENDS THE PLAY

SVAPNAVĀSAVADATTA.

NOTES.

ACT. I

P. 1. **स्वप्नवासव०**—The title of the play may be explained as वासवदत्तामधिकृत्य कृतं नाटकं वा॰दत्तं by affixing अण् according to अधिकृत्य कृते ग्रन्थे Pāṇ. IV. 3. 87; स्वप्नप्रधानं स्वप्नलक्षणं वा वासव॰ स्वप्नवा॰ the play wherin the dream plays a prominent part, or of which the special feature is a dream. Or it may be explained as स्वप्ने दृष्टा वासवदत्ता स्वप्नवासवदत्ता, सा एव अभेदोपचारात् (by a metaphorical transference of names) स्वप्नवासवदत्तं; here it will not do to say स्वप्नवासवदत्तामधिकृत्य कृतं नाटकं as that will give स्वप्नवासवदत्तं; *cf.* अभिज्ञानशाकुन्तलं the title of the best play of Kālidāsa.

नान्द्यन्ते ततः &c.--Bhāsa's plays, as a rule, begin with this stage-direction. The later plays from the time of Súdraka invariably begin with the नान्दी followed by नान्द्यन्ते सूत्रधारः. So it seems that the term नान्दी, in Bhāsa's time, when the drama was in its infancy, referred to the पूर्वरङ्ग (prelude) or the nine theatrical preliminaries of which Nāndī itself was one. These were probably performed behind the curtain by the Sūtradhâra of the पूर्वरङ्ग along with the other actors and to the accompaniment of vocal and instrumental music. नान्द्यन्ते means after the preliminary ceremony for pleasing the deities, that they should ward off obstacles, was gone through. ततः means immediately after. See com. p. 4. **सूत्रधारः**—*i. e.* the Sūtra. in his character as the नाटकसूत्रधार (as distinguished from the पूर्वरङ्गसूत्रधारः, the two might have been different persons also) also called स्थापक (and thus mentioned in the later treatises on dramaturgy) as is clear from the introduction here being called स्थापना by the poet himself. The stanza उदयनवेन्दु &c. is not therefore, like the usual benedictory stanza or stanzas of the later dramatists which formed the necessary Mangala also; for that was done before the entrance of the Sûtradhāra. It simply contains a blessing along with वस्तुनिर्देश. **सूत्रधार** is defined as--' नाट्यस्य यदनुष्ठानं तत्सूत्रं स्यात्सबीजकम् । रङ्गदैवतपूजाकृत् सूत्रधार उदी-

रित: ||' The definition of the नाटकसू० is 'वर्तनीयतया सूत्रं प्रथमं येन सूच्यते । रङ्गभूमिं समासाद्य सूत्रधारः स उच्यते ॥' नान्दी is explained as नन्दन्ति देवता अस्यां or नन्दिः आनन्दः तस्या इयं नान्दी; or नन्दयति देवद्विजनृपादीनिति। see Bha. Nāṭ. V. 98-103.

उदयनवेन्दु० &c.--Bhāsa seems to have followed the precept that the subject matter of a play should be hinted at in the introductory stanza. Hence the use of *Śliṣṭa* (paronomastic) epithets in the śl. and the consequent awkwardness or irregularity of the compound adjectives. उदय०—The const. is-उदयनवेन्दुसवर्णौ आसवदत्ताबलौ पद्मावतीर्णपूर्णौ वसन्तकम्रौ बलस्य भुजौ त्वां *i. e.* सामाजिकान् (the audience; sing. for the plural) पाताम्. उदयकालिकः नवेन्दुः उदयनवेन्दुः a comp. of the शाकपार्थिवादि class; समानः वर्णः ययोस्तौ सवर्णौ; ०वेन्दुना सवर्णौ ०सवर्णौ having the same colour as that of, *i. e.* reddish white like, the newly risen moon. आसवदत्ता०—दत्तः आसवः यस्यै सा आसवदत्ता; properly this should be दत्तासवा; but for the sake of श्लेष दत्त is made to take परनिपात (some latter in the comp.) the comp. being treated as one of the आहिताग्न्यादि class, by वा आहिताग्न्यादिषु । Pāṇ. II. 2. 37. आसवदत्ता अबला a woman (*i. e.* his wife) याभ्यां तौ °दत्ताबलौ. Balarāma's fondness for wine is well known; and it was usual for husbands in ancient times to give wine to their wives also when they quaffed it. The comp. may be also be dissolved as आसवेन दत्तमबलं याभ्यां तौ rendered feeble or drooping by the wine drunk. But this is not a good way as it will deprive the arms of their power of protection. पद्मावतीर्ण०—अवतीर्ण is a noun used for अवतारः । भावे क्तः (the p. participle forming an abs. noun), the descent *i. e.* presence in, of Padmá; तेन पूर्णौ full *i. e.* bountiful; or majestic with (Padmá meaning the goddess of splendour or beauty); beautiful. वसन्तकम्रौ०—कम्र lovely; from कम् to shine or love, and र which added to the roots नमँ, कम्प स्मि (नम्र, कम्प्र, स्मेर) &c. Pàṇ. III. 2, 167. वसन्ते (on account of the decorations suited to the season; see *infra.* p.30 प्रसाधितबलदेव &c. *v. l.*) कम्रौ. The name of Balarāma if remembered every day in the morning is said to remove difficulties; *cf.* ' हरिर्हरो हरिश्चन्द्रो हनुमांश्च हलायुधः । पञ्चैतान्संस्मरेन्नित्यं घोरसंकटनाशनम्' ॥ बलस्य—बल often stands for बलराम as भीम does for भीमसेन.

The poet has herein brought in, even at the sacrifice of perspicuity, the names of the four principal characters of the play, ***viz.*** the king Udayana, Vasantaka, his assistant in love matters, and the two queens, Vâsavadattâ and Padmàvatī. The figure by which this is done is called मुद्रालंकार; ' सूच्यार्थसूचनं मुद्रा प्रकृतार्थपरैः पदैः । ' It is somewhat strange that the poet should address the invocation here to Balarâma instead of to the usual deities, Śiva, Viṣṇu or the like. He does it probably to suggest that the arms of Udayana should grant protection to his subjects after regaining his kingdom and thus being powerful (बलमस्यातीति बलः बलवान् तस्य) by the acquisition of Padmâvatī. The first line is also so explained as to suit this suggested sense--thus उदयनं वाति (gets to) इति उदयनवाः; सा चासौ इन्दुसवर्णा च वासवदत्ता सा बलं ययोस्तौ, qualifying भुजा. But this is rather far-fetched.

This śl. it will be seen, has almost all the characteristics of the Nāndī of the later play-wrights; thus--it makes a reference to the moon; (2) invokes a blessing on the audience; (3) suggests the subject-matter; and (4) consists of 8 padas or words. *cf.* introd. stanzas of Pratimā, &c.

P. 2. **एवं**—Thus, *i. e.* in the way he had proposed to himself; see com. **आर्यमिश्रान्**—आर्याश्च ते मिश्राश्च । मिश्र is an honorific term and is always used in the plural; मिश्राः पूज्याः । पूज्ये मिश्रवचनं नित्यबहुवचनान्तम् । ' मरीचिमिश्रैर्दक्षेण ' इति विष्णुपुराणात् । आर्याः सुकुलादिसम्पन्नाः यदाह भरतः—'कुलं शीलं दया दानं धर्मः सत्यं कृतज्ञता । अद्रोह इति येष्वेतत्तानार्यान्संप्रचक्षते ।' यद्वा आराद्याता दूरं गताः ग्राम्यत्वादिदोषेभ्यः (*i. e.* respectable and polite) इत्यार्याः । Jag. on Mál. Mād. I. Another def. of आर्य, is—' कर्तव्यमाचरन्काममकर्तव्यमनाचरन् । तिष्ठति प्रकृताचारे स तु आर्य इति स्मृतः । ' इति वसिष्ठः । **विज्ञापयामि**--respectfully say to, or address. **अये**—here expresses surprise. The Sūtra. is surprised to hear some noise just has he was busy thinking out what to say to the audience but does not say it, his mind being called away by the noise. **व्यग्रः**—विगतमग्रं यस्मात् *lit.* one from whom the point is gone *i. e.* is solely occupied with or intent on. **शब्द इव**—Something like a sound (of speakers). As he was absorbed in his own thought he did not exactly catch the words of the speakers. **श्रूयते**—This form of the Prologue is also found in the Abhi., Bâla and Panch. **अङ्ग**—is a vocative particle often used without noun in the Vocative following it. Here the Sūtradhāra may be supposed to address the audience. **पश्यामि**--He means--I shall know it by listening to it attentively. This passage *viz.* एवं—to पश्यामि, which found in eight out of the thirteen plays of Bhâsa, is used by the poet as a device to introduce to the audience the character or characters about to enter and begin the play.

नेपथ्ये—नेपथ्य may mean here (1)the curtain; or (2) the tiring room. The word is derived as निनः (नि n. the eye) ने नेतुः (नि m. a leader) वा पथ्यम्. For other senses see our notes on the word at Śāk. p. 4. **आर्याः**—gentlemen, good people; this is simply a polite way of addressing the people. **विज्ञातं**—Known exactly or difinitely (वि). **मगधनाथस्य** —This was Darśaka, king of the Magadha country; see *Infra.* p. 6. **स्निग्धैः**—loving (*i. e.* who loved their master) and therefore trusty. **धृष्टं**—Boldly, with the tone of authority. **सर्वैः**—This is put in to show that the servants were showing no distinction in the discharge of their duty but blindly led by their loyalty to their master were asking all to move aside without distinction. This serves as the reason for the Sūtra. also to leave the stage, **तपोवन०**—The significance of this is that the presence of ascetics at least was harmless and they should not have been asked to move away. **स्थापना**—*lit.* that in which the topic of the play is established. This is what the later writers on dramaturgy call प्रस्तावना or आमुख. It was a simple thing in the days of Bhāsa, when the drama was in its initiatory stage and so in it the Sūtradhāra does not mention the poet's name or describe his family, hold conversation with the Natī or Mārisa, or the like; hence Bàṇa describes the plays of Bhāsa as सूत्रधारकृतारम्भाः. The Sthâpanā or प्रस्तावना here may be called of the kind प्रयोगातिशय; *cf.* for a similar introduction of the characters the Prologue of the Vik., and see our note thereon.

P. 3. **भटौ**—Two soldiers. Another reading is साधारणौ two ordinary men, *i. e.* servants. **उत्सरत उत्स०**—This way of proclaiming the entry of a royal personage is found in the Ùru. and Prat. p. 66 (ed. 1924) and occurs twice in the Pratijnāyaugandharāyaṇa. **ततः प्रविशतः** &c.—Yaugandharâyaṇa and Vāsavadattá who had entered the penance-grove in disguise hear the cry of उत्सारणा and enter. **परिव्राजकवेषः**—परित्यज्य सर्वे परितो वा व्रजतीति परिव्राजकः; a man who having renounced tbe world has become a Saṃnyāsin. परिव्राजकस्य इव वेषो यस्य. **यौगन्धरायणः**—युगन्धरस्य अपत्यं पुमान् यौगन्ध०; Yugandhara was the chief minister of सहस्रानीक, the father of Udayana. See **Introd.** **आवन्तिकावेषा**—अवन्त्यां (अवन्तीषु वा) भवा आवन्तिका a woman of Avantī (the capital, or of the country of Avantī), by adding वुञ् by Páṇ. IV. 2. 134, or by adding अण् (अवन्ती fem.) and then adding क as in the com.; see p. 8. तस्या इव वेषो यस्याः. **इहापि**—Even in this penance-grove) where उत्सारणा is not only not necessary but where one must behave humbly and with respect towards the sages). He makes this clear in the next śloka; or कुतः may be taken with त्रासः समुत्पाद्यते.

Śl. 3. **धीरस्य**—धियं रातीति धीरः; fr. धी and रा and affix क (अ); तस्य of one steady-minded, of self-possessed. *Cf.* Kum. I. 59. **आश्रम॰**—आश्रमं संश्रितः आश्रमसंश्रितः; Acc. Tat. comp. **वसतः** &c.—वने भवानि वन्यानि, तैः वन्यैः फलैः तुष्टस्य वसतः living, being contented with, &c. **त्रासः समुत्पाद्यते.**—Construe this with कुतः; or supply अतः after this. त्रासः समुत्पाद्यते अतः कः अयं उत्सिक्तः विनयादपेतः पुरुषः चलैर्भाग्यैः विस्मितः.......इदं निभृतं तपो॰ आज्ञया ग्रामीकरोति । **उत्सिक्तः**—Haughty, puffed up, विनयात् is connected with अपेत and should have been compounded (विनयादपेतश्चासौ पुरुषः च); but it is left out and so it is a case of सापेक्षत्वेऽपि गमकत्वात्समासः । see also com. **विस्मितः**—Proud by reason of or blinded by. For this sense, *cf.* विहगवाहनमात्रविस्मितो दूतः । Dv. p. 34, Panch. गन्धारविषयविस्मितशकुने p. 11. **भाग्यैः चलैः**—is put in to show that he has no reason to be proud as wealth is evanescent. *Cf.* ' अचिरांशुविलासचञ्चला ननु लक्ष्मीः फलमानुषङ्गिकम् । ' Kir. II. 19; also 39 (शरदभ्रचलाः श्रियः). **निभृतं**—Properly silent, noiseless (see Kum. III. 42); hence tranquil, peaceful. **तपोवनं**—तपःसाधनं तपोर्थं वा वनं तपोवनम्, and therefore a holy place. **ग्रामीकरोति**—Turns into (treats as) a village. **आज्ञया**—By giving orders to his servants to this effect; orders which are proper only in places inhabited by worldly men. See com. This shows the extreme impropriety of the act.

P. 4. **उत्सारयति**—Drives, expels himself from *i. e.* makes himself grossly guilty of an unrighteous deed. योऽधर्मे आत्मानं विनियोजयति—*V. l.* who directs or leads himself to the doing of an unrighteous deed. This is rather a tame reading and is not so strong as the one in the text, which means--He who is not really driving away others but himself from the path of righteousness (and hence, from heaven). अधमोद्दामाह्वानं was the reading given by C. Sastri in his first ed.—it means, अधमं base उद्दामं haughtily uttered च आह्वानं name यस्मिन् ; but the attendants did not do that; they rather addressed the men they were asking to move away as आर्याः and so it was rightly abandoned.

न ह्येवं वक्तुकामा—Supply आसम् . The nasal of the inf. is dropped before काम and मनस्. She means—I did not mean to ask—Who is this man that is clearing this way—does he know the consequence of his deed, &c. ? ; but " what sort of a man is he ? Will he ask me also to move out of the way, treating me as an ordinary woman? The addition of this clause, however, makes the sense obscure it had better been omitted. **उत्सारयितव्या**—One fit to be asked to leave the way; इति वक्तुकामा आसमिति शेषः ।

अनिर्ज्ञातानि—Not properly (as to their real nature) known. **दैवतानि**—देवा एव देवताः स्वार्थे तल् (ता) । देवता एव दैवतानि, by adding अ (अण्) again स्वार्थे (like प्रज्ञ एव प्राज्ञः). Read अपि after this. **अवधूयन्ते**—are despised, subjected to slight; what of human beings then, however great they may be). **अयं परिभवः**—never being subjected to such treatment before it is natural that Vâsavadattā should feel for the insult thus. **परिभवः**—slight, disrespect shown, or insult.

एष विषयः—This subject, this thing; *viz.* having the crowds similarly cleared off before her when she passed through the streets with all the pomp and dignity of a queen.

Śl. 4. **पूर्वं त्वयापि**—&c.—The sentence may be explained in several ways—(1) पूर्वं त्वयापि एवं अभिमतं यथा तथा (adv.) गतमासीत् formerly you too moved in this way in a manner desired by you (and you approved of it); (21 एवं गतं त्वया (तव) अपि अभिमतं आसीत् this manner of movement was desired even by you; पूर्वं त्वया त्वत्कृतमपि एवं अभिमतं esteemed by all गतं गमनं आसीत् (*see* com.) **श्लाघ्यं**—adv.; see com.; in a laudable or esteemable manner. **विजयेन भर्तुः**—*i. e.* when your husband will gain victory. **जगतः भाग्यपंक्तिः**—the series (course) of fortunes of the people. **कालक्रमेण**—According to the course of time (good or bad) **चक्रार०**—see com.; **अराः**—the spokes of a wheel. The same thought is expressed by Kâli. in his Meg.—' नीचैर्गच्छत्युपरि च दशाचक्रनेमिक्रमेण '। II, 49; *cf.* also ' सुखस्यानन्तरं दुःखं दुःखस्यानन्तरं सुखम् । सुखदुःखं मनुष्याणां चक्रवत्परिवर्तते ' ॥

P. 5. **काञ्चुकीयः**—The same as the कञ्चुकी of later dramatists so called on account of his wearing a long robe. In later dramas he is always introduced as complaining about his old age with its infirmities and his miserable lot. *Cf.* Śāk. V. 3, Vik. III, 1, Mudrā. III, 1, Anar. III, 1, &c. The form **काञ्चुकीय** is somehow got from **कञ्चुकिन्** by affixing छण् (ईय) to it; 'वेणुकादिभ्यः छण् वाच्यः ।' Vārtt. on Pāṇ. IV. 2. 138; see also com. The **कञ्चुकी** or chamberlain had charge of the king's harem; he was generally an old Brāhmaṇa, of acknowledged moral rectitude, virtuous, &c.; he is defined as—' ये नित्यं सत्वसम्पन्नाः कामदोषादिवर्जिताः । ज्ञानविज्ञानकुशलाः काञ्चुकीयास्तु ते स्मृताः ॥ मातृगुप्ताचार्यः; अन्तःपुरचरो वृद्धो विप्रो गुणगणान्वितः । सर्वकार्यार्थकुशलः कञ्चुकीत्यभिधीयते । जरावैक्लव्ययुक्तेन विशेद्गात्रेण कञ्चुकी ॥ '

S'l. 5. **नृपापवादं**—Blame that would be given to or the reproach that would be cast on, the king; for people would think that they were ordered that way by the king. **परुषं**—adj. used as a noun; harsh words or harsh treatment. **नगरपरिभवान्**—नगरोत्पन्नाः परिभवाः नगरपरिभवाः तान्; insults easy to be obtained in a city; the evils of city-life. **विमोक्तुं**—To give up, to avoid. **मनस्विनः**—प्रशस्तं मन एषामिति high-souled, wise, able to take a proper view of worldly life; *cf.* for a similar thought ' एते हि हृदयमर्मभिदः संसारभावा येभ्यो बीभत्समाना अरण्ये विश्राम्यन्ति मनीषिणः । ' Uttar. I. p. 10.

सविज्ञानं—विशिष्टं ज्ञानं विज्ञानं special knowledge, which enables one to see what is proper to be done and what is not; power of discrimination. **दर्शनं**—intellect, judgment; lit. the way of looking at things; it may also mean—his observation. **वत्से**—Yauga. in his character of an old ascetic addresses Vāsa. thus. **गुणवान्**—Full of merit, pleasing; he is pleased to see that his disguise is perfect as he quite passed for an ascetic. **आलापः**—The form of address **श्लिष्यते**—The root is here used intransitively and the Ātm. is irregular (आर्षः प्रयोगः); see com.; or the form may be considered as used impersonally, like ओदनः पच्यते (स्वयमेव); भिद्यते काष्ठम्; see Sid. Kau. on 'कर्मवत्कर्मणा तुल्यक्रियः ।' Pāṇ. III. 1. 87. See com.

P. 6. **गुरुभिः**—By elderly persons. He says this as it would have looked improper on his part to name the king; see com. **नामधेय**—is the same as नाम; the Tad. affix धेय is added to the words रूप, नाम and भाग without change of meaning. This shows that the king was young. **दर्शक**—King of Magadha and a contemporary of Udayana; king of Vatsa and of Mahāsena king of Avantî or Ujjain. He was the son of Ajātaśatru whose reign ended in *cir.* 475. B. C. and who according to the Purāṇas was succeeded by his son Darśaka (see V. A. Smith's A. H. of I. pp. 38-39, 3rd ed.). **महादेवीं**—This must have been the queen of Ajâtaśatru, residing in the penance-forest after the death of her husband. **राजगृहं**—The second capital of Magadha, the ancient one being गिरिव्रज. It was Bimbasāra who built Rājagṛha and made it his capital. Pāṭaliputra became the seat of government under Udaya, who succeeded Darśaka.

S'l. 6. **स्वैरं**—Adv.; स्वः ईरः (desire, prompting) यस्मिन्कर्मणि तद्यथा तथा; mark the Sandhi; see H. G. § 20. Excep. (c); according to their will, freely, without molestation. **तपोधनानि**—is in opposition with तीर्थोदकानि, समिधः &c. (एतानि) तपोधनानि (which form the wealth of penance *i. e.* ascetics). **तपोधनानां**—*v. l.* should be construed with उपनयन्तु gen. for the dat.; bring to the sages. Or इष्टानि should be supplied. This is not a good reading. **धर्मप्रिया**—see com ; the comp. may also be प्रियधर्मा; by the Vārtt. 'वा प्रियस्य' (प्रिय may come latter optionally in a Bah.); who loves religion *i. e.* who attaches a higher importance to Dharma than to her own dignity. **धर्मपीडा**—Obstruction of or hindrance to the religious performances and pursuits of the ascetics. तपस्विषु विषये धर्मपीडा नेच्छेत्. **इदं**—*i. e.* not to come in the way of, &c. *cf.* तपोवनवासिनामुपरोधो मा भूदिति एतावत्येव रथं स्थापय । Śāk. I. p. 17.

P. 7. **पुष्पकभद्रादिभिः**—Pspakabhadra seems to be an astrologer attached to the court of Udayana, and consulted by Yaugandharāyaṇa. **आदेशिकैः**—Astrologers; fr. दिश् with आ to order, *i. e.* tell authoritatively. See *infra.* p. 65.

S'l. 7. **सङ्कल्पात्**—संकल्प a definite idea or thought (formed in the mind) about an object (a thing or person) which is presented to the mind accordingly. **भर्तृदारा०**—see com.; he means—as I desire her to be the wife of my master, I regard her as a person belonging to or connected with me. I have an affectionate regard for her.

भगिनिकास्नेह:—Because she was herself राजदारिका, **अपि**—shows that she had also सपत्नीस्नेह, as her husband was to acquire supreme sovereignty owing to her being married to him. Such nobility of mind was a characteristic of many ancient Indian queens; *cf.* Māl V. 19.

P. 7. **अभिजना०**—अभिजनस्य (noble birth) अनुरूपं befitting to, in consonance with. **प्रविशति उपविष्टा तापसी**—this stage direction may appear to be strange; if she was उपविष्टा how could she enter; so here प्रविशति must be understood in the technical sense of 'is discovered (seated)' the curtain being lifted up or moved aside (the ancient stage must be supposed to have been provided with some such arrangement). We often meet with such stage-direction in Sans. plays; *cf.* ततः प्रविशत्यासनस्थः सचिन्तो राक्षसः Mud. II. p. 39. ततः प्रविशत्यासनस्थो राजा विदूषकश्च । S'âk. V. p 113. ततः प्रविशति भूम्यां निपतित...रामः । Uttar. III. &c., **तापसी**—A female ascetic is introduced here, as it would have been improper to begin the scene with the entrance of a male character, it being the object of the poet to bring Padmāvatī in contact with Yaugandharāyaṇa, that the latter might easily get an opportunity to consign Vāsavadattā to her care. **सा राजदारिका**—By सा she may mean—she whose marriage is to be brought about with my husband; or—who was referred to by the Chamberlain in his speech. **जाते**—*Lit.* one as good as just born, *i. e.* to be tenderly treated, hence a term of affectionate address like वत्से. **तपोवनानि नाम**—नाम as is well known. **अतिथि०**—अतति गच्छति इति अतिथि: one who travels; a guest coming to the house; fr. अत् and the Uṇādi aff. इथिन् ; some derive the word as नास्ति द्वितीया तिथिर्यस्य; *cf.* 'एकरात्रं तु निवसन्नतिथिर्ब्राह्मणः स्मृतः ।' Manu. III. 102. **गेहं**—Comp. for the idea 'यथेच्छं भोग्यं वो वनमिदं...फलं वा मूलं वा तदपि न पराधीनमिह वः ॥' Uttar. II. 1. **भवतु भवतु**—This repetition is characteristic of Bhāsa. **विश्वस्ता**—Full of confidence; I can feel quite at home here now.

भद्रमुखस्य—Lit. one of an auspicious face; the good or blessed one; this is a polite form of address like प्रियदर्शन, used by an elderly or superior person when addressing a younger person or a stranger.

Cf. 'भद्रमुख, एहि तावत् मोचयानेन दुर्मोक्हस्तेन' &c. S'āk. VII p. 187, where king Duṣyanta is so addressed by a तापसी. In dramas according to the Sāh. Dar. a prince is to be so addressed by inferior characters; see VI. 154 ('भद्रसौम्यमुखस्त्वेवमधमैस्तु कुमारकः'). Here the Tāpasī refers to king Darśaka.

प्रद्योतः—King of Avantī He was a powerful king and was called Mahāsena on account of his having a large and efficient army. He was also designated Chaṇḍamahâsena from his having obtained a boon from the gooddess Chaṇḍî. See our note on Pradyota, Meg. I. 33; and *cf.* 'महेन्द्रवर्मणो नप्ता जयसेनसुतो नृप । चण्डीवरान्महासेनः स चण्डाह्व-नृपोऽभवत् ॥' Bṛh. K. M. II. 24. **दारकस्य**—Pradyota had two sons: Gopâlaka and Pālaka; see *infra.* p. 133. **भवतु भवतु**—The repetition indicates her great joy. **आत्मीया**—a relation (being her sister-in-law). Vāsa. felt sure that Padmā.'s brother would not refuse a request coming from such a great king as her father and was glad that would avoid the marriage of Padmā. with her husband, while Yaugandha. would gain his object in that case also, the king of Magadha being thus related to her and therefore an ally of Vatsarāja. **अस्य बहु॰**—Inasmuch as the proposal came from the father of the son, while usually it is the daughter's father that so seeks such a favour **महत्तरे**—महार्हे (महार्हाणि) *V l.* of great worth, very high, exalted or highly worthy of each other.

P. 8. **आत्मानं**—Ourselves (the princess and her party). **अनुग्रहीतुं**—A grammatical irregularity, which must be explained away by taking अनुग्रहीतुं in a causal sense (अनुग्राहयितुं). **प्रदानेन**—*i. e.* the offer of the gift of; or प्रदानेन हेतुना; or ins. may be in the sense of the dat; प्रदानाय that I might give. **उपनिमन्त्र्यतां**—should be induced to approach (us); see com. **अनेन विस्रम्भेण**—By this intimacy or familiarity, *i. e.* the familiarity produced by the kind reception given to her. **जातविस्रम्भा**—here विस्रम्भ means confidence, trust (she has in your goodness; or that you will accede to her request). **धर्मार्थं**—धर्माय that you may discharge your religious duties with ease. This may also mean ' that she may get *dharma* or religious merit. The first is better, as containing no selfish motive. **अर्थेन**—Here अर्थ means प्रयोजन or the object one has in view; any thing that is desired. **उपनि॰**—respectfully invites you (भवतः—is the object which follows from the context). Mark the alliterations in this sentence.

S'l. 8. **यथानिश्चितं**—As resolved or determined upon; may be construed with वासः, or पारितवान्. **दीक्षां**—The vow of ब्रह्मचर्य or the student's period of Vedic studies. **देयं गुरोः**—&c.—In those days no monthly fees were charged, but a student paid the गुरुदक्षिणा on the completion of his course of studies, according to his means. **धर्माभिरामप्रिया**—A strange comp.; there are many such in Bhāsa's plays and which bear witness to the crudeness of his style. It may mean—(1) धर्मे धर्मो वा अभिरामा delight or delightful येषां ते धर्माभिरामाः, ते प्रिया यस्याः who likes the ascetics, *lit.* those who delight in religious rites; or (2) धर्मः अभिरामः attractive प्रियश्च यस्याः who takes delight in and loves religion; or धर्मेण अभिरामा charming, attractive चासौ प्रिया (dear to, liked by all) च. The style of the śl. is remarkably simple and homely and bespeaks a time when versification was simple (free from rich rhetorical ornament).

दिष्ट्या—Properly the inst. of दिष्टि, used as a particle expressive of joy, good luck, &c. She is glad because it is difficult to find an अर्थी in a penance. *Cf.* for a similar idea—'इत्यप्रार्थितलभ्यसर्वविषये दोषोऽयमेको वने दुष्प्रापार्थिनि यत्परार्थघटनावन्ध्यैर्वृथा स्थीयते ।' Nāg. IV. 2. **संतुष्ट०**—*i. e.* nobody here has got a desire to express. Mark how this one epithet vividly expresses the peaceful life led by the inmates of the hermitage; not being affected by desire. संतुष्टः रागद्वेषादिरहितः शान्तान्तरात्मा च तपस्विजनः यस्मिन्. **आगन्तुकेन**—Since he at once said that he was an अर्थी (one having something to ask for).

P. 9. **प्रोषितभर्तृकां**—प्रोषितः gone on a journey, भर्ता यस्याः सा; hence separated from her husband प्रोषित p. p. of वस् with प्र used actively. प्रोषित० is also one of the eight kinds of Nâyikās or heroines. See Rudrata's S'ṛingāratilaka, I. 131-32; Sāh. D. III. 84.

S'l. 9. **काषायं**—कषायेण रक्तं (dyed) काषायं, अण् (अ) being added in this sense. **प्रपन्नः**—Became a recluse; reddish garments being the badge of a Saṃnyāsin; *cf.* 'इमे काषाये गृहीते' Māl. V. p. 101. **दृष्टधर्मप्रचारा**—(1) whose rigid (प्र) observance of religious duties is well seen or marked; whose piety is wellknown; or (2) who well knows, or is conversant with, religious observances. And hence शक्ता &c. **चारित्रं**—चरित्रमेव चारित्रं purity of conduct. **शक्ता**—*i. e.* not by keeping guard over her but on others that might approach her with sinister motives.

निक्षेप्तुकाम:—desirous of delivering over or keeping as a deposit. Mark the meaning of क्षिप् with नि (used with the loc. of the person with whom a deposit is made.) *Cf.* निक्षेप.

क्रम:—a course of action, a step. **व्यपाश्रयणा**—request for support; from श्रि with वि, अप and आ; व्यपश्रि is also used in the Māyā. (व्यपश्रयिष्ये तावदेनं) and in the Panch. (व्यपश्रयिष्ये तावद्भवन्तं) in this sense.

S'l. 10. **सुखमर्थो भवेत्**—&c.—He means-One can very easily give away money or part with life, &c., but not with such ease undertake to guard a charge, सुखमर्थो भवेद्दातुं—Mark the idiomatic use of the *inf.* with a nom; supply शक्य: as done in the com; or the case may be taken as analogous to विषवृक्ष: स्वयं च्छेत्तुमसांप्रतं (अयुक्तं) भवेत् ; see Malli, on Kum II, 55. **प्रथममु०**—This brings out the nobility of mind of the princess, **भणति**—आज्ञापयति (आणवेदि) *V. l.* is better as more suited to the modesty of the princess. **आर्यात्मीयेदानीं संवृत्ता**—see p. 7, where Vāsa. makes a similar remark.

P, 10, **एषा गच्छामि म०**—occurs also in Prat. Yau. **अवसितं**—P, p, p of सो with अव; half has ended; *i. e.* the responsible business has been half accomplished. **समर्थितं**—settled after consultation, **परिणमति**—is taking its turn or attaining fruition. **प्रतिष्ठिते**—When he will be firmly set on his throne. The poet does not tell us what he means by this. It appears that Udayana had lost the whole of his kingdom, his capital only being left to him; see *infra*. कौशाम्बीमात्रं परिपालयामीति । p. 64, **उपनयत:**—As I shall take Vāsa. back to the king. **इह**—in this matter; or here (her ladyship *i. e.* Pad. here). **विश्वास०**—Here स्थानं has the sense of हेतु the cause of inspiring confidence in, *i. e.* will bear testimony to her chastity. This shows that Yaugandharāyaṇa was anxious to see that the king would have no reason to suspect the virtue of his queen during the period of her separation from him, Vide the extract from the Kathā. wherein Vàsa. shows her readiness to undergo the fire ordeal to prove her chastity, **यथा मन्त्रिभि: सह**—&c.—That Vàsav. should be placed under the care of Padmāvatī. For the deliberation of Yaug. with the ministers see extract from the Kathā. Tar, I.

S'l, 11, **पद्मावती**—&c.—Youg. bases his belief on the prediction of the seers; see *infra.* p. 65, According to the Kathā, :(Gunādhaya's Bṛh.) it was Nārada who foretold the calamity mentioned in the second line. He, however, did not predict Pad.'s marriage with Vatsarâja. Kṣemendra's Br. M. does not difinitely say that, but makes a passing reference to the prophecy that Pad.'s husband would become an imperial ruler. This shows that Bhāsa must have preceded Gunādhya. If we take the first line independently as done in the com., then we have to infer that Pad.'s marriage with Udayana was predicted by the seers. But we get the idea directly if the first two lines be construed as–यैः सिद्धैः नरपतेः विपत्तिः (राज्यभ्रंशरूपा) प्रथमं प्रदिष्टा तैः अथ पद्मावती नरपतेः महिषी भवित्री दृष्टा—Those seers who first foretold the mishap that was to befall our master (and which has been realised) have also told after that that &c. or यैः प्रथमं प्रदिष्टा नरपतेः विपत्तिः अस्माभिः दृष्टा तैः पद्मावती नरपतेः महिषी भवित्री प्रदिष्टा.

P, 11, तत्प्रत्ययात्—Having faith in that (their prediction), हि for, विधिः सुपरीक्षितानि सिद्धवाक्यानि उत्क्रम्य न गच्छति. The contains a general truth which supports the statement made in the previous line; the figure of speech, therefore, here is अर्थान्तरन्यास. He means,—This foreboding also of the आदेशिकs cannot be falsified.

ब्रह्मचारी—A vedic student; a bachelor undergoing a course of Vedic studies. ब्रह्म वेदः। तदध्ययनार्थं व्रतमपि उपचारात् ब्रह्म; ब्रह्म चरति चरितुं वा शीलमस्य। यद्वा ब्रह्म तपो ज्ञानं वा तच्चरत्यवश्यं; Pāṇ. III. 3. 170. The ब्रह्म॰ is introduced here to acquaint the audience with the reported destruction of queen in the fire at Làvāṇaka and the subsequent events that happened there. अभितः—All round; तपो॰ भवि॰—for he had unknowingly entered the environs of a penance forest.

S'l. 12. The śl. contains the various characterstic signs of a hermitage. विस्रब्धं—&c.—This shows that the deer belonged to a तपोवन; *cf.* 'विश्वासोपगमादभिन्नगतयः' &c. S'âk. I. 14, and 'नष्टाशंका हरिणशिशवो मन्दमन्दं चरन्ति' in the next śl. अचकिताः—without being frightened; this is unnecessary after विस्रब्धं and indicates the crude style of the śl; the description given here is less elegant than that by Kàli. referred to above. देशागतप्रत्ययाः—see com.; the deer were confident of safety as they knew that that was a region of peace and harmlessness. पुष्पफलैः समृ॰—An instance of सापेक्षसमास again, the whole should have been compounded as पुष्पफलसमृद्ध०; or, पुष्पफलैः उपलक्षिताः सहिता वा समृद्धविटपाः (with luxuriant branches). च दया-रक्षिताः—gives the reason why they were full of fruit, &c. *Cf.* Ragh. XIII. 46, 50; and 'नादत्ते प्रियमण्डनापि भवतां स्नेहेन या पल्लवं;' S'āk. IV. 9. भूयिष्ठं—For the most part, mostly; goes with वर्तन्ते and not with कपिलानि. गोधनानि—The cows formed the wealth of the ascetics being the sources of their sacrificial offerings; *cf.* 'गुरोरपीदं धनमाहिताग्नेः' &c.: Ragh. II. 44. Vasiṣṭha's Nandinī also was पाटला. (Ragh. I. 83). Tawny cows were considered more holy; *cf.* the स्मृति-अग्निचित् &c. quoted in the com. from Malli.'s com. on Ragh. XVII. 74. अक्षेत्र०—There were no field in sight in the surrounding regions, as the sages lived on wild corn; see Ragh. V. 9. अक्षेत्र may also mean uncultivated fields. बह्वाश्रयः—see com. for comp.; the smoke arose from various places as the sacred fire was simultaneously kindled in several huts. Or smoke issuing from many things, such as घृत, समिध्, तिल, तण्डुल &c. simultaneously burnt in the *Kuṇḍas*.

एष जनः—refers to the Chamberlain, who prominently attracts his attention. निर्दोषः—As there were ascetics he could enter without being open to the charge of intrusion. अये स्त्रीजनः—He then notices the women,—the Tāpasī along with Vāsa., Padmāvatî and Cheṭī (and hesitates to advance). Hence the Kânch. says—स्वैरं &c.

P. 12. हं—is a particle indicative of disapproval Ah (do you allow it). Probably she turns away her face after uttering this sound which elicits from Padmâ. the remark–" Oh, she avoids &c "

राजगृहतः—see *ante*. p. 6. The celibate was a native of Râjagṛha. श्रुतिविशेषणार्थं—For special or higher study of the Veda; or for acquiring distinction in Vedic studies. For Lāvāṇaka, see Introd. हा लावाणकं नाम – Lāvā., indeed (which I remember so very well). *Cf.* अभिमन्युर्नाम Pāṇ. II. नवीकृतः—A Chvi-form. At the mention of Lávâ. Vāsa. remembered all the incidents in connection with the plan formed by the ministers and her consequent separation from her dearly loved husband, which though temporary, caused poignant pain to her.

व्यसनं—A calamity. कथमिव–Yaugandharāyaṇa purposely feigns ignorance of the whole affair and asks the Brahmachārin about the events as Lāvāṇaka to lull at all suspicion about his true character, so that he may pass for a true recluse. He also wants to know what happened at Lāvā. after he had left it.

P. 13. अभिप्रेता—Loved. मन्दभागा—This shows that although she yielded to the persuasions of the ministers; it was not without pain inwardly felt, as every woman having a high sense of honour would surely feel.

अभ्यवपत्तुकामः—Wishing to get near, *i. e.* to rescue, her. सानुक्रोशत्वं—Tender heartedness towards or sympathy for; mark the meaning of अनुक्रोश (fr. अनुक्रुश् to cry or lament along with another) which is allied to the English sympathy (sun together and pathos suffering). दग्ध०—दग्धेभ्यः शेषाणि; see also com.

सकामः &c.—What she means is this–If the king swooned he suspected no fraud in the matter and believed that she was really dead. So Yaug. might succeed, as he desired, in persuading him to marry Padmā. when offered by her brother to him in marriage, there being no obstacle left. The sentence may also be taken as ironical. In this case the meaning is—knowing how deeply the king loved me. Yaug. formed this plan. The very news of my death has given such a shock to the king; the worse might follow; let Yau. gain his object at such a cost (as the end may be disastrous). And Kāli.'s similar words, *viz.* 'काम इदानीं सकामो भवतु येनासत्यसन्धे जने सखी' &c. lend support to this view. But the honorific epithet आर्य prefixed to यौग० shows that this could not have been meant. *Cf.* for a parallel 'राजा–(स्वगतम्) एवमस्मासु गृह्यमाणेषु स्वकार्यसिद्धिकामः सकामो भवत्वार्यः । ' Mud. III. p. 84. रोदिति &c.—This shows that Vāsa.'s eyes must have been filled with tears on hearing of the bitter grief caused to her husband by the sad news of her death.

अथ किमथ किम्—Mark how impatient Yau. is to prevent any suspicion being roused in the minds of the hearers about Vāsa. being connected with the king. *Cf.* for a similar precaution भीमसेनः—अर्जुन (which might have disclosed the identity of the Pāṇḍavas)—बृहन्नला—अथ किमथ किम् (you meant to say). अर्जुनपुत्रेण Pāṇ. III.

P. 14. ध्रियते—Supposed to be a pass. form of the root धृ having an act. force; or of धृ 6 Ā. He lives; *cf.* 'आर्यपुत्र, ध्रिये एषा ध्रिये' Uttar. III, p. 82: 'ध्रियते यावदेकोऽपि रिपुस्तावत्कुतः सुखम् । ' Śiś. II. 35.

S'l. 13. नैवेदानीं—इदानीं—now, when the king has been mourning the loss of his beloved wife so harrowingly. **तादृशा:**—like him, coming up to his standard of grief at the loss of a beloved. **चक्रवाका:**—चक्र इति संज्ञया उच्यते इति चक्रवाक: the ruddy goose; fr. चक्र+ वच् with aff घञ् (अ); or चक्र इति वाक: title, name यस्य; (for वाक thus used *cf.* Uttar. I. 1). The चक्रवाक is also called by such name as चक्राह्व, रथाङ्गनामन् &c. The Chakraváka pair is represented as the standard of connubial love and inability to bear separation from each other. **स्त्रीविशेषै:**—स्त्रीणां विशेषा: (most distinguished of) तै: वियुक्ता: (such as Aja, Rāma, &c.) **तथा वेत्ति**—knows her to be, regards her as, his all-in-all, being the highest pattern of feminine virtue. *Cf.* ' प्रियेषु सौभाग्यफला हि चारुता । ' Kuṃ. V. 1. **भर्तृस्नेहात्**—*cf.* 'न खलु स उपरतो यस्य वल्लभो जन: स्मरति । ' Māl. Mâdh. V. p. 111; and *infra.* 'उपरताप्यनुपरता' &c. VI. p. 59.

S'l. 14. **अनाहारे** &c.—The S'l. gives expression to the extreme loyalty and the sincere love Rum. bore to the king. **प्रतत०**—प्रतत continuous; क्षाम emaciated, grown lean, p. p. p. of क्षै. **संस्कारं**—decoration, such as applying unguents to the body, putting on ornaments, &c. **नृपति०**—is an adv. comp., see com., feeling equal pain with the king, feeling equally miserable as the king. This may also be taken as an adj. to संस्कार. **परिवहन्**—Bearing, the king attended to his body only so far as was necessary, *i. e.* he bathed, made the *tilaka* mark &c. but did not put on necklaces, &c.; *cf.* S'āk. ' प्रत्यादिष्टविशेषमण्डनविधि:' VI. 6. परिहरन् *v. l.* is perhaps better.

P. 15. **तस्याप्युपरम:**—*i. e.* he will also die after him. This is meant to assure Vāsa. that the king's safety would be sedulously attended to by Rumaṇvan.

भार:—Here भार refers to the two-fold heavy responsibility undertaken by the two principal ministers, *viz* (1) that of entrusting Vāsavadattà to the care of Padmāvatī, and (2) that of looking to the safety of the king in his bereavement—so essential for the successful execution of their plan.

S'l. 15. **अयं भार:**—This refers to the responsible task undertaken by Yaugandharāyaṇa; it was सविश्रम because he could enjoy ease of mind after committing Vāsa. to the safe keeping of Padmāvatī. **प्रसक्तस्तस्य** &c. see com. for construction; the responsibility devolving on him has proved to be arduous; or this may be construed as तस्य तु

भारः प्रसक्तः श्रमः—But the responsible task entrusted to him has been a source of continuous trouble to him. **तस्मिन्** &c ,—यत्र (यस्मिन्स्मण्वति) नृपः अधीनः (dependent on-on whose efforts and skill depends the life of the king) तस्मिन् सर्वमधीनं all other things including the success of our plan, depend upon him (Ruman.), the king being the most important person in the state. अधीन properly means इनमधिगतः one having a master, one dependent on; the comp. is by the Vārttika 'अत्यादयः' &c. on Pâṇ. II. 2. 18; hence dependent on, *cf.* ' अधीनो निघ्न आयत्तः' Amara. **अथ भो** &c.—is a question **पर्यवस्थापितः**—set right; composed or restored to his natural disposition. **हसितं**— and the other p. p. p that follow are used impersonally, the subject being मया (here I smiled with her) &c.

पर्युषितं—Stayed overnight, *i. e.* passed a night. **प्रोषितनक्षत्र०**—The simile here is somewhat faulty as the उपमेय (अमात्यs) and उपमान (नक्षत्रs) are of different genders (लिङ्गभेद). **किंनु खल्वपरा स्त्री**—this speech must be जनान्तिक (as nobody replies to her) being meant only for the ear of Padmávatī. Hereby the Cheṭī suggests that Padmà. might have her chance now.

P. 16. **आपृच्छामि**—should be आपृच्छे as प्रच्छ् with आ is Âtm. in this sense. **भवन्तौ**—He refers to the Kānch. and Yaugandharâyaṇa. **काञ्चु०**—तत्रभवत्या—should be अत्रभवत्या. **भगिनिका**—भगिनी एव भगिनिका, क being added स्वार्थे; *cf.* पुत्रिका. **उत्कण्ठिष्यते**—Will feel a longing or pine for; 2nd Fut. of उत्कण्ठ the denom. from उत्कण्ठ (उत्कण्ठते). **उत्कण्ठिष्यति**—For the justification of the Paras see com. **अभ्यन्तरं**—*i. e.* the inside of the hermitage.

S'l. 16. The description of sunset here is very natural and simple; the figure of speech here is स्वभावोक्ति. The idea expressed in the last two lines is in conformity with the primitive notion of the sun's falling from heavan and descending on the top of the setting mountain. **अवगाढः**—used actively, गाह् being a गत्यर्थक root, has entered water (for the purpose of bathing).

परिभ्रष्टः &c.—*Cf.* for the idea more elaborately worked out ' सन्ध्यामृष्टावशिष्टस्वकरपरिकरस्पष्टहेमारपङ्क्ति व्याकृष्यावस्थितोऽस्तक्षितिभृति नयतीवैष दिक्चक्रमर्कः ।' Rat. III. 5.

ACT. II

कुत्र भर्तृदारिका पद्मा०— Here we are to suppose that the Princess has returned to her residence in Rājagriha. **किं भणासि**—-This is what is technically called आकाशभाषितं (or a speech in the air) in which a character on the stage asks a person or persons not present on the stage a question and pretending to hear a reply to his querry repeats the same for the information of the audience with the words किं भणसि...इति; see com. **कन्दुकेन क्रीडति**—This seems to have been the favourite pastime of Indian princesses from the earliest times; *cf.* Kumā. I. 29, V, 19; Ragh. XVI. 83, Daś. ch. VI. p. 151, &c., Rája-śekhara has described it in his Vidh. II, 6-11.

उत्कृत०—qualifies मुखेन. उत्कृत raised up or placed on the ear (to prevent it from dangling about). **परिश्रान्त**—looking exhausted; or better take परिश्रान्त as a noun; परिश्रान्तेन परिश्रमेण रमणीयं दर्शनं यस्य तेन.

P. 18 **प्रवेशक**—is defined as 'तद्वदेवानुदात्तोक्त्या नीचपात्रप्रयोजितः । प्रवेशोऽङ्कद्वयस्यान्तः शेषार्थस्योपसूचकः ॥ ' D. R. It is an interlude which coming between any two acts indicates, like the Viṣkambhaka, parts of the story going forward, through the conversation of one or more low characters. For विष्कं० see *infra.* Act VI. A प्रवेशक can never appear at the beginning of the first Act.

हला—A particle of address for a female friend in plays, as हञ्जे is for a maid See com. **एष ते कन्दुकः**—Vāsa. wants to hand over the ball that had dropped down to her thinking that she might desire to play more. **भवत्विदानीं**—Let the play be so far *i. e.* end here. एतत्परिणामस्य एतावत् । **अधिकसञ्जातरागौ**—There is a pun on the word **राग** which is clear from Vāsavadattâ's words bellow. With their **राग** (1) redness increased (by handling the ball); (2) love (also hinted at) **परकीयौ इव**—(1) As if they belong to another, are not yours, being excessively red and so you cannot control their movement; (2) As if they are another's property (being inspired with love for another), and are not under your control; (referring to her intended marriage). The Prâkrit words केरअ or केरओ (also written as केरको) often occur in plays and appear to be used in the sense of " property or possession ", *cf.* 'जो सो वेस्साजणकेरओ अलंकारो ' Mrch. III. p. 81; ' तवस्सिणीए

केरआ अलंकारा;' *Ibid.* IX. p. 215. It appears that the word having originally this significance, being compounded with other words came to be regarded as an affix meaning 'belonging to'. इदमर्थस्य प्रत्ययस्य केर इत्यादेशो भवति । तम्हकेरो (युष्मदीयः); अम्हकेरो (अस्मदीयः); &c. Hemachandra.

कन्याभावरमणीयः—Because a maiden when married has no independence of action. *Cf.* ' क्रीडतु क्रीडतु । नैतत्सुलभं श्वशुरकुले । ' Pra. Yaug. II and for the idea ' रेमे मुहुर्मध्यगता सखीनां क्रीडारसं निर्विशतीव बाल्ये ।' Kum. I. 29; 'साहं पितृकुले...अविदितस्नेहशोकायासमनोहरं शैशवमतीतवती ।' Kād. p. 220-21. **निध्यायसि**— निध्यै means 'to look intently at or with a fixed gaze; *cf.* ' तेन राजर्षिणा विद्याधरदारिकोदयवती नाम चिरं निध्यातेति कुपितोर्वशी ।' Vik. IV. p. 91. "सोऽपि चिरं निध्यायति मां;' Māl. Mād. VII. p. 153. Padmāvatī thought that Vâsa. was looking at her steadfastly in order to laugh at her for her getting fatigued like that.

P. 19. **नहि नहि**—Vāsa. says—no; I look at you so intently because you appear more lovely to-day. सोहदि (शोभते) *v. l.* supply भवती; or it may go with मुखं. **वरमुखं**—There is also a double *entendre* on this; (1) I look at your excellent (charming) lace all round; take its view from all sides as it were; (2) In this case दे must be translated by त्वां; त्वामभितः about you. I fancy I behold the the bridegroom's face about you, *i. e.* your face has the loveliness of a maiden standing in the presence of the bridegroom, the colour of the face being due to blushing; the construction may also be वरमुखमभितः इव त्वां पश्यामि you look unnerved like one &c; you look charming like one whose marriage is at hand (the thought of approaching marriage giving the flush to the face). Padmâvatī understands this and says अपेहि &c. *Cf.* for a similar scene Śāk. I. Priyamvadâ's reference to Śakuntalā's marriage and the latter's retort ' एष तु तवात्मगतो मनोरथः ' p. 23.

भविष्यन्महा०—Vāsa. also retorts with equal grace, very well, here I remain quiet, if you do not like a reference to your marriage, *you* who are soon to be the daughter-in-law of the great king Mahâsena. This refers to the maid's reply to the तापसी अस्ति राजा.. ...दूतसम्पातं करोति. Here Vâsa. speaks of the marriage as certain, as Pad.'s brother was not expected to refuse family alliance with an illustrious and powerful king like Pradyota.

क एष महासेनो नाम—Pad., it seems, did not know that Pradyota was also named महासेन and hence her question. उज्जायिनीयः—उज्जयिन्यां भवः. बलपरि०—परिमाण measure, extent, largeness; निर्वृत्तं due to given rise to by. गुणानभि०—This is intended to bring out the nobility of Padmāvatī's mind. She loves merits, not so much beauty of form. सानुक्रोशः—Kind-hearted; who would love his wife. अयमपि जनः—Vāsa. here refers to herself. उन्मादितः—Of course before marriage. Vàsa. remembers how she also got passionately attached to him on hearing of his noble qualities.

P. 20. नहि नहि। दर्शनीयः—Vāsa.'s extreme love for her husband makes her impatient of even a doubt being expressed about her husband's handsomeness and she suddenly bursts into नहि नहि &c. समुदाचारः—Propriety of conduct. Bhāsa has used the word in this sense in Pra. Yau. (देवसमुदाचारः, अतिथिसमुदाचारः), and *infra.* p. 29. समतिक्रान्तः—'Because the question was how she knew that the Vatsa king was beautiful when she, as a Pativratā, avoided the sight of a stranger. दृष्टं—*i. e.* how to mend matters. उज्जयिनीयः—Vāsa. says this for a double reason:—(1) She could well believe the people of her own country; (2) He must be really attractive who is praised not only by his people but by the people of rival kingdom also. Padm. under stands this and endorses her view saying सर्वजनमनोभिरामं &c. सौभाग्यं—Properly the state of being fortunate (सुभगस्य भावः); hence here beauty, grace; *cf.* for this sense 'हिमं न सौभाग्यविलोपि जातम्'; Kum. I. 3; 'सौभाग्यमदेन वञ्चितं'; *Ibid.* V, 49. अथ कुशली—And after that (अथ) *i. e* the offer, is the king well. Did not the offer make him un-happy, was not his grief for his wife renewed? the *Dhatrī* of course takes this as a simple question. तस्य-तेन. प्रतीष्टा—Accepted; *cf.* for this sense ' देवस्य शासनं प्रतीष्य '; Śāk. VI, p. 141. अत्याहितं—Vāsa. again forgets that she is living *incognito* and ejaculates like this. The thought of her husband taking a second wife is too painful for her to bear. अत्याहितं—(1) as an exclamation—what an evil; oh alas! (2) A great calamity or misfortune. अतिशयेन आधीयते तन्निवारणार्थं मनो दीयते अस्मिन्निति; or अत्यन्तमाधीयते मनसि। तथा नाम &c.—Again she passes off the matter by giving a different colouring to it. 'I exclaimed so, because past experience has shown that he might prove indifferent to his second wife.'

P. 21. **आगमप्रधानानि**—Three meanings are possible. (1) आगम *i. e.* of sorrow; the befalling of a misfortune, प्रधान: chief *i. e.* overpowering येषां; the hearts of great men being tender are greatly overpowered by sorrow; sorrow makes a deep impression upon them; but are easily consoled or restored to their natural peace; (2) आगम: the teaching of the S'astras; they attach the highest importance to the teaching of the S'astras, which enables them to take a right view of things and &c. (3) **आगम:**—आगच्छतीति what comes to pass, what becomes necessary to be done, an emergency; as in the present case the regaining of the lost kingdom; they rise equal to the emergency that arises and so &c. Of these the first is the best and intended by the poet. For it seems to be the object of the poet to indicate contrast between the two phases of the mind of the great; *cf.* 'वज्रादपि कठोराणि मृदूनि कुसुमादपि । लोकोत्तराणां चेतांसि ।' Uttar. I. **अन्यप्रयोजनेन**—&c.—According to the Kathā. the Magadha king on learning how Vāsa. had perished in the flames sent his own messenger to Udaya at Làvâṇaka and offered Pad.'s hand to him. The poet has changed this for poetic effect. **विज्ञानवयो०**—These are the qualifications to be sought in a bridegroom; *cf.* Ragh. VI. 19, and 'कुलं च शीलं च सनाथतां च विद्यां च वित्तं च वपुर्वयश्च । एतान्गुणान्सप्त परीक्ष्य देया कन्या बुधैः शेषमचिन्तनीयम् ॥' **अनपराद्ध:**—Because महाराजेन दत्ता न तु स्वयमेव तेन वरिता (which she wanted to know to make sure of his constant love for her). **भट्टिनी**—The queen is so addressed by low characters: see Intro. **शोभनं नक्षत्रं**—Because it is the auspicious constellation of stars that is chiefly considered in determining the favourable time for marriage and the like. If the Nakṣatra be nót auspicious there is no further consideration of the *tithi* or *lagna*, *cf.* 'अद्यैव खलु गुणवन्नक्षत्रं'; Panch. अद्य नक्षत्रं शोभनमिति; Avi. **कौतुकमङ्गलं**—कौतुक the nuptial string-bracelet. The tying of the thread bracelet round the wrist (of the left hand of the bride) is one of the several ceremonies to be performed before the hand of the bride is actually taken by the bride-groom. *cf.* Nàrāyaṇa Bhatta 'तत: कण्ठदेशस्थसूत्रमधो निष्कास्य कुङ्कुमाक्तमूर्णायुक्तं कृत्वा तेन हरिद्राखण्डं बद्ध्वा तद्ध्रूवामहस्तप्रकोष्ठे वरो बध्नीयान्नीललोहितेति मन्त्रेण' (Rv. X 85, 28). *Cf.* कौतुकमालिकां *infra*. p. 23 where कौतुक means pertaining to the marriage. **अन्धीकरोति**—darkens, makes it gloomy on account of sorrow (not because she disliked Pad., but because she was to have now a share in her husband's love).

———

ACT. III.

आमोद—is used in its literal sense of joy all round, general merriment; festivity. **चतुःशालं**—see com ; or चतसृणां शालानां समाहारः, (also— शाली) by the Vārti. आबन्तो वा; a quadrangle or fourcornered hall enclosed by halls on the four sides. Such as buildings appear to have been much in vogue in ancient times; Bhāsa has used the word चतुशालं in his Avi., Châr. and Prat.; *cf.* also. ' अलं चतुःशालमिदं प्रवेश्य;' Mṛch. III. 8; 'मञ्जूषां गृहीत्वा चतुःशालतः कुब्जो निष्क्रामति' Māl. V. p. 89; 'आर्य, पाश्चाल्याश्चतुःशालमिदम्' Veṇ. I p. 13. **प्रमदवनं**–a garden exclusively for the use of the ladies or the harem; see com.; 'अथ वनं प्रमदपूर्वकम् । अन्तःपुरैकभोग्यं स्यात् । ' इति वृक्षारोपे । **भागधेय**—भाग एव भागधेयं; धेय is added to रूप, नाम and भाग स्वार्थे *i. e.* without change of meaning. **अत्याहितं**—see *supra* p. 20. **चक्रवाकवधूः**—see *supra* I. 13. **मनोरथेन जीवामि**—*cf* 'आशाबन्धः कुसुमसदृशं प्रायशो ह्यङ्गनानां सद्यःपाति प्रणयिहृदयं विप्रयोगे रुणद्धि । ' Meg. I. 9.

नीहार०—नीहारप्रतिहता with her brightness obstructed, *i. e.* obscured by **प्रतिपच्चन्द्र०**—is not a good reading, as the प्रति० is not clearly seen even when there is no mist. **भद्रक**—Auspicious, good.

P. 23. **प्रियङ्गुशि०**—*i. e.* the stone-slab-seat in the bower of the Pri. creeper. This creeper, also called फलिनि, श्यामा being of a lovely darkish colour (*cf* प्रियङ्गुश्यामाङ्गः Māl. Màd. III. 9) seems to have been a favourite of royal ladies; *cf.* Ragh. VIII. 61, It is described as having the gracefulness of a woman's body; see Meg. II. 44; Ṛit. III. 18. **कः कालः**—What a long time, that &c.; see com. Bhāsa very often uses this expression in his play.

अस्माकं भट्टिनी &c.—It is better to read the whole as one sentence; इति giving महाकुलप्र० &c. as the three reasons for making the request. She is महाकुल० and so may be expected to comply with the request; she is स्निग्धा and so will do it affectionately; and being निपुणा will do it adroitly. One ed. reads आवन्तिका after निपुणा; in this case the sentence must be taken as ending with इति; but the omission is better for the reason given above. **कौतुकमाला**—Here कौतुक means the marriage ceremony; nuptial garland; that is the garland to be worn by the bride at the time of the marriage. It is a wreath of Madhūka flowers intermixed with the sacred Dūrvā grass. See com. and *cf*. Ragh. VI. 25; Kum. VII. 14.

एतदपि मया &c. As a woman Vāsa. is pained to be forced to do what she would have faign avoided. According to Somadeva's account Vāsa. herself wreathed the garland for Pad. and also adorned her with the neverfading saffron mark. *cf*. 'अथासन्नविवाहायाः पद्मावत्या मनस्विनी। अम्लानमालातिलकौ दिव्यौ भूयांश्चकार सा ॥' The skill of weaving a garland that would never fade and making a mark that would ever remain fresh was imparted to Vāsa. by Udayana who had learnt it from the Nāgas. **अहो अकरुणा** &c.—occurs again at p. 47 *infra* and in Abhi. **मान्यच्चिन्त०**—The use of the absolutive with मा is against Pāṇ; perhaps the poet has used it on the analogy of अलं which is used with the inst. when it has a prohibitive force by 'अलंखल्वोः प्रतिषेधयोः प्राचां क्त्वा।' Pāṇ. III. 4. 18; 'अलं दत्वा; अलंखल्वोः किम्। मा कार्षीत्' S'id. Kau. There are many such archisms in Bhāsa. The reading अलमिदानीमन्यदनुचिन्त्य saves the difficulty; but the poet has again used मा similarly; see *infra*. pp. 28, 50. **अन्यत्**—Anything else; the maid seeing her remain pensive says this—Do not think of anything else; do not divert your thoughts to other things as that will cause delay. **मणिभूम्यां**—मणिभूमि lit. a house with a jewel-floor or pavement. It probably refers to a quadrangular bathing place (चतुष्क) having four pillars at the four corners; *cf*. Kum. VII. तां—वासो वसानामभिषेकयोग्यं नार्यश्चतुष्काभिमुखं व्यनैषुः ॥ (चतुष्कं चतुःस्तम्भगृहं Malli.) 'विन्यस्तवैदूर्यशिलातलेऽस्मिन्नाबद्धमुक्ताफलभक्तिचित्रे।' &c. 9. 10. **न शक्नोमि** &c.—I cannot think of anything else but of my helpless and pitiable condition. **कथं न शक्नोमि** &c.—How is it that I am not able &c., indicates her helplessness.

आम—In classical Prākrit it becomes आम; Sans. ओम्. **भर्तृदारिकायाः**—Gram. inaccuracy; should be दारिकायाम्.

P. 24. **भण भण**—Mark how eager Vāsa. is to hear her husband's praise; it fills her with rapturous joy. **शरचापहीनः काम०**—In the Avi. Magadhikā says—'अहमपि चिन्तयामि सशरीरो भगवान्कामदेव ईदृशो भवेदिति।' IV. In the Rat. Sāgarikā also speaks of उदयन as 'प्रत्यक्ष एव तत्रभगवान्कुसुमायुधः।' I. p. 25.

अयुक्तं परपुरुष०—*cf. supra* p. 12 परपुरुषदर्शनं &c.

वर्जयित्वा—Leaving out or putting aside. **आवर्ज्य** *v. l.*—Having emptied (lit. turned down) the basket of flowers. **औषधं**—a herb (plucked off from the earth); ओषधिरेव औषधम् । स्वार्थे अण् (अ) by 'औषधेरजातौ ।' Pāṇ. V. 4. 37. **अविधवाकरणं** and **सपत्नी०**—The names are probably invented by the poet. **न गुम्फितव्यं**—Mark the ready-wit of Vâs. with which she avoids the wreathing of the herb as that would mean her own destruction. **बहुशः**—In plenty; so as to have greater efficacy,

P. 25. **अविधवाभिः**—Only ladies with their husbands living can accompany the bride or the bridegroom when going to be married. See Kum. VII. 12.

परकेरओ—see *supra* note on परकीयौ p. 18; see com.

अविदा—indicates sorrow; अविद, is the form found in the प्राकृतसर्वस्व; so we should rather read अविद; probably it is a corrupt form of अव इह save me here; help. **अहं वि** is another reading:

ACT IV.

—:*:—

विदूषकः—Vasantaka, the king's नर्मसचिव. See Introd. **भो दिष्ट्या** &c.—In this soliloquy of the Vidū. his extreme love for his master, and fondness for eating and sleep are well brought out. The only thing that mars his joy is his inability to digest the dainty food he got in the palace. **अभिप्रेत**–As desired by the ministers and himself.

P. 29. **अनर्थसलिला०**—For comp. see com.; the अनर्थ meant is the expected destruction of his life by the king or his aversion to the pleasures of the world **दीर्घिकाः**—Pleasure–tanks, oblong in size, attached to the mansions of rich men and the palaces of kings. **उत्तरकुरुवासः**—A residence in the Uttarakurus. *i. e.* all the blessings attendant thereon. The Uttarakuru is the 7th of the nine divisions of the world lying to the north of Meru. Being the land of eternal beatitude and enjoyment it came to be regarded as a देवभूमि where the Apsarās (its exquisitely beautiful ladies) dwelt. It is twice referred to in Avi. IV.

" In the Aitareya Brâhmaṇa (VIII. 14) it is stated that the Uttarakurus lived beyond the Himālaya. In later works, the Mahābhārata (I. 17. 19. &c.) and the Rāmāyaṇa (IV. 44. 88 &c.) the land of the Uttarakurus has already become a mythical country. It is identified with Ottora Koma of Plotemy, and lassen places the country somewhere east of modern Kasgar. But we would place the Uttara. alluded to in the Ai. Br. somewhere north of the Himàlayan range, *i. e.* in Kashmir. " Dutt's His. of civilisation in Ancient India. Vol. I. pp. 120–1.

सुप्रच्छ०—And hence he should get sleep the more readily. **वातशोणितं**—generally called वातरक्त–A vitiated state of the blood due to the disturbance of वात, the second of the three humours in the body leading to gout or acute rheumatism. It is mentioned as of eight kinds, see com. **आमयपरिभूतं**—Overpowered, disturbed by disease. **अकल्यवर्तं**—Without the morning meal or breakfast. Vidū., whose fondness for sweet food is well known, is sorry that he could not eat anything in the morning, when he was sure to get a rich dish for his breakfast; or कल्यस्य नीरोगस्य वर्तः eating in such a way as not to get ill; अकल्य० in which one cannot eat without the fear of getting ill *i. e.* as much as one likes.

P. 27. **भवति**—Voc. sing.; भवती—Her ladyship (the queen). **सुमनो०**—Sam. Dwa ; सुमनावर्णकं *V. l.* Mālatī flowers and unguents. The expression occurs also in the Avi. **कोकिलानामक्षि०**—Mark the pun on the word परिवर्त, which means the turning from side to side of or revolving in one case and derangement in the other. The eyes of cuckoos are said to turn red in spring. But if the meaning be the passing of the pupil from one eye to the other then it is rather the crows and not the kokilās that are supposed to have one pupil only for both the eyes; and such confusion of things may well be expected from the Vidū.; *cf. infra.* अस्ति नगरं ब्रह्मदत्तं नाम &c p. 46.

ईदृश एव भव—Said in joke by the maid who knew how gluttonous the Vid. was. Be like that, so that you will not eat so voraciously and make yourself ill. **प्रमदवनं**— see *supra* p 22. **शेफालिका०**—गुल्मकाः clumps or clusters of; शेफालिका— शेरते शेफाः bees अस्यां;—is a small tree, Nyctanthes arbourtristes) with rough scabrous leaves but flowers that have a very sweet fragrance. Its delicate orange and white blossoms impart a very sweet perfume to the evening air and fall down in clusters. **प्रवालान्तरितैः**—intermixed with corals; because the stems of these flowers look like corals; *cf.* 'वृन्तैः क्षुद्रप्रवालस्थगितमिव तलं भाति शेफालिकानां;' Priya. II. 2. **आचिता०**—densely filled with.

P. 28. **अर्धमनःशिला०**—मनःशिला is red arsenic. पट्टक pieces or tablets. The comp. must be taken as in the com; अर्धं part of which (referring to the stems which are red) resembles &c; otherwise it is difficult to see the propriety of **अर्ध. मा अवचित्य**—see *ante* remark on मान्यचिन्तयित्वा p. 23. **अय्यपुत्तो** (आर्यपुत्रः) **इह** &c.—A grammatical irregularity. The cons. being passive we should expect **अय्यउत्तेन.** Or the use of the Nom. may be defended by supposing that in Prākrit the case of a word also, like its लिंग and वचन, depends on the will of the speaker, and that the Nom. be translated by the Inst. in Sanskrit. **संमानिता भवेयम्**—Because she expected her husband to congratulate her on her favourite trees being richly laden with flowers. *Cf.* the desire of Dhâriṇī in the Māl. to see the wealth of flowers of her favourite Aśoka tree in company of her husband. ('इच्छामि आर्यपुत्रेण सहाशोकवृक्षस्य प्रसूनलक्ष्मीं प्रत्यक्षीकर्तुम् ।' V. p. 91. **प्रियस्ते भर्ता**—you love your husband since you say so (expect to be complimented upon by your husband); or it may be taken as a question. Do you love your husband (so much as to think so) ?

उत्कण्ठिता—उत्कण्ठा अस्याः संजाता Mark the modesty and nobility of Pad.'s mind. She does not directly say 'yes' but answers like a well-bred maiden and her Cheṭī compliments her on this.

P. 29. **दुष्करं करोमि**—*i. e.* Being separated from my husband. **यथा मम**—Mark the girlish simplicity of Padmâvatī. **अतोऽप्यधिकं**—Vāsava's extreme love for her husband again makes her forget that she was living *incognito* and not tolerating Pad.'s querry, tells her that no other woman's love for her husband would approach hers She, however, displays a rare readiness of wit which enables her to explain away her blunders in a clever way. **परित्यजति**—परित्यजेत् would not have abandoned. **साधु**—eleverly, so as to induce him to teach you.

P. 30. **प्रचितपातित**—&c. For the comp. see com.; if वाद be translated by पात the meaning becomes somewhat obscure. It may be taken to mean:—on account of the scanty falling of the B. flowers those that had fallen being collected together or gathered. The reading नवविवर्धितविरलसम्पात० is the best.

Śl 1. In this śl. the king poetically expresses his inability tc account for the love he felt for Pad. when he had already bestowed al his love on Vāsavadattā. Construe—तदा उज्जयिनीं गते अवन्तिराजतनयां स्वैर दृष्ट्वा कामप्यवस्थां गते मयि कामेन &c. **स्वैरं**—At will, unchecked. Marl the Sandhi स्व + ईर् = स्वैरं by the Vârt. 'स्वादिरेरिणोः'. **पञ्च इषवः**—Sans. poets describe Kāma as armed with five arrows; they consist of flowers; hence he is also called कुसुमेषु. कुसुमसायक, कुसुमशर &c. *cf.* 'अरविन्दमशोकं च चूतं च नवमल्लिका। नीलोत्पलं च पञ्चैते पञ्चबाणस्य सायकाः।' Sometimes other kinds of arrows are also mentioned, *viz.* 'उन्मादनस्तापनश्च शोषणः स्तम्भनस्तथा। संमोहनश्च कामस्य पञ्च बाणाः प्रकीर्तिताः ॥' **सशल्यं**—शल्यैः सहितं all the five arrow-heads being yet in. What the king means this—since all the arrows were, yet there, none being withdrawn, Kāma must have used a sixth shaft to wound his heart anew; and this is wonderful. 'पथिकजनयुवतिलक्ष्यः पञ्चाभ्यधिकः शरो भव।' Śāk. VI. is compared by some as containing a similar idea, but there the meaning of पञ्चाभ्यधिकः is doubtful, see our note *ad loc.*

The same idea is more powerfully and elegantly expressed by S'rīharsa in his Ratnā. III. 3. **असन**—अस्यति रुतमित्यसनः *m.*, name of a tree also called पीतसाल and सर्जक. **सञ्चितं**—Bestrewed with. **कटुकसप्तच्छद**—सप्तच्छद having seven leaves per twig, hence also called सप्तपर्ण-पत्र &c., सप्तच्छद Alstonia scholares, is a large tree, having a very strong odour like that of the ichor of elephants and is often referred to by Sans. poets. *cf.* सप्तच्छदक्षीरकटु (fragrant) प्रवाहं Ragh. V. 48. **दारुपर्वतक**—A wooden structure resembling a hill. with bowers &c., similar to क्रीडापर्वतक. It occures in Av. **प्रसादित**—washed clean, probably the reading is प्रसारिद (प्रसारित) outstretched प्रसाधित (प्रसाधिद) 'decorated' is another reading here. The poet seems to be an admirer of Balarāma.

P. 31. **समाहितं**—Adv. in a well formed (compact) mass or line (in whatever situation it may be). समाहिता *V. l.*—adj. well formed.

S'l. 2. **ऋज्वायतां**—*i. e.* sometime moving straight in a mass, sometime isolated from one another. सप्तर्षिवंश—वंश family *i. e.* group; the constellation of Ursa-Major or Great Bear. **विरला**—As the group of birds in the front turned back and others followed, the whole mass became curved in shape and being compact looked like the Saptarṣis. **निर्मुच्यमान** &c.—*i. e.* when the slough is cast off. **विभज्यमाना**—The line was so long that when it moved away it looked like the boundary line of the sky being separated from it. **कोकनद**—means here a large white lotus. **अम्मो भर्ता**—We expect before this the stage direction दृष्ट्वा. **आर्ये, तव कारणात्**—Because herself she was anxious to see her husband, see *supra* आर्यपुत्रेण संमानिता भवेयं.

P. 32. **पद्मावती इहागत्य** &c.—Mark how the apparently careless Vidū. is often a keen observer of things. **कुसुमस्य**—Sing. for the pl., **विच्चिता**—*Cf. supra* प्रवालान्तरितैरिव &c. p. 27. **अवचित०**—अवचितानि कुसुमानि येभ्य:–from which some flowers have been plucked off; as the bunches of flowers were deprived of some of their flowers they could easily attract Vidú.'s notice. From this Vidū. concludes that Pad. must have visited the spot and plucked off the flowers, as no one else could have plucked them off without her order.

वसन्तकसंकीर्तनेन &c.—When Udayana had been captured by a stratagem and kept a prisoner in his place by king Pradyota of Ujjayinī, and asked to teach music to his daughter Vāsavadattā, Yaugandharāyaṇa his minister, accompanied by Vasantaka, went to Ujjayinī to effect his release. When he reached Ujjayinī, he by his magic power altered his appearance and also gave Vasantaka a deformed shape. Thus disguised they easily found access to the apartment of the princess. There Yaugan. revealed his identity as well as that of Vasan. to Udayana; and telling him how to make good his escape, left him leaving Vasan. in the palace for the entertainment of his master and of Vāsavadattā See Katha's. Tar. XII. 38-77. Here Vāsa. is put in mind of those days. See Priy. III, 6 and our note thereon. **शरत्कालतीक्ष्ण:**—The unbearableness of the heat of the autumnal sun is also referred to by S'rīharṣa. *Cf.* 'अहो अतिदारुणता शरदातपस्य;' Priy. I. p. 5; 'अधिकं खलु शरदातपेन संतप्तानि अद्यापि मेऽङ्गानि' &c., *ibid* III. p. 26. 'शरदातपजनितोऽयं मे सन्तापोऽधिकतरं बाधते ।' Nāg. II. p. 27.

मधुकरपरि०—should properly be परिनिलीनमधुकरां; so the comp. must be explained as belonging to the आहिताग्न्यादि class, wherein the adj. may optionally come latter in a comp.; *e. g.* आहिताग्नि: or अग्न्याहित:. see Pāṇ. II. 2. 37. **आकुलं कर्तुकाम:**—Wishing to throw into confusion, to upset everything '(referring to their plan to avoid the sight of the king).

अवलम्बलतां—अवलम्बभूता लता अव० the principal creeper at the entrance to the bower which also supported the other creepers that formed the bower. **मधुकर०**—is significant. The idea of the Cheṭī was that the bees being disturbed might move about and thus prevent the king from entering the bower.

P. 33. **अविधा**—Also written 'as अविहा is probably a corrupt form of अवेह (अव इह protect me here); hence used as a particle in the sense of help, help, when one is in distress; or 'hold hold' (do not do it) when there is some danger, &c. **दास्याःपुत्रैः**—*Lit.* the sons of a slave girl; hence used as a term of abuse or contempt; in this case the *aluk* is optional, by ' पुत्रे अन्यतरस्याम् ' Pâṇ. VI. 3. 22, so दासीपुत्रैः also will do; 'निन्दायां किम् । ब्राह्मणीपुत्रः' (alone); Sid. Kau This is Vidû.'s humorous way of referring to things or persons he does not like or wants to despise. *Cf.* ' एते दास्याःपुत्रा अर्थकल्यवर्ताः ' Mṛch. I. p. 13; 'दास्याः पुत्रं बन्धनहतकं' Priy. I. p. 6. 'एषा दास्याः सुतेन्दीवरिका;' ibid p 21.

S'l. 3. **कला**—uttering sweet but indistinct hums; as the bees were disturbed they moved about humming sweetly. Kāli, also describes the bees as drinking the wine of honey in the company of their mates; *cf.* ' मधु द्विरेफः कुसुमैकपात्रे पपौ प्रियां स्वामनुवर्तमानः । ' Kum. III. 36; *cf.* also Nāg. III 8 (पिबन्तः पर्याप्तं सह सहचरीभिर्मधुरसं &c.). **विषण्णाः**—disturbed, scared away. **वयमिव**—The king speaks here as a *Virahî* and says कान्तावियुक्ताः and not भार्यावियुक्ताः; Vāsa. was his Kāntà (the dearly loved one). His real view of his marriage with Padmâvatī is that expressed in V. 1. (पुनरागतदारभारः).

पादाक्रान्तानि &c.—This śl. is inserted here after T. Ganapati S'astri, as it is quoted in the Nâṭyadarpaṇa as from the S. Vaps., and as this seems to be its proper place. See foot-note. The learned S'āstrī thinks that its omission from the Mss. must be due to the oversight of the first copyist. **पुष्पाणि**—*i. e.* the stray S'ephālikā flowers lying on the ground near the stone-slab.

प्रकृतिस्थशरीरः—Vāsa. must have cast a hurried glance at the king and hence her remark and joy at the restoration of her lord health.

P. 34. **अविनयात्**—On account of the rudeness or impudent behaviour of—in that they trod heavily on the Kāśa flowers and caused the pollen to drop down unexpectedly. Mark Vāsa.'s ready-wittedness again.

शून्यमिदं &c.—Mark the poet's ingenuity introducing this scene. It serves the double purpose of impressing Vâsa. with the Heroe's unshaken love for her and of bringing out vividly the magnanimity of Padmāvatī and the utter absence of jealousy on her part as a सपत्नी. **प्रिया**—Object of real love; or it is equivalent to प्रियतरा. **बहुमान-संकटे**—The difficulty as regards the declaration of 'high regard for.' He means—you are putting me into an extremely awkward position—To say 'I love Vâsa. more' would be offending Padmāvatî To say 'I love Pad. more' would be going against my conscience.

यादृशे &c.—The sentence is incomplete; see com. **अहमपि** &c—for the fears that the king might easily speak against her, being supposed to be dead. **मुखर:**—given to heedless talking and hence would tell Pad. if I tell the truth.

सत्येन श०—This is a solemn form of taking an oath; *cf.* Shakes.—'by my troth' and 'शपामि सत्येन भयं न जाने।' Mad. Vyā. **संदष्टा**—bitten; that it should not get unruly—said joculary.

P. 35. **पुरोभागिता:**—पुरो भाग: अस्यास्तीति पुरोभागी (also—भाग:, fem. भागा); one who takes or claims a share first; hence one who wishes to have or insists on having a thing done first (this underlies a variety of meanings that the word has); hence पुरोभागिता here means—obstinacy of purpose or persistence in; or officiousness, forwardness. One who claims a share first is also jealous of another; hence पुरोभाग also means jealous, or envious of, unbearing; *cf.* 'प्राय: समानविद्या: परस्परयश:पुरोभागा: ।' Mâl. I. 20; for tha meaning of naughty, self-willed, *cf.* 'किं पुरोभागे स्वातन्त्र्यमवलम्बसे।' S'âk. V. p. 135.

का गति:—The King was helpless now that the Vidû. took his stand on his friendship with him.

Śl. 5. **माधुर्य**—Amiableness, sweetness of address; or the collective beauty or general attractiveness of form; *cf.* 'अहो मधुरमासां दर्शनम्' S'âk. I. p. 18. **तावत्** indeed; verily; न हरति तावत्; or fully (साकल्येन) तावन्न हरति.

वेतनं—Wages; hence compensation.

बहुगुण:—has brought many advantages, for it facilitated Pad.'s marriage with the king; secondly she had opportunities to know how noble-minded and innocent Pad. was; thirdly she had the satisfaction of hearing conversations about her lord; and fourthly she now heard actually from the lips of her husband how passionately she was still loved by him. **सदाक्षिण्य एव** &c.—One more instance of Padmā.'s nobility and utter freedom from jealousy. Even Vāsava. marks this and compliments her saying अहो अभिजातस्य &c.

P. 36. **विप्रलपितेन**—(1) Prattling or idle talk; (2) talking too much. **मा श्रुत्वा**—*i. e.* my real opinion. **महाब्राह्मण**—The king being in a vein of humour addresses Vidúṣaka as such. In later Sansk. this word came to have a bad meaning and was applied to an illiterate Brah. and in contempt.

प्रत्युद्गच्छति—Welcomes me saying. Some editions add वासवदत्ता after प्रत्युद्गच्छति; this is bad, as it spoils the sense. For Vasantaka is now praising Padmāvatī and his words अयं गुणः must refer to her. So if we read वासवदत्ता after प्रत्युद्गच्छति it must be taken as beginning a new sentence, the preceding sentence ending with प्रत्युद्गच्छति, with Padmāvatî as its subject, and the sentence will read as वासवदत्ता कुत्र नु खलु गत आर्यवसन्तक इति मां प्रत्युद्गच्छति (Vāsa. welcomes me merely by asking &c.) which has no sense, as Vāsavadattā is quite dead to Vidûṣaka.

स्मर इदानीं &c.—*i. e.* Keep it up very well in your memory, as you will have to repent one day for having said so.

P. 37. **अविधा**—has here the force of 'alas!' for its original meaning see *supra* P. 33.

S'l. 5. **व्याक्षिप्तं** — Drawn away from *i. e.* made oblivious of reality, and I thought I was living in the company of Vāsavadattā. **तथैव**—*i. e.* as when Vāsa. lived. **कथायोगः**—The course of conversation or story. She means—The king would have gone on talking about Vāsavadattā and said something more about her and thus forgotten his sorrow for some time more. **अप्रत्यक्षं**—and hence indicative of true love. **धारयतु**—supply आत्मानं.

S'l. 6. **दुःखं त्यक्तुं** &c.—Mark the use of दुःखं (adv.) with अनुरागः; it is to be explained like 'विषवृक्षोऽपि संवर्ध्य स्वयं च्छेत्तुमसांप्रतम् ।' Kum. II. 55, where Malli. says—स्वयं छेत्तुमसांप्रतमनर्हः; so here दुःखं is equivalent to असुकरः. He further observes 'असांप्रतमित्यनेन निपातेन' (adv.) 'अभिहितत्वाद् वृक्ष इति द्वितीयान्तो न भवति अनभिहिते कर्मणि द्वितीयाभिधा-

नात् । यथाह वामनः—'निपातेनाप्यभिहिते कर्मणि न कर्मविभक्तिः । परिगणनस्य प्रायिकत्वात् । ' *i. e.* as the relation of the object and verb is expressed here by the particle असांप्रतं विषवृक्ष is put in the Nomi. case; but when the relation is not expressed (Pāṇ. II. 3. 1–2) the object is put in the acc. case. For the full explanation see our note ad *loc.*; *cf.* for similar uses—'शक्यमालिङ्गितुं पवनः ।' S'āk. III. 5; 'नहि देहभृता शक्यं त्यक्तुं कर्माणि (pl.) अशेषतः ।' Bhag. XVIII. 21. Mah. Maho. Ganapati S'astri gives a stranga explanation of this, he says—' अनुरागः पद्मावतीविषयः प्रेमा ॥ दुःखं वासवदत्ताविरहव्यथां त्यक्तुं शमयितुं. (२) बद्धमूलः बद्धं रचितमर्थान्मया मूलं दृढावस्थानाधारो यस्य स तथाभूतः । जात इति शेषः । ' **स्मृत्वा स्मृत्वा**—A peculiarity of Bhāsa's style; properly स्मृत्वा has for its subject दुःखं; but this makes no sense; so it must be taken as equivalent to पुनः पुनः स्मरणेन.

P. 38. **यात्रा**—Course of nature; way of life. **विमुच्येत**—*v. l.* is better from a grammatical point of view. **प्राप्तानृण्या**—see com.; when tears are shed the debt of sorrow is paid off as it were. *cf.* 'शोकक्षोभे च हृदयं प्रलापैरेव धार्यते ।' Uttar. III. 29 and the introductory sentence to this—' सांप्रतिकमेवैतत् । कर्तव्यानि दुःखितैर्दुःखनिर्वापणानि । ' **मुखोदकं**—मुखार्थमुदकं (a comp. of the शाकपार्थिवादि class) water for (washing) the mouth. **बाष्पाकुलपट०**—full of tears and so concealed with a veil (as it were); see com; the reading बाष्पपटलान्तरितं means concealed with the mass of tears. But as it is difficult to imagine how the king could not have noticed the ladies passing away although his eyes were full of tears, it is better to translate this as ' covered with the hem of his garment wet of tears '. The Vidū. also says above that the face was moist with tears. T. Ganapati S'āstrī also says मार्जनवस्त्राच्छादितम्. **एतदिदम्**—Mark the Vidū.'s confusion on seeing Padmā. unexpectedly. He, however, soon recovers his self-possession and readiness of wit and explains away the matter in his next speech, वातनीतेन &c.

P. 39. **सदाक्षिण्यस्य**—Of one polite or respecting the feelings of others. Padmàvatī admires the desire of Vidū. to avoid saying anything that might have pained her. Or दाक्षिण्य may mean ' cleverness ' **जयत्वार्यपुत्रः**—Read after this इदं मुखोदकं (इदं मुहोदअं) left out by oversight. **अपवार्य**—the stage direction extends to राजा साधु वसन्तक.।

S'l. 7. **शरच्छशांक०**—The pollen of the Kāśa flowers is compared to the autumnal moon as it is very white. The epithet, however, has no propriety here. भामिनी A beautiful young woman having a (lustrous complexion). This s'l. is cited, as from the Svap., in Vāmana's Kāvy. Sūtras under व्याजोक्ति with the reading, शरच्चन्द्रांशु (which is better) and कृतं for मम. Daṇḍin cites the following as an instance of 'लेशालंकार-आनन्दाश्रु प्रवृत्तं मे कथं दृष्ट्वैव कन्यकाम्। अक्षि मे पुष्परजसा वातोद्धूतेन दूषितम् ॥' II. 267.

S'l. 8. **कामं**—Granted (admitting) that. **स्त्रीस्व०**—But after all, she is a woman, and may feel pained. **उचितं** &c.—Mark the Vidū.'s ingenuity again in extricating his master from an awkward situation. Padmā.'s sudden appearance had embarrassed the king and he could not have been long in her company with any grace. Vasan. sees this and thus comes to his master's rescue.

P. 40. **सत्कारो** &c.—He means—As the Mag. king honours you by giving you the precedence, so you too ought to honour him by being at his side. **प्रथमः**—Prime *i. e.* excellent. **कल्पः**—Thought, idea; constantly occurs in Sans plays.

S'l. 9. **गुणानां**—is used in the sense of excellent deeds or results; benefits; *cf.* for this sense—'उपरतस्य तु न कमपि गुणमावहति।' Kād. I. p. 265; 'गुणमहतां महते गुणाय (उत्कर्षाय Malli.) योगः।' Kir. X 25 **विज्ञातारः**–*i. e.* those who properly appreciate the good done and honour shown by them.

ACT. V

This Act is the outcome of the poet's fancy. The incidents mentioned herein are intended to bring the king and Vāsa. fancied to be seen in a dream, together.

केवलं &c.—Because she knew what love subsisted between the two.

P. 41. **समुद्रगृहके**—It is difficult to see what this exactly means. It was probably a summer-house or a pleasure-house surrounded by jets of water (मुद्राभिः सहितं समुद्रं गृहं) built in the palace garden. 'समुद्रगृहमित्युक्तं जलयन्त्रनिकेतनम्।' Hāravalī. It is mentioned in the poet's Prati. II. where Daśaratha is mentioned as lying in it. The Vidū. in Kāli.'s

Māl. IV. also places Mālavikā and her friend in a समुद्रगृह and goes to call the king. See Māl. p. 74. **समीरितस्य**—Excited; because he was at once put in mind of Vāsava. by the never fading माला and तिलक with which Padmā. was decked by Āvantikā. See the extract from the Kathā. (' अथासन्नविवाहायाः-अम्लानमालातिलकौ दिव्यौ भूयश्चकार सा ॥ '). **समीरितः**—The reading समीर्यमाणः mentioned by Prof. Devadhar qualifying ०दाहः is better.

P. 42. **आगतदारभारः**—indicates that he considered his second marriage as burdensome to himself; see com. **पद्मिनीं हिमहतामिव**— The comparison of a lotus-plant struck down by frost seems to have found favour with the later poet's; *cf.* ' हिमसेकविपत्तिरत्र मे नलिनी पूर्वनिदर्शनं मता । ' Ragh. VIII. 45; ' जातां मन्ये तुहिनमथितां पद्मिनीं वान्यरूपाम् । ' Megh. II. 23.

P. 43. **रूपश्रिया**—रूपस्य श्रीः the exuberance or splendour of beauty. **समुदितां**—Blazing or radiant with. Bhàsa generally uses this word in the sense of ' possessed of ' **मन्द इव**—something like मन्द, a little abated.

०सरुजोऽपि—See com; अपि is connected with मन्दः. **तथैव**—Just like Vāsavadattá. **अनुभूतदुःखः**—gives the reason why he expects a similar fate to overtake पद्मावती. The fig. of speech therefore is काव्यलिङ्ग (पदार्थहेतुक).

P. 44. **वैधेयः**—a fool or block-head; विधेयं विधानं तस्यायमधिकारी. One fit for executing orders or another's bidding; fr. विधेय+अ (अण्).

Śl. 3. **मुखतोरण०**—तोरण an arched door; also an outer door or gateway; ' तोरणोऽस्त्री बहिर्द्वारम् ' Amara. **लोल**—dangling about and (fallen down). **निशि**—and so not distinctly seen.

Śl. 4. **आस्तृतसमा**—May also be taken as ' किंतु) तथा आस्तृतसमा च; आस्तृतं ' (its being spread) समं यस्याः (such compounds are a peculiarity of Bhâsa); or ' आस्तृता चासौ समा च '. **क्लिष्टं**—spoiled, made dirty; for this sense *cf.* ' क्लिष्टेनोत्तमवाससा क्लिष्टं कौशेयवसनां; ' Rámà. Sund. XV XX; &c. **रोगे** सति when there is disease, *i. e.* one is ill. **शिरोपधानं**—शिर *m.* is of rare occurrence; see com. **रुजा**—रुजं *v. l.* is governed by प्राप्य getting ill. रुजा is better.

P. 45. **हों**—also हुं; a sound, used as a particle expressive of attention to a story, assent, &c. *Cf.* 'रामो नाम बभूव हुं तदबला सीतेति हुं' (said by Krisṇa.) &c. **इति करोतु**—Mark the child-like simplicity of Vidú.; उदकस्नानानि—Even in the mouth of the Vidū. this reading has no propriety. The other reading उदयज्ञानानि adopted by Mr. Bhide is better. उदय stands for उदयन and ज्ञानानि means marks or signs, (keeping up the memory) of Udayana It is natural for Vidū. to refer to the achievements of his master when in Ujjayinī Kālidâsa speaks of these in the Meg when he says 'प्रद्योतस्य प्रियदुहितरं वत्सराजोऽत्र जह्रे; अत्रोद्भ्रान्तः किल नडगिरिः—' &c. I. 34. This may also have the side-meaning of—'The means of knowing the rise of the heavenly bodies as Ujjayinī was noted for its observatories.

अवन्त्याधिपतेः—This apparently ungrammatical form must be explained as 'अवन्त्याः आ समन्तादधिपतिः अवन्त्याधिपतिः; or अवन्त्या हेतुना अधिपतिः,, अवन्या' being तृतीया हेत्वर्थे like गवां स्वामी, धन्येन धनी &c.; see com. **सुतायाः**—स्मृ in the sense of to remember with regret governs its object in the Gen.; see com. and A. G. § 113.

प्रस्थानकाले—*i. e.* When Udayana started clandestinely with Vâsava. from Ujjayinī to go to his capital.

S'l. 6. **उपदेशेषु**—During the times of instruction. **स्रस्तकोणेन**—While engaged in looking steadfastly at Vatsarāja Vāsa. did not notice when the fiddle-stick dropped from her hand; and quite unmindful of the fact she moved her hand in the air as though playing on the instrument.

P. 46. **नगरं ब्रह्मदत्तं नाम**—Vidū. confounds the name of the king with that of the city and ***vice versa.*** This apparent confusion is due to Vidū.'s characteristic forgetfulness. **ब्रह्मदत्त**—A king of Vārāṇasī, named Branmadatta is often referred to in the Jātaka stories. But he is not meant here. The king referred to must be a king of the Pânchāla race (who according to Prof. Bhide must have flourished about 300 years before Buddha) as Kâmpilya was the ancient capital of the Panchâla country where the Svayamvara of Draupadī was held. Kāmpilya corresponds with the Kāmpila of modern times, situated in the Doab on the old Ganges between Badāūn and Farukhabad. **ओष्ठगतं**—Deep-seated on the lips, so that his lips might utter the names correctly, being used to them even though his memory might fail him.

P. 47. **अकरुणाः खलु** &c—see *supra* p. 23. **एषा पद्मावती** &c.—

It is strange that Vásava. should have mistaken the king for Padmâvatī. It may be that the night being very chilly the king was covered with a mantle from head to foot. But again it is difficult to understand how Vāsava. could find out that she was ॰सुखनिश्वासा, if the nose and the mouth were covered up. **किं नु खलु** &c.—Although Vâsava. did not know that Udayana was there, she suddenly felt refreshed owing to the secret working of her mind that was linked with her husband's; *cf.* Kâli. ' मनो हि जन्मान्तरसंगतिज्ञम् ' Ragh. VII. 12. **एकदेश॰**—Because she had occupied half of the bed and left the other half for being occupied by her friend.

P. 48. **हम्**—expresses surprise. **महान्यौगन्ध॰**—For the discovery of the identity of Vâsava. would have upset the whole plan of Yaugandharāyana, although it had succeeded so far that the matrimonial alliance with the king of Magadha was formed. For Darśaka, the king of Magadha, would have been incensed on knowing the fraud played upon him and would have refused to help the ministers in winning back the lost kingdom of the Vatsa king. It was, therefore, absolutely necessary for Vâsava. to remain *incognito* until the enemy was vanquished and the Vatsa kingdom restored to Udayana. For Yau.'s plan see *supra* p. 10.

दिष्ट्या—Vāsava. was glad that she was not recognised.

आलपामि भर्तः &c.—The replies of Vāsa. must be considered as स्वगत or uttered in a suppressed voice. The king does not hear them. **इतः परं किम्**—may mean ' what ornament can I have beyond this *i. e* yourself ?"—that being the real ornament of woman. **विरचिकां**—According to the Kathâ. Virachikā was a female attendant of the harem with whom Udayana had a love intrigue. One day he addressed Vâsava. by her name and had to propitiate her by prostrating himself at her feet. See Kathâ II. 6. 65. 66.

P. 49. S'l. 7. **द्वारपक्षः**—The panel of a door **भूतार्थोऽयं** &c. may also be taken as ' अयं वासवदत्तादर्शनरूपः भूतार्थः ' (a reality) **मनोरथः** (a mere desire-fancy) **वा. धरते**—The correct form is **ध्रियते**. Bhása, however, uses the root as a root of the first Conj.; *cf.* ' नष्टाः शरीरे क्रतुभिर्धरन्ते' Panch. I 23; 'हतेषु देहेषु गुणा धरन्ते ।' Karn. 17. It is after this incident, *viz.* the King's seeing Vāsava. in a dream that the play is named **स्वप्न॰**, but not very appropriately or judiciously. See Intro **असम्भा॰**—The delusion of न improves the sense. With न the mean-ting will be '**इद तव वासवदत्तादर्शनं असंभावनीयं**' inconceivable **न; संभाव-नीयं** (can be conceived, explained) **एवं.**

P. 50. S'l. 9. **धन्यं** &c.—'**अप्रतिबोधनं धन्यं स्यात्.**' It will be a blessing not to be roused &c.;

विभ्रमोस्तु &c.—For in either case I shall long enjoy Vāsa.'s company.

अस्मिन्नगरे—The reading राजकुले should have been preferred. It seems that the presence of Avantikā in the place was kept off from the knowledge of the king and his attendants. Vidū. seems to have simply heard that there was a beautiful lady of Avantī in the apartment of the princess, and that she was a Yankṣiñī.

S'l 10. **नेत्रविप्रो०**—see com.; विप्रोषित entirely cast off **चारित्र्यं**–see *supra* I. 11. p 9.

S'l. 11. **संत्रस्तया**—Alarmed, flurried (at the thought of being discovered). **निपीडितः**—firmly sciezd; *cf.* for this sense **पाणि; बाल्ये बालेन पीडितः** Uttar VII. 5. *Cf.* with this rather tame description, Bhavabhūti's description of the effects produced on Rāma by the touch of S'ītā's hand—' आलिम्पन्नमृतयैरिव प्रलेपैः ' &c. III. 39. **रोमहर्ष**—The joy *i. e.* bristling up of the hair, horripilation (रोमाञ्च). This is one of the eight *sâtvika* bhâvas *viz.* 'स्तम्भप्रलयरोमाञ्चाः स्वेदो वैवर्ण्यवेपथू। अश्रुवैस्वर्य-मित्यष्टौ।' D. Rup.

मेदानीं &c.—Bhâsa's peculiarity; see *supra* note on मेदानीमन्य० p. 23. **अनर्थे**—Here अनर्थे may mean a calamity or misfortune; or what is without purpose (नास्ति अर्थः यस्मात्) or advantage.

P. 51. **आरुणि**—Nothing is known about this Āruñi. Somadeva in his Kathā. does not refer to him nor to the loss of the Vatsa-kingdom. It is, however difficult to imagine how Bhāsa could have invented name and incidents of such moment. So the story or the usurpation of the Vātsa country by some king Āruṇi by name must have been current in the day of Bhâsa; being an event of short duration it was not probably recorded by Gunādhya.

हस्त्यश्वरथ०--These were the four constituents of the ancient Indian army. As these are taken distributively there is no **समाहारद्वंद्व.** **विजयाङ्गानि**—विजयावहानि अङ्गानि (which stands for सेनाङ्गानि) विज-याङ्गानि the parts of the army each contributing to victory. **संनद्धानि**–*Lit.* armoured, fully equipped or ready for fighting.

भिन्नास्ते रिपवः—Separated by discord. This is one of the favourable circumstances for a canquerer to lead a campaign against his enemy. *Cf.* Kir. II. 52. (लघुवृत्तितया भिदां गतं—नृपस्य मण्डलं । &c.). and ' स्फीतं यदानुरक्तं च भवेत्प्रकृतिमण्डलम् । परस्य विपरीतं च तदा विग्रहमाचरेत् ॥' Kām. N. X. 28, also 30.

पार्ष्णी—The usual word is पार्ष्णिः *m.* (according to Amara) *m. f.* according to रन्तिदेव—' पार्ष्णिः स्त्रीपुंसयोः पादमूले स्याद् ध्वजिनीकटौ' It means the year of an invading king. The present word is derived from पार्ष्णि f. by adding the fem. ई by the Vārti. ' कृदिकारादक्तिनः '

विधानं कृतं—A conqueror must see that proper measures are taken to protect his own country from attack by a hostile king in his absence. See Kām. quoted in the com; and Ragh. IV. 26.

०प्रमाथजननं—जनयतीति जननं *fr.* जन् and अन् (ल्युट्) added कर्तरि (in the sense of the agent); प्रमाथस्य जननं (causing) प्रमाथजननं. **त्रिपथगात्रीन्** पथो गच्छतीति; or त्रयाणां पथां समाहारः त्रिपथं तेन गच्छतीति; *cf.* 'क्षितौ तारयते मर्त्यान्नागांस्तारयतेप्यधः । दिवि तारयते देवांस्तेन त्रिपथगा स्मृता' The course in the three worlds are called मन्दाकिनी, भागिरथी and भोगवती respectively.

S'l. 13. **नागेन्द्रतुरङ्ग** &c.—For comp. see com.; (1) fought by means of huge elephants and cavalry; (2) in which move sea-elephants and hippopotamuses. **विकीर्णबाणो०**—The volleys of arrows discharged by different warriors and flying at different heights or levels and hence resembling waves; unless we suppose so the comparison will not stand as the arrows fly in a straight and not in a curved line.

ACT VI.

—:*:—

P. 52. **काञ्चुकीयः**—This is the Chamberlain of Mahāsena sent to Udayana, who must be supposed to have returned to his capital after regaining his kingdom.

क इह &c.—The third act of Abhi. and the sixth of Prat. open similarly. **तोरण** (*m. n.*)—The outer gate of the palace. **अशून्यं**—*Lit.* not vacant; *i. e.* is in attendance at. **रैभ्य**—It is difficult to know who this रैभ्य was. But as he specially mentions him by way of introducing himself to the king it seems he was a well-known bard (fr. रेभः a praiser; रेभस्य अपत्यं पुमान्) or more probably an old trusty Kanch.. at the court of Mahāsena when Udayana was there. **अङ्गारवती**—So called because she was the daughter of a *daitya,* named अङ्गारक who, in the form of a boar decoyed Mahâsena to his den but was slain by him, by the help of his daughter. See Kathā. **अदेशकालः**—See com.; here the sense of अ is अप्राशंस्त्य impropriety or unfitness ('अप्राशस्त्यं विरोधश्च नञर्थाः षट् प्रकीर्तिताः ।'). **प्रतीहारस्य**—Of the person at the door; by using the *mas.* gender she intimates that neither she nor any other door-keeper can make the communication; or प्रतीहार may be taken in the sense of the message to be conveyed by a door-keeper. **नाम**—has the sense of 'possibly, I should like to know'.

सूर्यामुखप्रा०–It is difficult to know what the name of the palace really was. The text seems to be much corrupt here. According to Prof. Devadhar the name should be read as सुयामुनप्रा० (सुयामुणप्पा०—the reading found in the Mss. consulted by him); the palace commanding a good view of the Jamunā. सूर्यामुख may have also been सूर्याभिमुख० the palace facing the sun in the morning *i. e.* the east. सूर्यामु० according to M. M. Ganapatiśāstrî means—the palace having a wooden or stone image of सूर्या (the goddess presiding over a marriage) on its front wall. See com. Another meaning assigned by the S'āstrī to Sūryā is नवोढा (a maiden newly married). He says 'सूर्याया नवोढाया अर्थात्पद्मावत्याः मुखप्रासादं प्रासादपुरोभागं गतेन। देवक्या सूर्यया सार्धं (भाग० स्कं. १० अ. १) इति श्लोकव्याख्यायां सूर्यया नवोढया इति श्रीधरः।' Another reading is सय्यामुहप्पा० (शय्यामुखप्रा०) which may mean—The palace having the sleeping apartment in the front. **घोषवती**—'प्रशस्तः घोषोऽस्या विद्यते इति ।' *Lit.* having an enchanting sound. Name of the magic lute obtained by Udayana from Vasunemi, the brother of Vāsuki, whom he had saved from a S'abara when a boy. See Kathā. II. 1. 78-81. It was by this lute that Udayana charmed elephants and subdued them. The other two gifts obtained by him were the art of weaving an unfading garland and decorating the forehead with marks that never lost their freshness.

P. 53. **बाष्पपर्या०**—पर्याकुलोच्छूनमुखेन *v. l.*; उच्छून p. p. p. of श्वि with उत्; swollen; but this has no propriety. ०च्छूननेत्रेण would have been appropriate.

विष्कम्भकः—This is Viṣ. which shows in a few words the connection between parts of the story past and to follow, by means of the conversation of characters other than the chief ones. It is शुद्ध when carried on by one or more minor characters and मिश्र or mixed when expressed by characters minor and low. See com.

P. 54. S'l. 1. **श्रुतिसुखनिनदे**—Another reading is मधुरे; but मधुर after सुख is redundant. **विहगगण॰**—It is not a good way to take the com. as विहगगणेन रजसा &c. as the comp. becomes irregular; we may dissolve विहगगणस्य as in the com., or ॰गणोत्पन्नं रजस्तेन &c. **प्रतिभयं**—frightful; occurs constantly in the Mh. bhā. वनं प्रतिभयाकरं; Sāv. Up. V. 78; वनं प्रतिभयं शून्यं Nalopā. XII. 1. &c; it may be an adv., as in 'तां श्रिता. (शिवाः) प्रतिभयं ववासिरे' Ragh. X. 61, or an adj. qualifying अरण्यवासम्. Some read **अप्रतिभयं** adv. without being afraid of any one. अविद्यमानं प्रतिभयं यथा स्यात्तथा.

तपस्विन्या—is connected with ॰निपीडितानि &c. **खेद॰**—should better bave been खेदे (for symmetry with विरहे in the next line) स्तना॰. **वाद्यान्तरेषु**—अन्यानि वाद्यानि वाद्यान्तराणि तेषु in the intervals of musical tunes or notes. कथितानि—may mean—(1) our talks; or (2) instructions. **अलमिदानीं**—सन्तप्य—For a similar use *cf. infra* p. 50. अतिमात्रं सन्तप्य *V. l.* and 'अलमिदानीं महाराजोऽतिमात्रं सन्तप्य' Prati. II. **नवयोगा**—योग arrangement, construction, repaired by being furnished with new strings, &c.

P. 55. **किं न खलु** &c.—How possibly, indeed, is this that; or can it be indeed, that Mahā. &c. प्रियं मे &c—One more instance of Padmā.'s nobility of mind and utter absence of any feeling of jealousy. The king marks this trait of her character and says अनुरूपं &c. **वासवदत्ता॰**—Although she did not actually say this, it followed from her use of the word ज्ञातिकुल. **उदासीनमिव भ॰**—(1) It looks something like indifference (want of regard for the feelings of others) on your part; (2) I feel somewhat awkward (or disconsolate) as &c. **न श्लाघनीयं**—*V. l.* not commendable; something not to be approved of.

P. 56. **कलत्रदर्शनार्हे**—Because it is usual with Hindu parents to regard the second wife of a man as their own daughter; and *vice versa* (see Pad.'s speech below) and so their relatives also are entitled to see her. बहुदोषं—Because it bespeaks not only vanity, but also want of the knowledge of proper etiquette on the part of a man. ततोऽम्बा वा—That is the father and mother of Vāsa. whom she regards as her own parents.

S'l. 4. किं वक्ष्यतीति &c.—The same line occurs again in ś1. 15 below. महत् must be taken separately as an adv. modifying अवाप्य. The king thinks it was owing to adverse fate that he had a serious blow given to his merits in that he came to be regarded as a careless husband. Prof. Devadhar reads महदवाप्य. But even in this case महत् which has reference to magnitude and not intensity cannot appropriately be taken with उपघात. महद्भीतोऽपि sounds strange. ननु किं—is the emendation suggested by Prof. Devadhar, and followed here. The reading of the Triv. ed. is ण किं &c.; in this case न should be read separately; न एवम् । किं शक्यं &c.; or किं should be taken in the sense of किंचित्.

P. 57. S'l. 5. सम्बन्धि०—सम्बन्धी one connected by matrimonial alliance; *cf.* 'आत्मसम्बन्धो मागधः' Pratijñā. II. 8; 'सम्बन्धिनो वसिष्ठादीन्' Uttar. I. 19. यदि स्यात् &c.—The meaning is 'O Fate, you would have rendered every service to us, had there been the kingdom obtained by the king (as it has bean) and also the Queen safe! You have only half rendered the service.'

S'l. 6. राजवंश्याः—The descendants of *i. e.* Kṣatriyas belonging to royal families. उदयास्तमय—अस्तमयः fall; lit. setting; from अस्तं *adv.* and अयः (a noun from अय् to go); *cf.* for a similar idea 'उदयमस्तमयं च रघूद्वहादुभयमानशिरे वसुधाधिपाः ।' Ragh IX. 9. This shows that Pradyota was a powerful king and even the king of Magadha stood in fear of him. Prof. Devadhar finds a reference in the Majjhima Nikāya, according to which Ajātaśatru re-fortified Rājagṛha for fear of an invasion by Pradyota.

कांक्षितबान्धवः—The comp. it must be solved as कांक्षितश्चासौ बान्धवश्च । Some take it as कांक्षितं बान्धवं (relationship) यस्य or येन; but this is not satisfactory. We rarely find बान्धवं used in the sense of kinship. It is not the idea of 'kinship' but that of 'Kinsman' that is prominent here).

सर्वगतं—With reference to everything. The Chamberlain had a ray of hope that Vāsa. might still have been living (a hope faintly expressed in ś1. 5 above.

आसनादुत्थाय—Udayana naturally shows this high respect for Mahāsena, just to indicate to the Kanch. that the loss of the daughter of the man he held in such high respect could not have been due to any neglect on his part but to a sheer irony of fate.

वैदेहीपु०—We do not know who this princess of Videha was. It is usual with Bhàsa not to give names but to use such epithets as गान्धारीमातः, कौसल्यामातः &c., यादवीपुत्रः (Panch.) &c.; nothing is known about her to later history. The reference to the mother's name shows that she must have been well known for her Dāksiṇya (like Dilīp's Sudakṣiṇā) in Bhāsa's time.

P. 58. S'l. 7. **प्रायेण हि** &c.—A common idea in Sans. literature; *cf.* ' साहसे श्रीः प्रतिवसति ' Mṛch. IV. p. 89; ' अनिर्वेदप्राप्याणि श्रेयांसि ' Vik. p. 106; 'लभ्या धरित्री तव विक्रमेण' Kir. III. 17.

S'l. 8. **ननु यदुचितान्** &c.—This could not have been an idle compliment; king Pradyota might have helped in some way in the recovery of the Vatsa country. **उचित**—which rightfully belonged to me; my ancestral kingdom. **प्राप्तुं**—some such word as अशक्नवम् must be supplied after this.

S'l. 9. **अन्तःपुर**—अन्तः अभ्यन्तरे गृहमन्तःपुरं inner apartment; hence the occupants of the अन्तःपुर; the queens. **पुण्या**—shows what reverence Udayana has for the Queen. Not only this, but नगरदेवता the very goddess of the city. **प्रवासे**—my departure and absence from the city. **ईदृशं**—of this sort, *i. e.* marred by the death of Vāsavadattā.

P. 59. **अतिमात्रं**—अतिक्रान्ता मात्रा यस्मिन्कर्मणि beyond measure, exceeding. **मा संतप्तुं**— The use of मा with the inf. is against Pāṇ.; it seems to have been used here exactly like अलं; and Bhâsa uses the inf. with अलं, *cf.* ' अलमुपहतासु स्त्रीबुद्धिषु स्वमार्जवमुपनिक्षेप्तुम् । ' Pratimā I. Some read सन्तप्य; this shows that मा is used in the sense of अलं, *cf. supra,* Vidú.'s speech at p. 54. अलमिदानीं भवान् &c. at p. 50. मेदानीमनर्थं चिन्तयित्वा. **उपरताप्यनुप०**—*Cf. supra* भर्तृस्नेहात्सा हि दग्धाप्यदग्धा ।

S'l. 10. **तुल्यधर्मः**—We should rather have read तुल्यधर्मा; the form ०धर्म may be defended by the general maxim " समासान्तविधेरनित्यत्वात्. " **रुह्यते**—used irregularly for रोहति; or it may be looked upon as a case of कर्मवद्भाव (reflexive passive) like ओदनः पच्यते; see *ante* note on श्लिष्यते p. 3.

S'l. 11. **महासेनस्य दु०**—This is the first reason why I should have the highest regard for her; then again प्रियशिष्या, which she actually was. The wife was regarded in ancient times as the pupil of her husband who had to teach her the graceful arts; *cf.* 'प्रियशिष्या ललिते कलाविधौ।' Ragh. VIII. 67. **देहान्तरेष्वपि**—So how can I forget her in this life.

गोपालकपालकौ—Sons of Mahāsena. Pàlaka figures in Sûdraka's Mṛch. as the then reigning king of Ujjayinī. **अनग्निसाक्षि०**—साक्षाद्द्रष्टा साक्षी; fr. साक्षात् + इन्; अग्निः साक्षी यस्मिन्कर्मणि तद्यथा तथा; तथा न भवतीति अनग्निसाक्षिकं; *lit.* without keepnig the holy fire as a witness; hence without the formal marriage. It is an essential part of the Hindu marriage that the bridegroom should take oath never to let go the hand once seized by him; *cf.* 'वधूं द्विजः प्राह तवैष वत्से वह्निर्विवाहं प्रति कर्मसाक्षी।' Kum. VII. 83; see also Ragh. VII. 20. **वीणाव्यपदेशेन**-under the guise of, *i. e.* apparently for the purpose of teaching her how to play on the lute. **चपलतया**—through overhastiness or impatience; it does not mean here 'rashness.' **विवाहो निर्वृत्तः**—*i. e.* to give solemnity to your elopement. There is a reference to this marriage in the Prat. Yau. in the words—'क्षत्रधर्मेणोद्दिष्टस्ते दुहितुर्विवाहः । किमिदानीं हर्षकाले सन्तप्यसे। तच्चित्रफलकस्थयोर्वत्सराजवासवदत्तयोर्विवाहोऽनुष्ठीयताम्।' Act. IV.

P. 60. **चित्रगतं गुरुजनं**—Because Vàsavadattā was the senior queen. One more instance of Padmâ.'s nobility of mind and sense of duty. **हम्**—shows 'surprise' here. **सदृशी खलु** &c.—is a question Śl. 13. **स्निग्धस्य**—स्निग्ध properly oily or unctuous; hence affectionate, charming, attractive. **इदं च** &c.—Here the king blames Agni for want of discretion.

आर्यपुत्रस्य प्रतिकृतिं दृष्ट्वा—Because if her husband's picture bore a perfect resemblance to him then she would conclude that Vāsas.' picture too was a perfect representation of her.

प्रहृष्टोद्विग्नां—First delighted and then dejected. Her उद्वेग might have been due to the thought that the king might grow somewhat cold towards her in case Āvantikā's true identity were discovered; or to the thought that the king might be disappointed in case Āvantikā were found to be really a Brāh. lady, and not Vāsavadattā, inspite of the close resemblance she bore to the picture. See śl. 14 below.

तदार्या पश्यतु—आर्या the nurse. *Let* the nurse see; for, she would not expose herself to the sight of a stranger. The other reading आर्या मया सहागतां &c. is to be rejected for this reason.

S'l. 14. अन्या—being of the Brāhmaṇa class.

P. 62. भवितव्यं—supply तेन. अभ्यन्तर०—formalities to be observed when a guest is received in the inside of the palace.

S'l. 15. कामं—may mean—At will, according to my desire; or (2) granted that. किं वक्ष्यतीति &c.—has occurred before; see S'l. 4.

साक्षिमत्—Adv.; साक्षिमद्यथा तथा like बलवत् in 'बलवदपि शिक्षितानां' &c. S'āk. I. 2; accompanied by, *i. e.* in the presence of. अधिकरणं—The court; the officers (standing as witnesses). देवि प्रविश &c.—This, as well as the sentence महासेनपुत्री खलु &c. below, shows that the king is overhasty; he does not wait to ascertain the truth from the Brāhmaṇa.

S'l. 16. भारतानां—भरतस्य गोत्रापत्यानि पुमांसः भारताः; तेषां कुले. The race of Bharata was held in the high esteem and loved by the people. Here he appeals to his exalted birth and proceeds in the manner of a climax: to add to this you are विनीत; not only that, ज्ञानवान् and शुचि (who put your knowledge into practice): and aobve all राजधर्मस्य देशिकः.

यवनिका—The curtain; some take it to mean 'a veil'; but that is not the meaning here; in the first place the king says संक्षिप्यतां and not अपनीयतां as is done by Râma when asking Sītâ to remove her veil–मैथिलि अपनीयतामवगुण्ठनं in Pratimā I; and further on again we have देव्यः अवगुण्ठनमपनयन्ति; Act III, Secondly the *Dhâtrī* marks closely the features of Āvantikâ and recognises in her her princess Vāsavadattā; this she could not have done had the latter been veiled. So we must suppose the Avantikā was placed behind the curtain and the nurse was asked to go there; the latter on beholding her at once exclaims 'अहो भर्तृदारिका &c.' जयतु स्वामी—Yaug. now doffs his disguise and appears in his true character.

P. 64. S'l. 17. किं नु &c.—The king does not know how far to believe the testimony of his own eyes; he gives the reason for this in the second half. अनयाप्येवमे०—The reference is to the Vāsa. scene in Act V. wherein she replaces the king's hand on the bed and suddenly leaves him, the king only, catching glimpse of her.

S'l. 28. मिथ्योन्मादैः—The king means my actions as one उन्मत्त were मिथ्या; as now proved, as they were caused by your carrying away the queen without my knowledge and which as I see now were meant to mislead the enemy.

सखीजन०—न तु गुरुजन०. अविघवे—It is somewhat strange that Vāsa. should address her as अवि० instead of using some such word as भगिनी; perhaps by addressing her as अवि० she wants to draw her attention prominently to the fact that it was she who enabled the king to support his life; otherwise he could not have outlived the shock her death had given him. **अर्थिस्वं नाम**—Here नाम has the sense of 'a pretended' action. I was presented to you as one belonging to a supplicant, and hence you treated me in that way. See com.

कौशाम्बीमात्रं—He means—I did all this to enable you to rule over the whole country (practically governed by me as your trusted chief minister); see com. परिपालयसि *v. l.* would be better.

P. 65. **पुष्पकभद्रा०**—See *supra* p. 6. **स्वामिनो देवी** &c.—The sentence is very suggestive—(1) She was sure to be your queen; (2) She would bear testimony to Vâsava.'s chastity being her constant companion; see *supra* 'इहात्रभवती मगधराजपुत्री विश्वासस्थानं' p. 10; (3) Vāsava. would mark how noble-minded Padmā. was and would conceive a sisterly affection for her though her, co-wife; (4) Being placed in a royal palace Vāsa. would not be ill at ease for want of the comforts of life she was accustomed to enjoy. **अहो शठः**—The King calls Rum.; of course humorously a शठ (a clever cheat) because he did not give him the slightest inkling of the plan to carry away the Queen and keep her in hiding, but kept him under the delusion that she was consumed by fire until the last moment.

भरतवाक्यं—The stanza containing an expression of good wishes, &c., repeated by the actors (भरतs); see com. Bhāsa's plays, like the later plays, end with the *Bharatavâkya.* But with Bhāsa like his prologue, it is a simple thing, and very short. The Bharatavākya of almost all the later play-wrights is introduced by some such words as 'किं ते भूयः प्रियमुपकरोमि । किमतः परमपि प्रियमस्ति तथापीदमस्तु ।'

S'l. 19. **इमां** &c.—This Vākya is also found in Abhi. VI. 35. Avi. VI. 22, Bāla. V. 20, Dut. Vâk. V. 56, Panch. R. III. 26 and Prat. Yau. IV. 26. **एकातपत्राङ्का** see com., A white silken umbrella was the badge of universal sovereignty. (सार्वभौमत्व); *cf.* 'एकातपत्रं जगतः प्रभुत्वं' Ragh. II. 47. **राजसिंहः**—A compliment to the reigning sovereigns.; no particular King seems to have been meant.

APPENDICES I.

The Subh asitas occurring in the play.

अनतिक्रमणीयो हि विधिः ।	३७
अयुक्तं परपुरुषसंकीर्तनं श्रोतुम् ।	२४
अस्य स्निग्धस्य वर्णस्य विपत्तिर्दारुणा कथम् ।	६०
आगमप्रधानानि सुलभपर्यवस्थानानि महापुरुषहृदयानि भवन्ति ।	२१
एवमनिर्ज्ञातानि दैवतान्यप्युत्सार्यन्ते ।	४
कः कं शक्तो रक्षितुं मृत्युकाले । &c.	५९
कालक्रमेण जगतः परिवर्तमाना चक्रारपंक्तिरिव गच्छति भाग्यपंक्तिः ।	४
गुणानां वा विशालानाम् &c.	४०
तपोवनानि नामातिथिजनस्य स्वगेहम् ।	७
दत्तं वेतनं परिखेदस्य ।	३५
दुःखं त्यक्तुं बद्धमूलोऽनुरागः । &c.	३७
न परुषमाश्रमवासिषु प्रयोज्यम् ।	५
न हि सिद्धवाक्यानुत्क्रम्य गच्छति विधिः सुपरीक्षितानि ।	११
परस्परगता लोके दृश्यते रूपतुल्यता ।	६१
प्रद्वेषो बहुमानो वा संकल्पादुपजायते ।	६
प्रायेण हि नरेन्द्रश्रीः सोत्साहैरेव भुज्यते ।	५८
सत्कारो हि नाम सत्कारेण प्रतीष्टः प्रीतिमुत्पादयति ।	४०
सदाक्षिण्यस्य जनस्य परिजनोऽपि सदाक्षिण्य एव भवति ।	३९
सर्वजनमनोभिरामं खलु सौभाग्यं नाम ।	२०
सर्वजनसाधारणमाश्रमपदं नाम ।	१२
सविज्ञानमस्य दर्शनम् ।	५
साक्षिमन्न्यासो निर्यातयितव्यः ।	६३
स्त्रीस्वभावस्तु कातरः ।	३९
अतिचिरं कन्दुकेन क्रीडित्वाऽधिकसंजातखेदानि &c.	१८

II

Peculiar Grammatical Constructions &c.

III
The Metres used in the Play, their Definitions and Schemes.

1. Sanskrit verse is regulated by quantity, and not, as in English, by accent. A पद्य (stanza) consists usually of four पाद्s (quarters). A पाद् is regulated either by the number of syllables (अक्षरs), or of syllabic instants (मात्राs). When the पाद्s are all similar, it is called a समवृत्त, to which type most of the metres conform. There are अर्धसमवृत्तs, wherein the first quarter corresponds to the third, and the second to the fourth. called respectively the *odd* (विषम) and *even* (सम) quarters. A third class comprises विषमवृत्तs, but these are very seldom used.

9. The vowels अ, इ, उ. ऋ and ऌ are short, and the rest long. The quantity of a syllable is determined by its vowel. A syllable with a short vowel is called लघु ('light'), and a syllable with a long vowel is called गुरु ('heavy') But a लघु syllable is considered as गुरु if it is followed by an *anusvâra*, is a *visarga* or a conjunct, consonant or when it comes at the end of a पाद्.*

c. A set of three successive syllables is called a गण (foot). Marking a short syllable as ⏑ and a long one as—, the different गणs,‡ which are 8 in number, may be exhibited as follows:— य ⏑ – –; र – ⏑ –; त – – ⏑; भ – ⏑ ⏑; ज ⏑ – ⏑; स ⏑ ⏑ –; म – – –; and न ⏑ ⏑ ⏑. In the definitions which are given below, a short syllable is indicated by the letter ल and long one by ग.

There are only 57 ślokas in this play in eleven different metres, of which 26 are in the अनुष्टुप् metre. These are given below with their difinitions and schemes.

Def.— ' श्लोके षष्ठं गुरु ज्ञेयं सर्वत्र लघु पञ्चमम् । द्विचतुःपादयोर्ह्रस्वं सप्तमं दीर्घमन्ययोः ॥ ' There are many varieties of this; but the one defined above is the most common. Each pāda has eight syllables, of which the sixth is long and the fifth short; and the seventh is short in the second

* सानुस्वारश्च दीर्घश्च विसर्गी च गुरुर्भवेत् ।
वर्णः संयोगपूर्वश्च तथा पादान्तगोऽपि वा ॥

‡ आदिमध्यावसानेषु य-र-ता यान्ति लाघवम् ।
भ-ज-सा गौरवं यान्ति म-नौ तु गुरुलाघवम् ॥

and the fourth padas and long in the first and third. The rest of the syllables may be either short or long.

अनुष्टुप्—(Also called Śloka)—

I. 2, 7, 10, 15; IV. 6, 8, 9, 10; V. 6, 7, 8, 9, 10, 11; VI. 3, 6, 7, 9, 11, 12, 13, 14, 16, 17, 18, 19.

आर्या—यस्याः पादे प्रथमे द्वादश मात्रास्तथा तृतीयेऽपि । अष्टादश द्वितीये चतुर्थके पञ्चदश साऽऽर्या ॥ This belong to the class of metres regulated by मात्राs. The four pādas contain respectively 12, 18, 12 and 15 Mātrâs

I. 1; IV. 3, 5.

उपेन्द्रवज्रा—उपेन्द्रवज्रा जतजास्ततो गौ । 11 syllables. Sch.—ज त ज ग ग. V. 13.

उपजातिः—स्यादिन्द्रवज्रा यदि तौ जगौ गः । उपेन्द्र० (see above) अनन्तरोदीरितलक्ष्मभाजौ पादौ यदीयावुपजातयस्ताः । Upajâti is a mixture of one or two pādas of इन्द्र० and उपेन्द्रवज्रा. इन्द्र० has 11 syllables in each quarter. Sch. त त ज ग ग.

शालिनी—मातौ गौ चेत् शालिनी वेदलोकैः । 11 syllables; the pause at 4th syll. Sch.—म त त ग ग.

I. 13; N. 7; VI. 10.

वैश्वदेवी—बाणाश्वैश्छिन्ना वैश्वदेवी ममौ यौ । 12 syllables; pause at the fifth syll. Sch.—म म य य.

I. 9.

वसन्ततिलका—उक्ता वसन्ततिलका तभजा जगौ गः । 14 syllables; pause at the 8th syll.; Sch.—त भ ज ज ग ग.

I. 4, 6, 11; IV. 2; V. 1, 2, 3; VI. 2, 4, 5, 15.

शिखरिणी—रसै रुद्रैश्छिन्ना यमनसभला गः शिखरिणी । 17 syllables; pause at the 6th syll. Sch,—य म न स भ ल ग.

I. 14, 16.

हरिणी—नसमरसला गः षड्वेदैर्हयैर्हरिणी मता । 17 syllables; pause at the 6th and 4th sylls. Sch.—न स म र स ल ग.

VI. 8.

शार्दूलविक्रीडितं—सूर्याश्वैर्यदि मः सजौ सततगाः शार्दूलविक्रीडितम् । 19 syllables; pause at the 12th syll. Sch.—म स ज स त त ग.

पुष्पिताग्रा—अयुजि नयुगरेफतो यकारो युजि च नजौ जरगाश्च पुष्पिताग्रा । Odd *pâdas*—12 syllables; sch. न न य र. Even pādas 13 syllables; sch. न न ज र ग. This is an अर्धसमवृत्त.

I. 5; VI 1.

IV

Stanzas attributed to Bha'sa in the Anthologies.

दग्धे मनोभवतरौ बालाकुचकुम्भसंभृतैरमृतैः ।
त्रिवलीकृतालवाला जाता रोमावली वल्ली ॥

सदुक्तिकर्णामृते

पेया सुरा प्रियतमामुखमीक्षणीयं
ग्राह्यः स्वभावललितो विकटश्च वेषः ।
येनेदमीदृशमदृश्यत मोक्षवर्त्म
दीर्घायुरस्तु भगवान् स पिनाकपाणिः ॥
तीक्ष्णं रविस्तपति नीच इवाचिराढ्यः
शृङ्गं रुरुस्त्यजति मित्रमिवाकृतज्ञः ।
तोयं प्रसीदति मुनेरिव चित्तमन्तः
कामी दरिद्र इव शोषमुपैति पङ्कः ॥

शार्ङ्गधरपद्धतौ

बाला च सा विदितपञ्चशरप्रपञ्चा
तन्वी च सा स्तनभरोपचिताङ्गयष्टिः ।
लज्जां समुद्वहति सा सुरतावसाने
हा कापि सा किमिव किं कथयामि तस्याः ॥

सुभाषितावल्याम्

कपोले मार्जारः पय इति कराँल्लेढि शशिन-
स्तरुच्छिद्रप्रोतान्बिसमिति करी संकलयति ।
रतान्ते तल्पस्थान् हरति वनिताप्यंशुकमिति
प्रभामत्तश्चन्द्रो जगदिदमहो विप्लवयति ॥

शार्ङ्गधरपद्धतौ

कठिणहृदये मुञ्च क्रोधं सुखप्रतिघातकं
लिखति दिवसं यातं यातं यमः किल मानिनि ।
वयसि तरुणे नैतद्युक्तं चले च समागमे
भवति कलहो यावत्तावद्वरं सुभगे रतम् ॥

सुभाषितावल्याम्

कृतककृतकैर्मायासख्यैस्त्वयास्म्यतिवञ्चिता
निभृतनिभृतैः कार्यालापैर्मयाप्युपलक्षितम् ।

भवतु विदितं नेष्टाहं ते वृथा किमु खिद्यसे
ह्यहमसहना त्वं निःस्नेहः समेन समं गतम् ॥

सुभाषितावल्याम्

विरहिवनितावक्त्रौपम्यं बिभर्ति निशापति–
र्गलितविभवस्याज्ञेवाद्य द्युतिर्मसृणा रवेः ।
अभिनववधूरोषस्वादुः करीषतनूनपा–
दसरलजनाश्लेषक्रूरस्तुषारसमीरणः ॥

सदुक्तिकर्णामृते

यदपि विबुद्धैः सिन्धोरन्तः कथंचिदुपार्जितं
तदपि सकलं चारुस्त्रीणां मुखेषु विलोक्यते ।
सुरसुमनसः श्वासामोदे शशी च कपोलयो–
रमृतमधरे तिर्यग्भूते विषं च विलोचने ॥

सूक्तिमुक्तावल्याम्

दुःखार्ते मयि दुःखिता भवति या हृष्टे प्रहृष्टा तथा
दीने दैन्यमुपैति रोषपरुषे पथ्यं वचो भाषते ।
कालं वेत्ति कथाः करोति निपुणा मत्संस्तवे रज्यति
भार्या मन्त्रिवरः सखा परिजनः सैका बहुत्वं गता ॥

सुभाषितावल्याम्

प्रत्यासन्नविवाहमङ्गलविधौ देवार्चनव्यग्रया
दृष्ट्वाग्रे परिणेतुरेव लिखितां गङ्गाधरस्याकृतिम् ।
उन्मादस्मितरोमलज्जितरसैर्गौर्या कथंचिच्चिरा-
द्बद्धः स्त्रीवचनात्प्रिये विनिहितः पुष्पांजलिः पातु वः ॥

सदुक्तिकर्णामृते

अस्या ललाटे रचिता सखीभिः विभाव्यते चन्दनपत्रलेखा ।
आपाण्डुरक्षामकपोलभित्तौ-अनङ्गबाणव्रणपट्टिकेव ॥

दयिताबाहुपाशस्य कुतोऽयमपरो विधिः ।
जीवयत्यार्पितः कण्ठे मारयत्यपवर्जितः ॥

शार्ङ्गधरपद्धतौ

The story as told in the Katha'saritsa'gara which may be compared with the theme of the Play.

लावाणकनाम्नि तृतीये लम्बके

प्रथमस्तरङ्गः ।

निर्विघ्नविश्वनिर्माणसिद्धये यदनुग्रहम् ।
मन्ये स वव्रे धातापि तस्मै विघ्नजिते नमः ॥ १ ॥
एवं स राजा वत्सेशः क्रमेण सुतरामभूत् ।
प्राप्तवासवदत्तस्तत्सुखासक्तैकमानसः ॥ २ ॥
यौगन्धरायणश्चास्य महामन्त्री दिवानिशम् ।
सेनापती रुमण्वांश्च राज्यभारमुदूहतुः ॥ ३ ॥
स कदाचिच्च चिन्तावानानीय रजनौ गृहम् ।
निजगाद रुमण्वन्तं मन्त्री यौगन्धरायणः ॥ ४ ॥
पाण्डवान्वयजातोऽयं वत्सेशोऽस्य च मेदिनी ।
कुलक्रमागता कृत्स्ना पुरं च गजसाह्वयम् ॥ ५ ॥
तत्सर्वमजिगीषेण त्यक्तमेतेन भूभृता ।
इहैव चास्य संजातं राज्यमेकत्र मण्डले ॥ ६ ॥
स्त्रीमद्यमृगयासक्तो निश्चिन्तो ह्येष तिष्ठति ।
अस्मासु राज्यचिन्ता च सर्वानेन समर्पिता ॥ ७ ॥
तदस्माभिः स्वबुद्ध्यैव तथा कार्यं यथैष तत् ।
समग्रपृथिवीराज्यं प्राप्नोत्येव क्रमागतम् ॥ ८ ॥
एवं कृते हि भक्तिश्च मन्त्रिता च कृता भवेत् ॥ ९ ॥
वयं राजहितं कुर्मः साधयामास्य मेदिनीम् ॥ १० ॥
परिपन्थी च तत्रैकः प्रद्योतो मगधेश्वरः ।
पार्ष्णिग्राहः स हि सदा पश्चात्कोपं करोति नः ॥ ११ ॥
तत्तस्य कन्यकारत्नमस्ति पद्मावतीति यत् ।
तदस्य वत्सराजस्य कृते याचामहे वयम् ॥ १२ ॥
छन्नां वासवदत्तां च स्थापयित्वा स्वबुद्धितः ।
दत्त्वाग्निं वासके ब्रूमो देवी दग्धेति सर्वतः ॥ १३ ॥
नान्यथा तां सुतां राज्ञे ददाति मगधाधिपः ।
एतदर्थं स हि मया प्रार्थितः पूर्वमुक्तवान् ॥ १४ ॥

नाहं वत्सेश्वरायैतां दास्याम्यात्माधिकां सुताम् ।
तस्य वासवदत्तायां स्नेहो हि सुमहानिति ॥ १५ ॥
सत्यां देव्यां च वत्सेशो नैवान्यां परिणेष्यति ।
देवी दग्धेति जातायां ख्यातौ सर्वं तु सेत्स्यति ॥ १६ ॥
पद्मावत्यां च लब्धायां संबन्धी मगधाधिपः ।
पश्चात्कोपं न कुरुते सहायत्वं च गच्छति ॥ १७ ॥
ततः पूर्वां दिशं जेतुं गच्छामोऽन्याश्च तत्क्रमात् ।
इत्थं वत्सेश्वरस्यैतां साधयामोऽखिलां भुवम् ॥ १८ ॥
कृतोद्योगेषु चास्मासु पृथिवीमेष भूपतिः ।
प्राप्नुयादेव पूर्वं हि दिव्या वागेवमब्रवीत् ॥ १९ ॥
ईदृंशि राजकार्याणि भवन्ति तदिदं वयम् ।
देवीदाहप्रवादेन कार्यं धैर्येण कुर्महे ॥ २० ॥
इत्येतान्निश्चितमते श्रुत्वा यौगन्धरायणात् ।
रुमण्वानब्रवीदेवं तर्हि यद्येष निश्चयः ॥ २१ ॥
तद्गोपालकमानीय देव्या भ्रातरमादृतम् ।
संमन्त्र्य च समं तेन सम्यक्सर्वं विधीयताम् ॥ २२ ॥
एवमस्त्विवति वक्ति स्म ततो यौगन्धरायणः ।
तत्प्रत्ययाद्रुमण्वांश्च चक्रे कर्तव्यनिश्चयम् ॥ २३ ॥
अन्येद्युर्मन्त्रिमुख्यौ तौ दूतं व्यसृजतां निजम् ।
गोपालकं तमानेतुमुत्कण्ठाव्यपदेशतः ॥ २४ ॥
कार्यहेतोर्गतः पूर्वं तद्दूतवचनाच्च सः ।
अगाद्गोपालकस्तत्र स्वयं मूर्त इवोत्सवः ॥ २५ ॥
आगतं तदहश्चैनं स्वैरं यौगन्धरायणः ।
निनाय सरुमण्वत्कं गृहं गोपालकं निशि ॥ २६ ॥
तत्र चास्मै तदुत्साहं शशंस स्वचिकीर्षितम् ।
यत्पूर्वं मन्त्रितं तेन सर्वं सह रुमण्वता ॥ २७ ॥
स च राजहितैषी सन्दुःखावहमपि स्वसुः ।
गोपालकोऽनुमेने तत्कर्तव्यं हि सतां वचः ॥ २८ ॥
सर्वमेतत्सुविहितं देवीं दग्धामवेत्य तु ।
प्राणांस्त्यजन्कथं रक्ष्यो वत्सेश इति चिन्त्यताम् ॥ २९ ॥

सदुपायादिसामग्रीसंभवे किल सत्यपि ।
मुख्यमङ्गं हि मन्त्रस्य विनिपातप्रतिक्रिया ॥ ३० ॥
इति भूयोऽपि तत्कालमुक्ते तत्र रुमण्वता ।
उवाचालोचिताशेषकार्यो यौगन्धरायणः ॥ ३१ ॥
नास्त्यत्र चिन्ता यद्राजपुत्री गोपालकस्य सा ।
कनीयसी स्वसा देवी प्राणेभ्योऽप्यधिका प्रिया ॥ ३२ ॥
एतस्य चाल्पमालोक्य शोकं वत्सेश्वरस्तदा ।
जीवेत्कदाचिद्देवीति मत्वा धैर्यमवाप्स्यति ॥ ३३ ॥
अपि चोत्तमसत्त्वोऽयं शीघ्रं च परिणीयते ।
पद्मावती ततो देवी दर्श्यते चाचिरादिति ॥ ३४ ॥
एवमेतद्विनिश्चित्य ततो यौगन्धरायणः ।
गोपालको रुमण्वांश्च ततो मन्त्रमिति व्यधुः ॥ ३५ ॥
युक्त्या लावाणकं यामः सह देव्या नृपेण च ।
पर्यन्तो मगधासन्नवर्ती हि विषयोऽस्ति सः ॥ ३६ ॥
सुभगाखेटभूमित्वाद्राज्ञश्चासांनिधानकृत् ।
तत्रान्तःपुरमादीप्य क्रियते यदि चिन्तितम् ॥ ३७ ॥
देवी च स्थाप्यते नीत्वा युक्त्या पद्मावतीगृहे ।
छन्नस्थिताया येनास्याः सैव स्याच्छीलसाक्षिणी ॥ ३८ ॥
एवं रात्रौ मिथः कृत्वा मन्त्रं सर्वेऽपरेऽहनि ।
यौगन्धरायणाद्यास्ते प्राविशन् राजमन्दिरम् ॥ ३९ ॥
तत्रैवमथ विज्ञप्तो वत्सराजो रुमण्वता ।
देव लावाणकेऽस्माकं गतानां वर्तते शिवम् ॥ ४० ॥
स चातिरम्यो विषयस्तत्र चाखेटभूमयः ।
शोभनाः सन्ति ते राजन्नडघासाश्च सुग्रहाः ॥ ४१ ॥
बाधते तं च नैकट्यात्सर्वं स मगधेश्वरः ।
तत्तत्र रक्षाहेतोश्च विनोदाय च गम्यताम् ॥ ४२ ॥
एतच्छ्रुत्वा च वत्सेशः समं वासवदत्तया ।
क्रीडैकलालसश्चक्रे गन्तुं लावाणके मतिम् ॥ ४३ ॥
निश्चिते गमनेऽन्येद्युर्लग्ने च प्रकल्पिते ।
अकस्मान्नारदमुनिः कान्तिद्योतितदिङ्मुखः ॥ ४४ ॥

अवतीर्य नभोमध्यात्प्रदत्तनयनोत्सवः ।
शशीव स्वकुलप्रीत्या तं वत्सेश्वरमभ्यगात् ॥ ४५ ॥
गृहीतातिथ्यसत्कारः पारिजातमयीं स्रजम् ।
प्रीतः स च मुनिस्तस्मै ददौ प्रह्वाय भूभृते ॥ ४६ ॥
विद्याधराधिपं पुत्रं कामदेवांशमाप्स्यसि ।
इति वासवदत्तां च सोऽभ्यनन्दत्कृतादरः ॥ ४७ ॥
ततश्चोवाच वत्सेशं स्थिते यौगन्धरायणे ।
राजन्वासवदत्तां ते दृष्ट्वा हन्त स्मृतं मया ॥ ४८ ॥
युधिष्ठिरादयोऽभूवन्पुरा ते प्रपितामहाः ॥ ४९ ॥
ते च मे सुहृदोऽभूवंस्तत्प्रीत्या चाहमागतः ।
त्वां द्रष्टुमिह वत्सेश तदिदं शृणु वच्मि ते ॥ ५० ॥
यथैतन्मे कृतं वाक्यं कुर्यास्त्वं मन्त्रिणां तथा ।
अचिरेण च कालेन महतीमृद्धिमाप्स्यसि ॥ ५१ ॥
कंचित्कालं च दुःखं ते भविष्यति न च त्वया ।
तत्रातिमोहः कर्तव्यः सुखान्तं भविता हि तत् ॥ ५२ ॥
सम्यगेवमभिधाय तत्क्षणं वत्सराजमुदयस्य भाविनः ।
भङ्गिसूचनविधौ विशारदो नारदो मुनिरदर्शनं ययौ ॥ ५३ ॥
सर्वे च तस्य वचसा मुनिपुंगवस्य
यौगन्धरायणमुखाः सचिवास्ततस्ते ।
संभाव्य सिद्ध्युदयमात्मचिकीर्षितस्य
संपादनाय सुतरां जगृहुः प्रमत्तम् ॥ ५४ ॥

ति महाकविश्रीसोमदेवभट्टविरचिते कथासरित्सागरे लावाणकलम्बके
प्रथमस्तरङ्गः ।

द्वितीयस्तरङ्गः ।

ततः पूर्वोक्तया युक्त्या वत्सराजं सवल्लभम् ।
यौगन्धरायणाद्यास्ते निन्युर्लावाणकं प्रति ॥ १ ॥
स राजा प्राप तं देशं सैन्यघोषेण मूर्च्छता ।
अभिवाञ्छितसंसिद्धिं वदन्तमिव मन्त्रिणाम् ॥ २ ॥
तत्र प्राप्तं विदित्वा च वत्सेशं सपरिच्छदम् ।
अवस्कन्दभयाशङ्की चकम्पे मगधेश्वरः ॥ ३ ॥

यौगन्धरायणोपान्तं सद्बुद्धिर्विससर्ज च ।
स दूतं सोऽपि सन्मन्त्री कार्यज्ञोऽभिननन्द तम् ॥ ४ ॥
वत्सेश्वरोऽपि निवसंस्तस्मिन्देशे दवीयसीम् ।
आखेटकार्थमटवीमटति स्म दिने दिने ॥ ५ ॥
एकस्मिन्दिवसे तस्मिन् राजन्याखेटकं गते ।
कर्तव्यसंविदं कृत्वा गोपालकसमन्वितः ॥ ६ ॥
यौगन्धरायणो धीमान्सरुमण्वद्वसन्तकः ।
देव्या वासवदत्ताया विजने निकटं ययौ ॥ ७ ॥
तत्र तां राजकार्येऽत्र साहाय्ये तत्तदुक्तिभिः ।
प्रह्वामभ्यर्थयामास भ्रात्रा पूर्वं प्रबोधिताम् ॥ ८ ॥
सानुमेने च विरहक्लेशदायि तदात्मनः ।
किं नाम न सहन्ते हि भर्तृभक्ताः कुलाङ्गनाः ॥ ९ ॥
ततस्तां ब्राह्मणीरूपां देवीं यौगन्धरायणः ।
स चकार कृती दत्त्वा योगं रूपविवर्तनम् ॥ १० ॥
वसन्तकं च कृतवान्काणं बटुकरूपिणम् ।
आत्मना च तथैवाभूत्स्थविरब्राह्मणाकृतिः ॥ ११ ॥
तथारूपां गृहीत्वाथ तां देवीं स महामतिः ।
वसन्तकसखः स्वैरं प्रतस्थे मगधान्प्रति ॥ १२ ॥
तथा वासवदत्ता सा स्वगृहान्निर्गता सती ।
अगाच्चित्तेन भर्तारं पन्थानं वपुषा पुनः ॥ १३ ॥
तन्मन्दिरमथादीप्य दहनेन रुमण्वता ।
हा हा वसन्तकयुता देवी दग्धेत्यघोष्यत ॥ १४ ॥
तथा च दहनाक्रन्दौ समं तत्रोदतिष्ठताम् ।
शनैः शशाम दहनो न पुनः क्रन्दितध्वनिः ॥ १५ ॥
यौगन्धरायणः सोऽथ सह वासवदत्तया ।
वसन्तकेन च प्राप मगधाधिपतेः पुरम् ॥ १६ ॥
तत्रोद्यानगतां दृष्ट्वा समं ताभ्यामुपाययौ ।
पद्मावतीं राजसुतां वार्यमाणोऽपि रक्षिभिः ॥ १७ ॥
पद्मावत्याश्च दृष्ट्वैव ब्राह्मणीरूपधारिणीम् ।
देवीं वासवदत्तां तां दृशोः प्रीतिरजायत ॥ १८ ॥

सा रक्षिणो निषिध्यैव ततो यौगन्धरायणम् ।
आनाययद्राजकन्या ब्राह्मणाकृतिमन्तिकम् । १९ ॥
पप्रच्छ च महाब्रह्मन्का ते बाला भवत्यसौ ।
किमर्थमागतोऽसीति सोऽपि तां प्रत्यभाषत ॥ २० ॥
इयमावन्तिका नाम राजपुत्रि सुता मम ।
अस्याश्च भर्ता व्यसनी त्यक्त्वेमां कुत्रचिद्गतः ॥ २१ ॥
तदेतां स्थापयाम्यद्य तव हस्ते यशस्विनि ।
यावत्तमानयाम्यस्या गतान्विष्याचिरात्पतिम् ॥ २२ ॥
भ्राता काणबटुश्चायमिहैवास्याः समीपगः ।
तिष्ठत्येकाकिनीभावदुःखं येन न यात्यसौ ॥ २३ ॥
इत्युक्त्वा राजतनयामङ्गीकृतवचास्तया ।
तामामन्त्र्य स सन्मन्त्री द्रुतं लावाणकं ययौ ॥ २४ ॥
ततो वासवदत्तां तां स्थितामावन्तिकाख्यया ।
वसन्तकं चानुगतं तं काणबटुरूपिणम् ॥ २५ ॥
सहादाय कृतोदारसत्कारा स्नेहशालिनी ।
पद्मावती स्वभवनं विवेश बहुकौतुकम् ॥ २६ ॥
तत्र वासवदत्ता च प्रविष्टा चित्रभित्तिषु ।
पश्यन्ती रामचरिते सीतां सेहे निजव्यथाम् ॥ २७ ॥
आकृत्या सौकुमार्येण शयनाशनसौष्ठवैः ।
शरीरसौरभेणापि नीलोत्पलसुगन्धिना ॥ २८ ॥
तामुत्तमां विनिश्चित्य महार्हैरात्मनः समैः ।
पद्मावती यथाकाममुपचारैरुपाचरत् ॥ २९ ॥
अचिन्तयच्च काप्येषा छन्ना नूनमिह स्थिता ।
गूढा किं द्रौपदी नासीद्विराटवसताविति ॥ ३० ॥
अथ वासवदत्तास्याश्चक्रे देव्याः प्रसङ्गतः ।
अम्लानमालातिलकौ वत्सेशात्पूर्वशिक्षितौ ॥ ३१ ॥
तद्रूपितां च दृष्ट्वा तां माता पद्मावतीं रहः ।
पप्रच्छ मालातिलकौ केनेमौ निर्मिताविति ॥ ३२ ॥
ऊचे पद्मावती चैनामत्र मन्मन्दिरे स्थिता ।
काचिदावन्तिका नाम तया कृतमिदं मम ॥ ३३ ॥

तच्छ्रुत्वा सा बभाषे तां माता पुत्रि न तर्हि सा ।
मानुषी कापि देवी सा यस्या विज्ञानमीदृशम् ॥ ३४ ॥
देवता मुनयश्चापि वञ्चनार्थं सतां गृहे ।
तिष्ठन्त्येव तदा चैतामत्र पुत्रि कथां शृणु ॥ ३५ ॥
इत्थमासीन्मुनिस्तत्र तदेषावन्तिकापि ते ।
तद्वदेव स्थिता कापि तत्त्वमाराधयेरिमाम् ॥ ३६ ॥
इति मातृमुखाच्छ्रुत्वा पद्मावत्यन्यरूपिणीम् ।
तत्र वासवदत्तां तां सुतरां बह्वमन्यत ॥ ३७ ॥
सापि वासवदत्तात्र निजनाथविनाकृता ।
तस्थौ विधुरविच्छाया निशीथस्थेव पद्मिनी ॥ ३८ ॥
अत्रान्तरेऽतिदूरासु भ्रान्त्वाखेटकभूमिषु ।
वत्सराजश्चिरादागात्सायं लावाणकं पुनः ॥ ३९ ॥
भस्मीकृतमपश्यच्च तत्रान्तःपुरमग्निना ।
देवीं दग्धां च शुश्राव मन्त्रिभ्यः सवसन्तकाम् ॥ ४० ॥
श्रुत्वैव चापतद् भूमौ मोहेन हृतचेतनः ।
तद्दुःखानुभवक्लेशमपाकर्तुमिवेच्छता ॥ ४१ ॥
क्षणाच्च लब्धसंज्ञः सञ्जज्वाल हृदये शुचा ।
आविष्ट इव तत्रस्थदेवीदाहेक्षणाग्निना ॥ ४२ ॥
विलपन्नथ दुःखार्तो देहत्यागैकसंमुखः ।
क्षणान्तरे स नृपतिः संमृत्यैतदचिन्तयत् ॥ ४३ ॥
विद्याधराधिपः पुत्रो देव्यास्तस्या भविष्यति ।
एतन्मे नारदमुनिर्वक्ति स्म न च तन्मृषा ॥ ४४ ॥
कंचित्कालं च दुःखं मे तेनैव मुनिनोदितम् ।
गोपालकस्य चैतस्य शोकः स्वल्प इवेक्ष्यते ॥ ४५ ॥
यौगन्धरायणादीनां न चैषामतिदुःखिता ।
दृश्यते तेन जाने सा देवी जीवेत्कथंचन ॥ ४६ ॥
इयं किमपि नीतिस्तु प्रत्युक्ता मन्त्रिभिर्भवेत् ।
अतो मम भवेज्जातु तया देव्या समागमः ॥ ४७ ॥
तत्पश्याम्यत्र पर्यन्तमित्यालोच्य स भूपतिः ।
निदधे हृदये धैर्य बोध्यमानश्च मन्त्रिभिः ॥ ४८ ॥

गोपालकश्च संदिश्य तद्यथावस्तु तत्क्षणम् ।
प्रजिघाय ततश्चारं धृतिहेतोरलक्षितम् ॥ ४९ ॥
एवं गते स्ववृत्तान्ते लावाणकगतैस्तदा ।
गत्वा मगधराजाय चारैः सर्वं निवेदितम् ॥ ५० ॥
स तद् बुद्ध्वैव कालज्ञो वत्सराजाय तां सुताम् ।
दातुं पद्मावतीमैच्छत्पूर्वं तन्मन्त्रिमार्गिताम् ॥ ५१ ॥
ततो दूतमुखेनैनमर्थं वत्सेश्वराय सः ।
यौगन्धरायणायापि संदिदेश यथेप्सितम् ॥ ५२ ॥
यौगन्धरायणोक्त्या च वत्सेशोऽङ्गीचकार तत् ।
प्रच्छादितैनदर्थं स्याद्देवी जात्विति चिन्तयन् ॥ ५३ ॥
ततो लग्नं विनिश्चित्य तूर्णं यौगन्धरायणः ।
तस्मै मगधराजाय प्रतिदूतं व्यसर्जयत् ॥ ५४ ॥
त्वदिच्छाङ्गीकृतास्माभिस्तदितः सप्तमे दिने ।
पद्मावतीविवाहाय वत्सेशोऽत्रागमिष्यति ॥ ५५ ॥
शीघ्रं वासवदत्तां च येनासौ विस्मरिष्यति ।
इति चास्मै महामन्त्री संदिदेश स भूभृते ॥ ५६ ॥
प्रतिदूतः स गत्वा च यथासंदिष्टमभ्यधात् ।
ततो मगधराजाय स चाप्यभिननन्द तम् ॥ ५७ ॥
ततः स दुहितृस्नेहनिजेच्छाविभवोचितम् ।
विवाहोत्सवसंभारं चकार मगधेश्वरः ॥ ५८ ॥
सा चाभीष्टवरश्रुत्या मुदं पद्मावती ययौ ।
प्राप वासवदत्ता च तद्वार्ताकर्णनाच्छुचम् ॥ ५९ ॥
सा वार्ता कर्णमागत्य तस्या वैवर्ण्यदायिनी ।
प्रच्छन्नवासवैरूप्यसाहायकमिवाकरोत् ॥ ६० ॥
इत्थं मित्रीकृतः शत्रुर्न च भर्तान्यथा त्वयि ।
वसन्तकोक्तिरित्यस्याः सर्वाव विदधे धृतिम् ॥ ६१ ॥
अथासन्नविवाहायाः पद्मावत्या मनस्विनी ।
अम्लानमालातिलकौ दिव्यो भूयश्चकार सा ॥ ६२ ॥
ततो वत्सेश्वरस्तत्र संप्राप्ते सप्तमेऽहनि ।
ससैन्यो मन्त्रिभिः सार्कं परिणेतुं किलाययौ ॥ ६३ ॥

मनसापि तदुद्योगं विरही स कथं स्पृशेत् ।
देवीं लभेय तामेवमित्याशा न भवेद्यदि ॥ ६४ ॥
प्रत्युद्ययौ च तं सद्यः सानन्दो मगधेश्वरः ।
प्रजानेत्रोत्सवं चन्द्रमुदयस्थमिवाम्बुधिः ॥ ६५ ॥
विवेशाथ स वत्सेशो मगधाधिपतेः पुरम् ।
समन्तात्पौरलोकस्य मानसं च महोत्सवः ॥ ६६ ॥
विरहक्षामवपुष मनःसंमोददायिनम् ।
ददृशुस्तत्र नार्यस्तं रतिहीनमिव स्मरम् ॥ ६७ ॥
प्रविश्य मगधेशस्य वत्सेशोऽप्यथ मन्दिरम् ।
सनाथं पतिपत्नीभिः कौतुकागारमाययौ ॥ ६८ ॥
तत्र पद्मावतीमन्तर्ददर्श कृतकौतुकाम् ।
स राजा पूर्णवक्त्रेन्दुजितपूर्णेन्दुमण्डलाम् ॥ ६९ ॥
तस्याश्च मालातिलकौ दिव्यावालोक्य तौ निजौ ।
एतौ कुतोऽस्या इत्येवं विममर्श स भूपतिः ॥ ७० ॥
ततः स वेदीमारुह्य तस्या जग्राह यत्करम् ।
तदेवारम्भतां प्राप तस्य पृथ्व्याः करग्रहे ॥ ७१ ॥
प्रियवासवदत्तोऽयमिदं शक्नोति नेक्षितुम् ।
इतीव वेदीधूमोऽस्य बाष्पेण पिदधे दृशौ ॥ ७२ ॥
अग्निप्रदक्षिणे ताम्रं तदा पद्मावतीमुखम् ।
विज्ञातभर्त्रभिप्रायं कोपाकुलमिवाबभौ ॥ ७३ ॥
मुमोच स कृतोद्वाहः कराद्वत्सेश्वरो वधूम् ।
न तु वासवदत्तां तां तत्याज हृदयात्क्षणम् ॥ ७४ ॥
ततस्तथा ददौ तस्मै रत्नानि मगधाधिपः ।
निर्दुग्धरत्नरिक्तेव पृथिवी बुबुधे यथा ॥ ७५ ॥
साक्षीकृत्य च तत्कालमग्निं यौगन्धरायणः ।
अद्रोहप्रत्ययं राज्ञो मगधेशमकारयत् ॥ ७६ ॥
प्रदत्तवस्त्राभरणः प्रगीतवरचारणः ।
प्रनृत्तवरनारीकः प्रससार महोत्सवः ॥ ७७ ॥
उदयापेक्षिणी पत्युः सुप्तेवालक्षितस्थिता ।
तदा वासवदत्ताभूद् दिवा कान्तिरिवैन्दवी ॥ ७८ ॥

अन्तःपुरमुपायाते राज्ञि वत्सेश्वरे ततः ।
देवीसंदर्शनाशङ्की कृती यौगन्धरायणः ॥ ७९ ॥
मन्त्रभेदभयादेवं मगधेश्वरमभ्यधात् ।
अद्यैव नाथ वत्सेशः प्रयाति त्वद्गृहादिति ॥ ८० ॥
तथेत्यङ्गीकृतं तेन तमेवार्थं तदैव सः ।
व्यजिज्ञपद्वत्सराजं सोऽपि तच्छ्रद्दधे तथा ॥ ८१ ॥
अथोच्चचाल वत्सेशो भुक्तपीतपरिच्छदः ।
मन्त्रिभिः सममादाय वधूं पद्मावतीं ततः ॥ ८२ ॥
पद्मावत्या विसृष्टं च सुखमारुह्य वाहनम् ।
तयैव च समादिष्टैस्तन्महत्तरकैः सह ॥ ८३ ॥
आगाद्वासवदत्तापि गुप्तं सैन्यस्य पृष्ठतः ।
कृतरूपविवर्तं तं पुरस्कृत्य वसन्तकम् ॥ ८४ ॥
क्रमाल्लावाणकं प्राप्य वत्सेशो वसतिं निजाम् ।
प्रविवेश समं वध्वा देवीचित्तं तु केवलः ॥ ८५ ॥
एत्य वासवदत्तापि सा गोपालकमन्दिरम् ।
विवेशाथ निशीथे च परिस्थाप्य महत्तरान् ॥ ८६ ॥
तत्र गोपालकं दृष्ट्वा भ्रातरं दर्शितादरम् ।
कण्ठे जग्राह रुदती बाष्पव्याकुललोचनम् ॥ ८७ ॥
तत्क्षणे स्थितसंविच्च तत्र यौगन्धरायणः ।
आययौ सरुमण्वत्कस्तया देव्या कृतादरः ॥ ८८ ॥
सोऽस्याः प्रोत्साहविश्लेषदुःखं यावद्व्यपोहति ।
तावत्पद्मावतीपार्श्वं प्रययुस्ते महत्तराः ॥ ८९ ॥
आगतावन्तिका देवि किमप्यस्मान्विहाय तु ।
प्रविष्टा राजपुत्रस्य गृहं गोपालकस्य सा ॥ ९० ॥
इति पद्मावती सा तैर्विज्ञप्ता स्वमहत्तरैः ।
वत्सेश्वराग्रे साशङ्का तानेवं प्रत्यभाषत ॥ ९१ ॥
गच्छतावन्तिकां ब्रूथ निःक्षेपस्त्वं हि मे स्थिता ।
तदत्र किं ते यत्राहं तत्रैवागम्यतामिति ॥ ९२ ॥
तच्छ्रुत्वा तेषु यातेषु राजा पद्मावतीं रहः ।
पप्रच्छ मालातिलकौ केनेमौ ते कृताविति ॥ ९३ ॥

सावोचदथ मन्देहे न्यस्ता विप्रेण केनचित् ।
आवन्तिकाभिधा यैषा तस्याः शिल्पमिदं महत् ॥ ९४ ॥

तच्छ्रुत्वैव च वत्सेशो गोपालगृहमाययौ ।
नूनं वासवदत्ता सा भवेदत्रेति चिन्तयन् ॥ ९५ ॥

प्रविवेश च गत्वा तद्द्वारस्थितमहत्तरम् ।
अन्तःस्थदेवीगोपालमन्त्रिद्वयवसन्तकम् ॥ ९६ ॥

तत्र वासवदत्तां तां ददर्श प्रोषितागताम् ।
उपप्लवविनिर्मुक्तां मूर्तिं चान्द्रमसीमिव ॥ ९७ ॥

पपाताथ महीपृष्ठे स शोकविषविह्वलः ।
कम्पो वासवदत्ताया हृदये तूपपद्यत ॥ ९८ ॥

ततः साप्यपतद् भूमौ गात्रैर्विरहपाण्डुरैः ।
विललाप च निन्दन्ती तदाचरितमात्मनः ॥ ९९ ॥

अथ तौ दंपती शोकदीनौ रुरुदतुस्तथा ।
यौगन्धरायणोऽप्यासीद्बाष्पधौतमुखो यथा ॥ १०० ॥

तथाविधं च तच्छ्रुत्वा काले कोलाहलं तदा ।
पद्मावत्यपि तत्रैव साकुला तमुपाययौ ॥ १०१ ॥

क्रमादवगतार्था च राजवासवदत्तयोः ।
तुल्यावस्थैव साप्यासीत्स्निग्धमुग्धा हि सत्स्त्रियः ॥ १०२ ॥

किं जीवितेन मे कार्यं भर्तृदुःखप्रदायिना ।
इति वासवदत्ता च जगाद रुदती मुहुः ॥ १०३ ॥

मगधेशसुतालाभात्तव साम्राज्यकाङ्क्षिणा ॥
कृतमेतन्मया देव देव्या दोषो न कश्चन ॥ १०४ ॥

इयं त्वस्याः सपत्न्येव प्रवासे शीलसाक्षिणी ।
इत्युवाचाथ वत्सेशं धीरो यौगन्धरायणः ॥ १०५ ॥

अहमत्र विशाम्यग्नावस्याः शुद्धिप्रकाशने ।
इति पद्मावती तत्र जगादामत्सराशया ॥ १०६ ॥

अहमेवापराध्यामि यत्कृते सुमहानयम् ।
सोढो देव्यापि हि क्लेश इति राजाप्यभाषत ॥ १०७ ॥

अग्निप्रवेशः कार्यो मे राज्ञो हृदयशुद्धये ।
इति वासवदत्ता च बभाषे बद्धनिश्चया ॥ १०८ ॥
ततः स कृतिनां धुर्यो धीमान्यौगन्धरायणः ।
आचम्य प्राङ्मुखः शुद्धि इति वाचमुदैरयत् ॥ १०९ ॥
यद्यहं हितकृद्राज्ञो देवी शुद्धिमती यदि ।
ब्रूत भो लोकपालास्तन्न चेद्देहं त्यजाम्यहम् ॥ ११० ॥
इत्युक्त्वा विरते तस्मिन्दिव्या वागुदभूदियम् ॥
धन्यस्त्वं नृपते यस्य मन्त्री यौगन्धरायणः ॥ १११ ॥
यस्य वासवदत्ता च भार्या प्राग्जन्मदेवता ।
न दोषः कश्चिदेतस्या इत्युक्त्वा वागुपारमत् ॥ ११२ ॥
आकर्ण्य तन्मुखरिताखिलदिग्विभाग-
मामन्द्रनूतनघनाघनगर्जितश्रि ।
उत्कंधराश्च सुचिरं विहताभितापाः
सर्वेऽपि ते स्फुटविडम्बितनीलकण्ठाः ॥ ११३ ॥
गोपालकसहितोऽपि च राजा यौगन्धरायणाचारितम् ।
स्तौति स्म वत्सराजो मेने पृथ्वीं च हस्तगताम् ॥ ११४ ॥
दधदथ नृपतिः स मूर्तिमत्यौ निकटगते रतिनिर्वृती इवोभे ।
अनुदिनसहवाससानुरागे निजदयिते परमुत्सवं बभार ॥ ११५ ॥

इति महाकविश्रीसोमदेवभट्टविरचिते कथासरित्सागरे लावाणकलम्बके द्वितीयस्तरङ्गः ।

Index of Important Words

(The figures refer to pages of this edition.)